STARTING AND RUNNING

A PROFITABLE

INVESTMENT CLUB

THE OFFICIAL GUIDE FROM

THE NATIONAL ASSOCIATION OF INVESTORS CORPORATION

STARTING AND RUNNING A PROFITABLE INVESTMENT CLUB

THOMAS E. O'HARA AND KENNETH S. JANKE, SR.

THREE RIVERS PRESS • NEW YORK

Published by Three Rivers Press, New York, New York.
Member of the Crown Publishing Group.

Random House, Inc. New York, Toronto, London, Sydney, Auckland
www.randomhouse.com

THREE RIVERS PRESS is a registered trademark and the Three Rivers Press colophon is a trademark of Random House, Inc.

Printed in the United States of America

Library of Congress Cataloging-in-Publication Data available upon request.

ISBN 0-8129-3008-8

10   9   8   7   6

A MESSAGE FROM THE CHAIRMAN OF NAIC's BOARD OF ADVISORS

*I*nvestment clubs have existed in the United States for more than a century. The oldest known investment club began operation in Texas in 1898.

Most of the early clubs were built around a combination of like social interests and a desire to try one's wings in the blue skies of investment and speculation. There was little, if any, attempt to establish uniform principles for guidance or education of members.

The modern investment club movement began in Detroit in 1940 because circumstances dictated a serious attitude toward investment results. Frederick C. Russell, unable to find a job and desiring to buy a small business, decided to form an investment club as the vehicle for accumulating capital. He became the inspiration for the investment club movement.

Being a serious undertaking, the Mutual Investment Club of Detroit, at my suggestion, determined to do three things: (1) invest every month, (2) reinvest all dividends, and (3) buy growth companies. Each principle in itself was adopted for the purpose of safety, but the three in combination produced aggressive results over the years.

Having observed the Mutual Investment Club of Detroit for over 50 years and the growth of the investment club movement, I believe it is possible for most people to achieve a goal of investing $20,000 in stock over 20 to

30 years by budgeting $20 to $25 a month for such a purpose. Russell's club members had realized a gain of more than $200,000 each by 1982 on $10 to $20 a month invested. This contributed to the education of their children, better housing, and supplements to retirement years.

The behavior of investment club members during the stock market declines has been essentially professional. Most uneducated investors panicked and suffered losses.

Seeing the progress of the Mutual Investment Club and noting the ways in which the club members advanced in their family finances and businesses, we first discussed the creation of a national association in 1949.

On October 20, 1951, the National Association of Investment Clubs (NAIC) was founded at the Rackham Building, Detroit, with the Mutual Investment Club of Detroit and three other Michigan clubs as charter members. One objective of the Association was to transform investment clubs into a vast, nationwide educational project. This emphasis on education is one essential difference between the early days of the investment club movement and the modern-day clubs.

Having found a vigorous interest in investment club work abroad, NAIC took the lead in establishing the World Federation of Investment Clubs on July 8, 1960, in London. The founding associations were: NAIC, United States; NAIC, Great Britain; the National Bureau voor Beleggings Studieclubs, the Netherlands; and the Federation of New Zealand Investment Clubs.

Realizing the vital significance of the widespread ownership of industry and its dependence on effective investment education, NAIC launched the Investment Education Institute in February, 1961. The International Investment Education Institute was established in London in August, 1996. Investment education worldwide has been gradually broadening from its investment club base to include growing numbers of individual investors.

With billions of dollars going into pension funds for retirement years, with world industrialization requiring increasing supplies of capital, with inflation making us all conscious of the need to maintain purchasing power, and with Japanese competition and their concept of government, business, and labor cooperation creating trade tension, the question of who owns industry is of deep significance. Capitalism can exist only to the extent that equity money is made available to business—small, medium, and large—in all areas, here and abroad. Capitalism will work better if people (1) understand investing, (2) are educated to invest successfully, and (3) intelligently provide capital to expanding industries. Investment education is essential to good citizenship in the modern world.

George A. Nicholson, Jr. (1908–1996)
Chairman of the Advisory Board
National Association of Investors Corporation

ACKNOWLEDGMENTS

NATIONAL ASSOCIATION OF INVESTORS CORPORATION

INVESTMENT EDUCATION FOR INDIVIDUALS AND CLUBS SINCE 1951

711 W. Thirteen Mile Rd. · Madison Heights, Mich. 48071
(248) 583-6242 (NAIC)
NAIC website: http://www.better–investing.org

NAIC is a Michigan Not-for-Profit Corporation founded by and served by a group of volunteer officers whose sincerity, diligent service, and devotion to sound investment principles have produced the tremendous growth and success of the Investment Club movement and made it an outstanding force for investment education.

Board of Advisors
James L. Agee, Chairman
Helen J. McLane

Trustees
Thomas E. O'Hara, Chairman
Kenneth S. Janke, Sr., President and CEO
Lewis A. Rockwell, Secretary
Robert W. Hague, Treasurer
Warren B. Alexander
Donald E. Danko
Lorrie Gustin
Elizabeth N. Hamm
Richard A. Holthaus
Kenneth R. Lightcap

Leroy F. Mumford
Peggy L. Schmeltz
Ralph L. Seger, Jr.
Sharon L. Vuinovich

**National Investors Association
Board of Directors**
Officers
Ruth C. McPhetridge, Chairman
Rose C. Kapranos, President
Evonne A. Hurst, Vice President, Council and Membership
Stephen W. Beer, Vice President, Budget/Finance
Shirley Knudsen, Treasurer
Elizabeth A. Sinnock, Secretary

Douglas Gerlach
Hans D. Steinke
G. Ken Wood
   Associate Directors
Nancy Crays
Kenneth A. Halwas, Ph.D.
Steve Martin
Phyllis G. Pawlovsky
Linda K. Penfold
Bob Schaelchlin
Leslie A. Wilkinson
Bart Womack
   Directors Emeriti
Richard Kenfield
John M. Paterson

**NAIC Corporate Advisory
Committee**
John D. Tyson, Chairman
Lisa Kikora, Vice Chairman
Sandy Upperman, Secretary
Jonathan W. Borraem, Treasurer
John Baker
Guttie Carr
Marsha Gordon
J. Kevin Helmintoller
Mike Klodnicki
Mark Rozelle
Barbara VenHorst

CONTENTS

STARTING AND RUNNING

A PROFITABLE

INVESTMENT CLUB

LEARNING AND EARNING WITH AN INVESTMENT CLUB

*E*veryone interested in the stock market wants to find the key to consistently profitable investing. There is a way. In forming an investment club, you are joining hundreds of thousands of other men and women who are following the profitable path of learn-by-doing investing in common stocks. You share with them the opportunity to enhance your knowledge of business and investing; accumulate a significant amount of capital over time; and have fun, too.

What is an investment club? It's a group of like-minded people interested in investing in the stock market. They agree to a few basic investing goals and principles, and they each take on part of the job of research. The modest investment of each individual, the limited time each puts into research, and the devotion to four basic principles collectively add up to a formidable investing force.

But why the stock market? The chart from the Ibbotson Study (Figure I-1) demonstrates quite clearly that few investments compare with stocks in rate of return. What's more, stocks are easily bought and sold and have a universally recognized value.

WHAT MEMBERSHIP CAN MEAN

You can make more money through your investment club than you might have thought possible. Of course, in the first year or two, many clubs show

3

Figure I-1

Comparison of Total Returns on Different Kinds of Investments

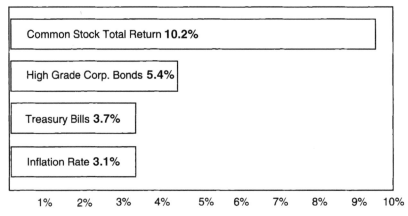

This sixty-nine-year study (1926–1994) from Ibbotson Associates clearly shows that common stocks have been twice as profitable as corporate bonds. What is more, common stocks have earned enough to outpace inflation by almost three times.

losses or only small gains. However, as members become more knowledgeable and the amount of money under management grows, gains often begin to increase exponentially.

Consider someone who joined the Mutual Investment Club of Detroit, the granddaddy of the investment club movement, shortly after its formation in February 1940 (Figure I-2). After paying in $20 monthly for five years, he interrupted that schedule for two years. He then resumed his contributions, making up some back payments.

Almost forty-one years later, at normal retirement age, he had paid in $8,120. His share of club assets amounted to $158,962. This savings program enabled him to spend most of his income throughout his working years while accumulating, by means of small but regular investments, a substantial supplement to his pension and Social Security income.

The knowledge of investing he had gained through his club enabled him also to invest wisely for his own personal account, adding to his modest fortune. (Typically, when a club forms, only two members own personal portfolios. After five years, almost all do. Currently, nine out of ten NAIC club members buy securities for their own accounts in addition to making club investments.)

Figure I-2

A History of the Mutual Investment Club of Detroit

Year Ended Dec. 31	Total Deposit by Members	*Earnings from Both Dividends & Sales of Securities* Dividends	*Sales*	Accumulated Total Deposits & Reinvested Earnings	Withdrawals	Liquidating Value Feb. 28 of Following Year
1941	$ 800			$ 800		$ 812
1942	1,920			1,920		1,915
1943	3,220			3,220		3,405
1944	4,860			4,860		8,847
1945	5,080			5,080		9,844
1946	5,080	$ 1,489*		6,569	$ 2,519	15,347
1947	5,620	978		8,087		11,854
1948	7,310	1,004	$ 693	11,474	825	12,401
1949	9,761	1,196	(525)	14,794	200	13,439
1950	8,741	1,100	167	15,041	3,000	20,690
1951	10,190	1,670	2,513	20,673	800	27,471
1952	11,460	1,433	1,937	25,313		33,222
1953	15,025	1,690	806	31,374	1,606	43,233
1954	18,430	2,073	(459)	36,393	7,631	50,125
1955	21,770	2,200	3,618	45,551		75,975
1956	26,642	2,991	7,707	61,123	5,689	85,001
1957	30,542	3,355	2,600	70,978		94,121
1958	35,282	3,074	3,737	82,529		91,323
1959	35,935	3,367	3,114	89,663	6,695	132,690
1960	40,885	3,701	11,012	109,326		151,515
1961	45,470	4,369	174	118,454	1,026	171,655
1962	49,870	3,731	2,867	129,452	5,000	188,738
1963	53,960	4,568	2,311	140,421	1,000	172,577
1964	57,085	4,258	3,621	151,425	800	211,801
1965	61,685	6,069	6,102	168,196		246,738
1966	59,040	5,599	5,146	176,296	21,302	268,829
1967	62,308	6,411	1,500	187,196	8,142	270,994
1968	67,056	10,139	21,968	224,330	17,340	386,558
1969	75,327	11,815	2,967	247,383	5,175	535,604
1970	84,083	11,696	3,498	271,333	2,955	394,434
1971	93,493	11,541	2,599	294,883		439,849
1972	90,819	11,524	(2,092)	301,641	43,658	436,413
1973	97,219	9,560	13,493	331,094		430,081
1974	103,584	12,241	3,026	351,726	3,925	382,959
1975	108,983	15,621	429	374,175	14,300	470,675
1976	115,076	13,840	2,739	396,847	13,000	503,916
1977	112,250	18,443	6,779	419,243	29,000	478,418
1978	118,589	22,073	5,378	453,033	12,000	559,419
1979	126,860	24,630	70,183	556,117	15,000	759,038

Figure I-2 (Continued)
A History of the Mutual Investment Club of Detroit

Year Ended Dec. 31	Total Deposit by Members	Earnings from Both Dividends & Sales of Securities		Accumulated Total Deposits & Reinvested Earnings	Withdrawals	Liquidating Value Feb. 28 of Following Year
		Dividends	Sales			
1980	133,640	19,003	67,171	649,035	25,750	915,726
1981	142,136	24,122	80,542	762,231	38,086	891,196
1982	145,716	25,988	1,653	783,452	25,750	1,124,038
1983	167,952	26,767	33,127	875,582	7,210	1,235,893
1984	195,954	29,328	10,937	943,846	78,280	1,474,266
1985	211,659	31,094	55,283	966,018	10,300	1,600,543
1986	211,489	25,761	62,904	1,064,513	386,094	1,754,924
1987	233,159	22,390	48,356	1,266,832	90,640	1,602,599
1988	248,524	41,562	102,943	1,386,702	105,957	1,729,620
1989	262,530	47,838	29,916	1,478,462	109,150	1,682,569
1990	275,130	59,865	55,951	1,606,878	105,321	1,833,368
1991	291,045	58,594	47,842	1,729,229	106,295	2,109,917
1992	310,797	56,987	30,002	1,835,980	41,928	2,377,930
1993	331,777	51,541	65,089	1,973,580	59,988	2,413,378
1994	371,802	55,065	113,798	2,182,468	23,800	2,701,399
1995	425,960	59,581	100,593	2,396,800	445,285	3,002,181
Totals	$425,960	$874,925	$1,095,915	$2,396,800	$1,881,412	$3,002,181

* The amount of dividends shown here is the accumulation from the beginning of this club through 1946. Note that the club members invested $425,960 in 56 years, withdrew $1,881,412, and had a liquidating value of $3,002,181 as of February 29, 1996, the 56th anniversary of the club's founding.

Figure I-3
Building Your Nest Egg

Rate of Return	Years				
	5	10	20	30	40
3%	$19,442.50	$42,027.23	$ 98,736.83	$175,258.12	$ 278,512.39
5	20,486.83	46,778.79	123,823.89	250,717.91	459,713.57
8	22,190.01	55,249.70	177,884.17	450,088.55	1,054,284.37
10	23,424.71	61,965.61	229,709.07	683,797.60	1,913,034.07

Use this table to see how much you would save over a period of years at various rates of return if you invested $300 a month.

SET YOUR OBJECTIVE

The National Association of Investors Corporation (NAIC) recommends that your investment objective should be to double your money every five years. To do so, you must achieve an average 14.9 percent compounded annual growth rate. This same growth will not come every year, but you should expect to achieve that average from one stock market peak to the next. In the past ten years, NAIC's surveys have seen the average club exceed that figure three times. In the 1995 sampling of 629 clubs, the average club (which was nearly nine years old) had earned 12.3 percent over its lifetime.

Of course, you need not meet the typical return of NAIC members to prosper. Figure I-3 shows what you can accumulate over various spans of time at different rates of return by investing $300 monthly. An 8 percent return is

Figure I-4
Taking the Long-Term View: The Ibbotson Associates Study

This Ibbotson Associates study covers 1926–1994. Over time, certain trends appear, mainly that stocks have the highest annual return (12.2% for small-company stocks and 10.2% for large-company stocks) compared with long-term government bonds (4.8%), Treasury bills (3.7%), and inflation (3.1%). Source: © Stocks, Bonds, Bills, and Inflation 1995 Yearbook™, Ibbotson Associates, Chicago (annually updates work by Roger G. Ibbotson and Rex A. Sinquefield). Used with permission. All rights reserved.

Figure I-5

Taking the Long-Term View: The Dow Jones Industrial Average
(1920–1994)

Long-term trends provide a great deal of information for the investor. Perhaps the most important observation for the investor to make is that stock prices have followed an upward trend for approximately 200 years. Second, prices do fluctuate. Downward trends can continue for a while, but the overall movement has been upward. Of course, you want your investments to keep pace with or, better

a conservative objective, since the stock market overall has attained a long-term annual growth of roughly 10 percent. Were you to invest $300 monthly for 20 years at 8 percent, you would amass total capital of $177,884. In 30 years, you would wind up with $450,088.

To make consistent overall returns, you will need to invest in down markets, when virtually all stocks are underpriced, as well as in up markets, when most stocks are fully valued. And at all times, good stock selection is vital.

YOUR CLUB ACCOUNT HELPS BUILD YOUR PERSONAL ACCOUNT

For many people, the investment club is their introduction to the stock market. If you're one of these people, your club experience will lead you to open a personal investment account in addition to your club shares, and here you will build your individual portfolio.

Figure I-5 (Continued)
Taking the Long-Term View: The Dow Jones Industrial Average
(1920–1994)

*yet, outperform inflation. The records suggest that stock prices do indeed exceed the rate of inflation
over time. As a club member, you will purchase stocks when they are high and low. But the general
upward trend will most likely continue, and investors will benefit from that trend. The important
thing is not to concentrate on the short term, but to keep the total picture in mind.*

Having a personal account doesn't mean you should abandon membership in an investment club. Continuing club membership can be very valuable. Members look at stocks at least once a month, which serves as a reminder
to pay attention to their own personal portfolios as well. Many investment
ideas come from club meetings, even for the most experienced investor.

The Mutual Investment Club of Detroit celebrated its fifty-fifth an-
niversary in 1995. Some of the original members still participate actively, despite the fact that their personal portfolios have grown to substantial sums.
Investment club membership can be a lifelong experience. Through the club,
experienced help is at hand.

It only works, though, if you can stick with it. Twenty-five percent of
new investment clubs are out of business within two years, victims of poor
member selection and a "get rich quick" mentality. Everyone needs to agree at
the outset to common goals, meaning entering into a long-term program
with a long-term investment philosophy. (See Figures I-4 and I-5.) Short-
term trading simply doesn't work in an investment club.

LOOK FOR INVESTMENT IDEAS

With this book, you and your fellow club members will gain ideas on selecting investments. If you also become a member of NAIC, you will receive additional useful information, including NAIC's monthly publication, *Better Investing.* Over the years, securities featured in the magazine's "Stock to Study" feature have on average met NAIC's goal of doubling their value within five years. Your broker may have suggestions for you as well. But don't accept anyone else's word as final. Using NAIC's tools, after learning how from this book, you and your fellow members should make your own informed judgments about what and when to buy and sell. Tips are great, but put every stock to the test of the NAIC Stock Selection Guide and Report before making a purchase.

This book will show you how to organize your club properly and guide its operation through the years to come. Left to its own devices, your club might falter and fall back on highly speculative concepts. In adhering to the principles we present, you will follow the same time-tested techniques used by many others to finance their children's educations, travel the world, and avoid money worries in retirement.

Investing the NAIC Way

CHAPTER 1

A PROVEN INVESTMENT PHILOSOPHY

*T*here is no rapid route to riches. Today's most successful investment clubs—
with assets of hundreds of thousands of dollars, a million dollars, or more—
started out, years ago, with only a few dollars. Most of the members in those
clubs had no previous stock market experience, and their investment funds
were limited, as was the time available to devote to club activities. Yet they've
achieved results that would make many professional investors envious.

You can apply the same philosophy that has made them prosperous. All
you need is patience to follow a few tested and proven standards, while avoiding the traps so many investors fall into. David Babson, the noted investment
counselor, has written:

> It is surprising how few investment portfolios are based on a consistent philos-
> ophy aimed at meeting long-term objectives. Most are merely collections of se-
> curities assembled over time for a variety of reasons which seemed compelling at
> the moment of purchase, but are no longer clearly remembered.
>
> Even among those investors who develop a basic plan, far too many do not
> stick with it through thick and thin. In periods of pessimism, they end up sell-
> ing stocks when they should be buying. And when optimism prevails, they be-
> come lured by rumors, greed or bad advice into speculating when they should
> be investing.

With the basic principles recommended by NAIC and practiced by successful clubs in the past, you can apply a consistent philosophy aimed at long-

term, proven investment objectives. Since 1951, these simple rules have led investors to consistently superior results. Here they are.

Principle 1: Invest Regularly, Regardless of the Market Outlook. When you start investing, you may be nervous about timing. What if you commit your capital and the market immediately heads south? Could there be another Black Monday—or worse—after your money is invested?

Time and experience will help allay these fears. The market's overall trend for decades has been upward, at an average annual compound rate of about 10 percent—despite intermittent cycles of boom, recession, depression, and recovery. Once you recognize the rhythm of market cycles, fluctuations will no longer distract you; instead, you'll welcome market dips as buying opportunities.

Investors minimize risk when they purchase shares they intend to hold as long as the business operates successfully. In contrast, speculators who try to forecast near-term market fluctuations magnify their risk tremendously. We've found that one quarter of all investment clubs go out of business within the first twenty-four months because of conflict between those who believe in long-term investing and those advocating speculative trading. Be sure your members agree on a long-term philosophy before you get started.

Principle 2: Reinvest All Earnings. Put your investment earnings back into the market. This will let you maximize your profits through compounding, so you'll earn more than you would have just by keeping your original capital at work. In the examples presented in coming chapters, you will see the amazing effect of compounding made possible by reinvestment.

Principle 3: Invest in Growth Companies. Buy shares in businesses whose sales and earnings are moving ahead faster than the gross domestic product, and whose records suggest they will be far more valuable five years in the future. We'll show you later how to identify growth companies with the best potential.

Principle 4: Diversify to Reduce Risk. Some of your selections will be great successes, while others will post disappointing results. Since it is impossible to predict the future with certainty, you cannot expect every outcome to reach your forecast. With diversification, you need only realize an average advance that meets your goal; an occasional mistake will not prove disastrous.

Diversification is a basic principle in investing. The idea is that, because you cannot possibly know which stocks will perform better or worse than average, you cannot afford to put all your money into one company, or even in companies within a single industry. You have to spread the risk—and the opportunity. Only by diversifying will you be able to realize your average return objective with lower risk. It's true that diversification also limits the upside potential, but that's important in order to balance risk and opportunity.

By applying these four principles, you will be in an especially good position to succeed as an investor. You should also seek out an experienced investor who subscribes to this philosophy and is equipped to serve as your club's coach. The individual might be an experienced investment club member, an individual investor, or your broker.

THE FOUR PRINCIPLES IN ACTION

Here's an example of how the principles work in a real situation. Everyone who approaches the stock market begins with the question: Is the market today high or low? This question is more complex than it seems at first glance. Perhaps the market is high compared with last week or last month, but lower than a year ago. Maybe it will prove to be low now compared with its level a year ago. Maybe it will prove to be low now compared with its level a year hence. But who knows? It is virtually impossible to find someone who has built a fortune over a lifetime by forecasting short-term movements in the market. In contrast, millions have found purchasing sound stocks regularly to be a profitable pursuit, as the market has advanced over the long term. That's where our investing principles come in.

When you make regular purchases with a set sum, regardless of the market's level, you are utilizing an idea called *dollar cost averaging.* You'll buy more shares when prices are depressed, and fewer when they are high. That's because when prices are lower, your investment dollars get more shares for the same amount; and when those same shares are more expensive, the set amount buys fewer shares (Figure 1-1).

When is it time to sell? When you buy carefully, very seldom should you sell. When you own quality companies with continuing high growth potential, you should continue to hold. When a company becomes grossly overpriced, you should take one quarter to one third of your profits. We'll talk about how to recognize overvalued stocks in more detail later. However, when you purchase a company whose growth is driven by management, you may hold it for as long as that management remains in control. One company widely held by NAIC members has just completed forty-nine successive years of increasing sales and earnings per share.

Figure 1-1
Regular Investing Can Lower Your Average Cost per Share

Price/Share Mo.	1	2	3	4	5	6	7	8	9	10	11	12	13	14	15	16	17	18	19	20	21	22
(1)	$20	$20	$20	$20	$20	$20	$20	$20	$20	$20	$20	$20	$20	$20	$20	$20	$20	$20	$20	$20	$20	$20
(2)	1.333	1.250	1.176	1.250	1.333	1.429	1.538	1.429	1.333	1.429	1.538	1.667	1.818	1.667	1.538	1.667	1.538	1.429	1.333	1.250	1.176	1.111

(1) Monthly Investment - $440 Invested (2) Shares Purchased Monthly

31.232 Shares at $18 = $562.18

If you invested $20 each month in a particular stock, the fluctuating nature of the stock, the fluctuating nature of the stock market would allow your $20 investment to buy more of the stock at some times and less of the stock at others. However, because of the nature of dollar cost averaging, you are at an advantage. Your average cost per share is actually lower over time. The figures on the bottom line show the number of shares purchased each month with the $20 fixed amount of investment. The $440 invested over a twenty-two-month period bought 31.232 shares. At the latest price of $18, the 31.232 shares are worth $562.18. As you continue to invest, your advantage will increase.

16

But why dollar cost average in the first place? Why not just "buy low and sell high?" The answer is that you don't know with foresight when those situations really exist. Hindsight tells all, but as investors, you don't have that luxury. Combining dollar cost averaging with the policy of reinvesting all of your dividends will let you, over time, buy more shares low and fewer shares high without the benefit of hindsight.

SETTING INVESTMENT GOALS

Your club's goal should be to attain average growth in prices and dividend income of 14.9 percent, compounded annually. At this rate, you will double the value of your holdings every five years. Still, an 8 percent per year increase over an extended period of time would be an excellent result.

An important component of your increase in value is dividends. Your aim should be to realize a 4 to 6 percent yield over time on your investment from dividend income, particularly in the early part of the business cycle, when stock prices tend to be lower and yields consequently higher. Often this will prove difficult, perhaps even impossible, but keep that standard in mind. Remember, it's a standard, not a hard-and-fast rule.

When you join or start an investment club, plan to stay a member until your retirement years. A fifteen-member club in which each member pays in $20 per month should reach a worth of $22,190 in five years. The longer you invest, and the wiser your choices, the better your results will be. The compound interest table (see Figure I-3) shows how the value of $300 invested monthly at varying rates of return for different periods of time can grow.

Club members who begin their program in their twenties and maintain it until their departure from the labor force forty years later could amass $1,913,034 at a rate of return of 10 percent, barring withdrawals over the four decades, especially if those clubs follow our advice to invest in growth companies. It is thrilling to invest in companies and see them subsequently grow in size, stature, and, of course, value. Buying shares in such concerns, whose sales and earnings outperform those of business as a whole, typically means you will reap a higher price for your shares.

This increased price stems not only from growing earnings, but also from the propensity of investors to pay a premium for growth. Growth company shares typically sell at higher price/earnings multiples than do other issues. Be aware that a company must attain growth over a period of years to warrant the growth designation. Growth comes in a number of ways. It comes when an industry is new and has a new market to satisfy. It may come from a new product. Growth may also be produced by vigorous, talented, driven management. It is the last type of growth that is the most dependable and long lasting. A five-year history should be minimum, to ensure that the company is established and that management has encountered varying conditions in which to prove its mettle. A short period of growth may be a lucky accident, not the indication of management drive that we are looking for.

The charts in Figure 1-2 show how the consistent growth records of American Home Products and Sigma Aldrich have been accompanied over the years by higher prices.

CHOOSING GROWTH STOCKS

From the charts in Figure 1-2 the investor can readily see that when sales increase nearly every year and earnings per share follow roughly the same pattern, the price of the stock usually continues to advance. That is what all of us are seeking. NAIC believes that the investor profits most dependably by placing money in a company whose history suggests that it will be worth substantially more five years in the future.

Growth in a business comes in many ways. For example, there are growth industries. These occur where a new product, material, or service is offered and the companies satisfying this need grow as they fill the new market. In some cases, such as electronics, the growth seems likely to continue indefinitely, spurred by the steady development of new products. Some new products offer growth for just a few years. Sometimes the growth comes from a new use for an old product. The investor who understands where the growth is coming from is in a good position to understand how long it may continue and the potential in the investment.

NAIC members have found that the most reliable growth is a result not so much of the industry as of a management that is driven to produce growth. Such growth can last the lifetime of the management. And some such managements are able to instill a growth culture in their corporations that will be carried on for years after the originating management is gone. A well-known example is Minnesota Mining and Manufacturing. The idea of replacing the product line with new items within a short time span has carried forward from one management to the next and has given the company an outstanding

Figure 1-2

Two Companies Showing How Sales and Earnings Growth Rises

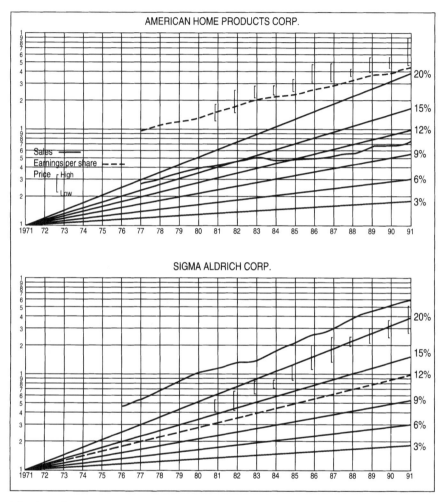

The charts for American Home Products Corp. and Sigma Aldrich Corp. document the consistent growth in sales and earnings per share that identify a company as a good prospective investment.

record of growth. The two companies in Figure 1-2 are other examples of this sustained growth.

NAIC's Stock Selection Guide ("the Guide") is designed to help you recognize this kind of management. Such a management produces a fairly consistent increase in sales and earnings per share, superior pre-tax margins, and high earnings on invested capital. These features are clearly shown in the Guide. When the investor identifies the features, the remaining job is to figure out a reasonable price. That's the purpose of the third section of the Guide.

Diversify to reduce risk. Most investment clubs purchase eight to twelve stocks in the first year. Later, they concentrate on increasing their ownership of the best performers and substituting better stocks for the laggards. How many stocks should your club own? No more than you can remain informed about. Clubs under ten years of age are likely to own no more than twenty to twenty-five stocks; twelve issues should be sufficient diversification for a relatively new club. Your main concern is not how many or how few stocks you own, but that each has the qualifications enabling it to be worth substantially more at the next market peak.

These totals presuppose an active membership. One active member can probably keep current on four stocks. If only two or three members are thus involved, the club's portfolio will clearly be restricted in size.

As part of the diversification process, we recommend including big, small, and medium-sized companies in your portfolio. Large companies (generally those with annual sales of $4 billion or more) tend to have a more predictable rate of growth and offer more resistance to price decline during down markets. On the other hand, small companies (those with sales of $400 million or less) are able to achieve more rapid rates of growth. Their shares may advance sharply in buoyant markets. When the market goes down, their prices tend to fall more than the average amount. The in-between companies provide further balance and range of market interest.

Historically, there have been extended periods when, in spite of increasing sales and earnings, stock prices remained virtually unchanged. In such periods, while the market overall may stand still, groups of stocks will attract attention. A range of large, medium, and small companies offers your club sufficient variety in securities so that something in your portfolio will get market attention and thus help keep interest in your club alive during a dull period.

In selecting stocks for your club's portfolio, try to put one fourth of your holdings in major companies in major industries and another fourth in small companies. The latter companies can be selected from corporations headquartered in your area, making it easier for you to obtain information concerning them.

The remaining half of the portfolio should be mid-sized companies. Aim for growth potential of 5 to 7 percent a year among the major companies, and at least 12 percent among the small concerns. The mid-range organizations should offer a 7 to 12 percent rate. If these guidelines are followed, your overall portfolio should return 10 to 12 percent in price appreciation. This, coupled with dividends, will enable you to attain the 14.9 percent overall gain we suggest you seek. The amount of the portfolio apportioned between different-sized companies will vary as stock prices change. We are not aiming at a precise percentage in each size holding but a reasonable holding in each size level.

KEY FACTORS IN INVESTMENT ANALYSIS

Club members should agree that no stock will be purchased without advance analysis. Members are not expected to become professional stock analysts—although many investment club members have done so. However, you should become proficient in applying a few essential tests to enhance your prospects for success and reduce your risk in buying and selling stocks.

As you pursue your goal of achieving 100 percent appreciation within five years, your members should analyze every prospective purchase for (1) the company's management capability, as evidenced by growing sales and earnings, pre-tax profit margin, and superior return on stockholders' equity; and (2) a reasonable current share price that can be expected to rise as financial results improve in the future.

Management Capability. The drive of a corporation's management is the single most influential element of growth. When investment clubs give undue attention to industry outlook ("Health care is bound to grow") or the product of a company ("Fat-free food ingredients are certain winners"), they ignore, to their later regret, that only the best-led companies succeed over the long run. Growth is most reliable when it is produced by good management.

Apply these three tests of management:

1. *Rate of growth.* Other factors being equal, over the long term an investment is likely to increase in value at about the same rate that sales grow. The companies you select as possible investments for your club should be those whose sales have increased at least at the expected rate for their size as described earlier. Further, each company should offer the promise of continuing advances.

2. *Pre-tax profit margin.* This margin is calculated by deducting costs from sales and then dividing the result, profit before taxes, by sales:

Pre-tax Profit

$$\frac{(\text{Sales} - \text{Costs})}{\text{Sales}} = \% \text{ Pre-tax Profit}$$

Comparison with other companies in the same industry will show whether the margin is average, better than typical, or under par. Obviously, a higher margin is preferable. Warning bells should ring if the margin is far above the averages of other companies. That could mean there's a distortion in the way profits are being reported, and chances are the high rate won't be repeated. If the high margin is for real, competition will be quickly attracted.

3. *Earnings on stockholders' equity.* Another mark of good management is a high percentage of earnings on stockholders' equity (which is net earnings divided by the sum of the value of preferred stock, common stock, and retained earnings). Compare the company being considered with others in the same industry. The same caveat applies as before: An unusually high rate of return may indicate distortion in the numbers or a temporary advantage.

You will learn to apply other means of appraising management as your investment experience grows. These three basic tests should be employed from the outset on every stock you study.

Another important basic to keep in mind in your review is share price. Quality and growth potential mean nothing in a security if you pay an exorbitant price. Use the Stock Selection Guide in assessing the high and low limits of the stock's price over the next five years (see Chapter 9). Then relate current price to this range and to your objective of doubling your money.

There are three ways to test for reasonableness of price:

1. *Earnings per share.* Earnings should be growing on a per-share basis at approximately the same rate as sales. Under occasional market conditions, you will find growing companies—particularly smaller ones—that can be bought for no more than the sum of the estimated earnings per share for the next five years. This situation is rarely found, but when it is, you may have an exceptional buying opportunity.

2. *Dividends.* Generally speaking, a quality growth company pays out no more than half of its earnings; the remainder is retained to help build the business. If you as an investor can expect over the years a dividend yield of 4 to 6 percent on the price paid for the stock, with retained earnings devoted to fueling growth, you can also anticipate stock price appreciation. When the stock you're considering has a track record of rapid growth in sales and earnings per share, be content with a relatively modest payout. The company can probably achieve greater value for you in building the business than you can attain elsewhere with your dividends.

3. *Price range.* Study the price range of the stock over the past five years. If you review the lows, you'll get a sense of where the stock might be bought at some point during the year to come. Looking at the highs, you'll see where the stock might be sold, should the club wish to sell. Although this is admittedly a rough test, it gives you a good general guideline for recognizing an excessively high current price.

In the world of investments, as elsewhere, rewards reflect the quality and quantity of the effort you and your fellow investors expend. You get out of investment club study just what you put into it—no more and no less.

As you continue to develop your investment background, you should know that there are two broad procedures used by investors to select stocks and decide when to invest and when not to. One is called the *fundamental procedure,* and the other is called the *technical procedure.* Investors usually choose one or the other procedure for their method of operation, but some combine parts of the two procedures. In the fundamental approach, the investor studies the company, its industry, and its market and tries to understand what makes the company run and what its future will be. The technician pays more attention to the stock market and stock price rather than to the individual company, expecting to make more money from the price movement caused by different stock market forces than by the progress achieved by a particular company through business processes. Both of these procedures enable investors to make money, but there are great differences.

In the fundamental approach, the investor is looking for companies to grow and increase in value over a long time period. The pie gets bigger and everyone benefits—customers, employees, and shareowners. Three companies widely held by NAIC members are good examples of fundamental growth. NAIC members started buying these companies fifteen to twenty years ago

Figure 1-3
Reinvesting Dividends

Month	Amount Paid In	Dividend Added	Total Invested	Shares Purchased	Total Shares Owned
1	$ 20	—	$ 20.00	1.333	1.333
2	20	$ 0.27	20.27	1.267	2.600
3	20	—	20.00	1.176	3.776
4	20	—	20.00	1.250	5.026
5	20	1.00	21.00	1.400	6.426
6	20	—	20.00	1.428	7.854
7	20	—	20.00	1.538	9.392
8	20	1.88	21.88	1.563	10.955
9	20	—	20.00	1.333	12.288
10	20	—	20.00	1.428	13.716
11	20	2.74	22.74	1.749	15.465
12	20	—	20.00	1.667	17.132
13	20	—	20.00	1.818	18.950
14	20	3.79	23.79	1.983	20.933
15	20	—	20.00	1.538	22.471
16	20	—	20.00	1.667	24.138
17	20	4.83	24.83	1.910	26.048
18	20	—	20.00	1.428	27.476
19	20	—	20.00	1.333	28.809
20	20	5.76	25.76	1.610	30.419
21	20	—	20.00	1.176	31.595
22	20	—	20.00	1.111	32.706
	$440	$20.27	$460.27	32.706	@$18 = $588.71

Dividend is $0.80 per share per year, $0.20 per quarter. Stock is bought at prices shown in preceding chart.

You can compound your earnings even more quickly by reinvesting dividends. The additional amount earned is small at first but grows to sizable sums as you continue to invest. Plus, when you take into consideration that many companies increase their dividends regularly, you begin to see the power of dividend reinvestment. If you look at column 3 of the chart, you can see how the amount earned increases at each dividend payment. In this case, the investor ended up with 32.706 shares in twenty-two months—about 1½ shares more than in the example in Figure 1-1.

with the expectation that they would continue to grow, and the companies are now many times the size they were when the clubs made their first purchases. The companies are AFLAC, McDonald's and RPM. Clubs started to buy McDonald's when it had a couple hundred stores; now it has thousands. Its stock price has multiplied many times. We have seen clubs' portfolios showing the cost per share of AFLAC at 75 cents. Recently it has sold as high as $45. Members have thousands of shares of RPM that they bought for 20 cents and that are now selling for $17. Members, of course, hold many other companies as well. The company whose growth is driven by management can produce tremendous results for the investor. NAIC's stock study procedures are designed to help you identify such companies.

In the technical approach, the goal is usually to catch fairly quick price moves. These moves are caused more often by conditions in the stock market itself than by the nature of the individual security, although there are technical procedures involving market factors concerning only one particular company. Usually profits of 20 to 50 percent are taken when they become available, and holding the stock for long-term growth is not contemplated. The result is that the first investors to start following a trend and the first to bail out reap the largest profits. The latest in and the slowest out make less or lose. (See Figure 1-3.)

A study performed by Dr. Jess H. Chua and Richard S. Woodward at the University of Calgary under the auspices of the Salomon Brothers Center for the Study of Financial Institutions found that individuals who followed short-term, technical techniques over a sixty-year test period had to be right 80 percent of the time to achieve the same results as the investor who bought good-quality growing companies, held them for long periods of time, and made few changes. Based on the experience of NAIC, this is the type of procedure that the great mass of individuals can learn, follow, and benefit from greatly.

The stock study program detailed in this book has proven beneficial to investors for half a century. If you resolve now to utilize the program consistently, your club will reap rewards as well.

CHAPTER 2

FINDING COMPANIES TO STUDY

In launching your investment program, your club's first challenge is identifying suitable stock candidates for purchase. Your plan is to invest in growth stocks. Remember the definition of a growth company: one whose earnings per share and sales are growing at a rate higher than that of the economy as a whole. With thousands of public companies available, where should you start?

FINDING GROWTH COMPANIES

Growth stems from management. While growth companies are normally found in growing industries, they are also located in stagnant and declining industry groups. Growth of sales and earnings happens to almost everyone in a growth industry and is not as reliable a factor in identifying a growth management as in other situations. When growth stops, there is a shakeout, and poorly managed companies go bankrupt.

When buying into companies in rapidly growing industries, try to select the best-managed companies within those industries. Usually those are the ones with the highest pre-tax profit margins and earnings on invested capital. While this is a logical method, it can be dangerous. Growth industries frequently attract many marginal performers that start strong but are destined to decline during periods of severe competition. Ordinarily, a shakeout period follows, where a third of the industry is lost or absorbed by the stronger units. Only after such a shakeout period does the ultimate leader emerge. All companies tend to have good figures in the first stage of a new industry.

A more practical approach is to look for companies, regardless of industry, where management has achieved a growth of 10 percent or more compounded annually. This method entails less risk, since your attention is focused on able management within one company rather than on a strong industry with ever-changing companies, the real leader of which might not yet be firmly established.

Each month, *Better Investing,* NAIC's own magazine, features a "Stock to Study," which has been selected because it appears to possess the potential to double in price within five years. Companies mentioned by columnists in the magazine may also prove worthy of investigation. Members of NAIC's Computer Group also receive *BITS.* It contains articles on individual companies, a monthly NAIC Growth Screen, and an annual "Superscreen" on the top 200 companies held by NAIC members.

USING BUSINESS PUBLICATIONS

Your reading of business and financial publications will bring to your attention companies that merit exploration. *The Wall Street Journal, Barron's, Business Week, Fortune,* and *Forbes* are among the helpful sources.

Many advisory services are dedicated to the monitoring of stocks with prospects of growing value. NAIC's own Investor Advisory Service has an outstanding record. It presents Stock Selection Guides and comments on three growth stocks each month. Two other services are *Growth Stock Outlook,* published by Charles Allmon, and Standard & Poor's *The Outlook,* which highlights 200 fast-growing companies each month. Both may be available at your local library. Members with computers may access the NAIC website, the NAIC Forum on CompuServe, or the SEC's EDGAR database. In addition, NAIC Software offers a database with frequent updates on 3,500 publicly held companies, including those that are most popular among long-term investors.

Don't overlook the importance of "backyard" investment opportunities. Local companies featured in your own community's paper could offer outstanding potential not yet recognized by the world at large.

Your broker or other business acquaintances, including suppliers and customers, and your friends who work in different industries in your own and other areas can offer suggestions worth pursuing.

PUT IDEAS TO THE NAIC TEST

The source of an idea is not important; how you react to it is crucial. No purchase should be made at any time without formal analysis. Logical thought, not raw emotion, leads to success in the market. A great story does not produce a profitable investment. There has to be a management capable of producing growing earnings per share.

A mistake frequently made by new and inexperienced clubs is concentrating on so-called cheap stocks—those selling at a low price per share. Members deem it advantageous to own more shares for their monthly contributions. Of course, stocks may or may not be "cheap" at any price; it depends on what you're getting for your money. From the very beginning of your investment activity, emphasize the purchase of quality stocks at a reasonable price.

In performing your analysis of stocks, you'll be using the NAIC tools described later in this book. It's also important to obtain a copy of each company's annual report to review as a prospective stockholder. The next chapter tells you how.

THE NAIC LOW-COST INVESTMENT PLAN

NAIC offers a valuable service to its members, enabling them to reinvest earnings and additional funds in additional partial shares of stock with little or no expense—a feature critical to success if your club intends to follow the reinvestment recommendation. To learn the details of this program, contact NAIC and the information forwarded will be accompanied by a complete list of companies in the program. The current list of NAIC Low-Cost Investment Plan companies is also found in *Better Investing* each month.

Under the program, you pay NAIC a one-time $7 charge for each stock purchased, to meet set-up and handling expenses. Some companies charge a small fee for each purchase you make, but most do not—every dollar goes to the purchase of shares. Certain companies even sell you stock at a discount from market or reinvest your dividends at a discount. Once your initial purchase is received by NAIC, you will receive the Plan prospectus with full details of the cost associated with each company. You can make changes or terminate the program at any time.

There are three advantages to investing in one or more of the dozens of companies comprising NAIC's Low-Cost Investment Plan:

Figure 2-1
Results from NAIC's Low-Cost Investment Plan

Time Period	Amount Invested at $100/Quarter	Dividends Received	*Total of Shares*	
			Bought	Now Owned
1st Q	$ 122.07	$ 0.27	6.2470	6.2470
2d Q	100.00	1.69	5.7582	11.9852
3d Q	100.00	3.24	6.5177	18.5029
4th Q	100.00	5.00	6.9399	25.4428
2d year	400.00	41.02	22.1677	47.6105
3d–5th years	1,200.00	307.16	58.4990	106.1095
6th–10th years	2,000.00	1,176.97	81.9142	188.0237
Totals	$4,022.07	$1,535.35	188.0237	188.0237

NAIC's unique Low-Cost Investment Plan is perfect for a new club that doesn't want to spend lots of money in transaction fees. With only a $7 set-up fee, your club will show a profit more quickly. The initial purchase of one share was $22.07. At the end of five years, the stock was selling at $32 and the portfolio value amounted to $3,395.50 on an investment of $2,022.07. After ten years, the stock price was $52.50, for a value of $9,871.24 on an investment of $4,022.07.

1. Information on all Plan companies is readily available for your investment analysis.

2. As a Plan participant, you will be following NAIC's proven philosophy by investing a set amount regularly, reinvesting your dividends, and buying into companies with characteristics suggesting that they can be worth substantially more five years in the future.

3. The low costs associated with the Plan will permit your club to show a profit more quickly than if your club, rather than the company, were paying the commissions. NAIC has joined the dividend reinvestment programs of a number of corporations. You pick the company in which you wish to invest. Send your money to NAIC. Once your initial purchase is registered, you'll send future investments directly to the corporation's transfer agent.

You will be surprised at how quickly your monthly payments and reinvested dividends grow into sizable holdings of the stocks you have selected. Figure 2-1 shows what would have happened had you elected to invest $100 per quarter for the last ten years in one Plan company. The initial dividend was 27 cents quarterly, and it increased five times, to 43 cents quarterly by the end of the decade of investing.

CHAPTER 3

ANNUAL REPORTS: THE BALANCE SHEET

*T*he annual report constitutes an essential piece of information concerning any company. Typically, the report includes financial highlights for two years, although tables of financial statistics may cover ten or more years of performance. The more years presented, the more easily you can spot and follow financial trends.

The annual report inevitably includes the President's "Message to Stockholders," which reviews the past year and looks ahead to the next. Financial statements are always included, along with an independent auditing firm's certification. Financial statements include a balance sheet and income statement, as well as a statement of cash flows. Reports usually also include narrative sections focusing on different product lines, research activities, foreign operations, and other subjects of interest to would-be and current owners of the business, often accompanied by photographs.

You may not derive much meaning from the financial statements when you begin analyzing them because of the terminology barrier. What is a "current ratio?" What does "shareholders' equity" mean? We'll help you clear this hurdle in the next few chapters as we explain basic financial terms every investor should know. You'll discover that all you need to put these ratios and terms to good use is simple arithmetic. You'll even discover that many companies have done at least some of the calculations for you, offering key ratios for your immediate interpretation.

BALANCE SHEET TERMINOLOGY

The balance sheet reports the financial condition of a company at a specific point in time. You can evaluate the company's solvency, or ability to meet its debts, by studying the balance sheet.

Assets are properties and accounts owned by the company, while liabilities are the debts and claims against the company. The difference between assets and liabilities is called shareholders' equity. The balance sheet is so named because it shows the two sides of the company's condition. On one side are the assets; on the other are liabilities and shareholders' equity. The two sides are always equal in total value:

$$Assets = Liabilities + Shareholders' Equity$$

Shown in Figure 3-1 is the balance sheet for a (fictitious) firm, Manic Manufacturing Company, as of December 31, 199X. Let's look more closely at the meaning of the key terms found on this balance sheet and the relationship of various entries.

Current assets constitute assets owned by the company that can be converted into cash within a year. They will not necessarily be converted; the word "current" defines these assets as "liquid," or readily available. Current assets are listed in the order of their "closeness to cash," meaning ease of convertibility. Since "cash" is immediately available for use, it ranks first. In this example, cash on hand and in the bank equals $4,500,000.

Accounts receivable is the sum of accounts due from customers for goods already sold. Practically all business transactions are conducted on a credit basis, with payment due at the end of thirty or sixty days. On occasion, the company encounters slow payers; in some instances, accounts prove to be uncollectible. For this reason, companies establish a reserve for bad debts. The amount of accounts receivable shown on the statement represents the amount due from customers minus the reserve for bad debts. Manic's accounts receivable balance is $6,750,000.

Inventories are the balances of materials at various stages of manufacture: raw materials, work in process, and finished goods. Inventory balances are considered current assets on the theory that, on average, they will be sold, or

Figure 3-1

Manic Manufacturing Company Balance Sheet,
December 31, 199X

CURRENT ASSETS

Cash	$4,500,000
Accounts receivable—less	
allowance for doubtful assets	6,750,000
Inventories	22,500,000
Total current assets	$33,750,000

PROPERTY, PLANT, AND EQUIPMENT

Cost	$40,000,000	
Accumulated depreciation	7,300,000	
Net property		32,700,000
Total assets		$66,450,000

CURRENT LIABILITIES

Accounts payable	$3,000,000
Accrued taxes	2,000,000
Accrued wages, interest, and other expense	1,225,000
Total current liabilities	$6,225,000

LONG-TERM DEBT

Mortgage bonds	$12,000,000	
Debentures	6,000,000	
Total long-term debt		$18,000,000

SHAREHOLDERS' EQUITY

Preferred stock, 100,000 shares,	
$100 par value	$10,000,000
Common stock, 6,750,000 shares,	
no par value	20,000,000
Amounts contributed above stated value	
(arising from sale of stock)	7,000,000
Retained earnings	5,225,000
Total shareholders' equity	$42,225,000
Total liabilities and shareholders' equity	$66,450,000

"turned over," within one year or less. Inventory balances will not be converted into cash until the goods are sold and the resulting receivables are collected. Being furthest from cash, inventories rank last in the list of current assets.

     Companies usually value their inventories at cost or market value, usually using the lower of the two figures or values suggested by their auditors with the intent of presenting an inventory value that is consistent, conservative, and in line with economic facts as well as with tax law. Manic values its inventories at $22,500,000.

In some cases (although not in this example), companies list securities among their assets. Some companies invest surplus cash in short-term government bonds and other investments. Since these holdings are closer to cash than either accounts receivable or inventories, securities follow cash in the ranking of current assets and are normally reported at their cost value. An accountant's note will show the other value if any adjustments are made to the cost of securities.

The terms *fixed assets, long-term assets,* and *property, plant, and equipment* are used interchangeably. These are capital assets owned by the company that are expected to be employed on a continuing basis and not converted into cash within a year. Included are land, buildings, office equipment, production machinery, delivery trucks, and other long-term assets.

Except for land, all fixed assets are depreciated over a prescribed recovery period set by tax law. Depreciation is a means of writing off expensive capital assets over a period of years. It is reported by way of a reserve for depreciation. This appears as a reduction to capital asset values on the balance sheet, so that the final amount shown is the net value of assets minus accumulated depreciation. For example, if a machine is purchased for $1,000,000 and is subject to depreciation over a period of seven years, a portion is deducted from the value each year for depreciation until the full purchase price is deducted.

For some types of assets, companies are allowed to deduct a higher amount in the first few years and less later on. Companies also have the option to claim the same amount of depreciation each year—*straight-line depreciation.* For example, suppose that some machinery a company bought cost $140,000 and has a recovery period of seven years. Applying the straight-line method, the company would be allowed to deduct one seventh of the cost, or $20,000, each year. At the end of seven years, the asset will be fully depreciated and its book value will be zero.

If and when the company sells that equipment, it has to "recapture" the depreciation it paid. That means it will have to pay tax on its profits. Since the book value is zero after the equipment is fully depreciated, the sales price of the fully depreciated machinery in the example above would be fully taxable—at capital gains rates. For example, let's say the company sells the machinery after it's fully depreciated for $90,000:

Cost	$140,000
Less: depreciation	−140,000
Book value	$ 0
Sales price	$ 90,000
Taxable profit	$ 90,000

Manic values its property, plant, and equipment at cost ($40,000,000) minus accumulated depreciation ($7,300,000), resulting in a net property value of $32,700,000.

Depletion is a term you'll encounter on some balance sheets. It is similar to depreciation, but recognizes the exhaustion of a natural resource. Lumber companies set up depletion accounts for their timberlands, and oil companies claim accumulated depletion on their oil reserves.

By combining the total current assets and net property of Manic, we find the company's total assets to be $66,450,000.

LOOKING AT LIABILITIES

Let's look now at the other side of the balance sheet: liabilities and stockholders' equity.

Current liabilities include debts that come due within one year. That includes the next twelve payments on any long-term loan. Mortgages or debentures are usually payable periodically over a number of years. Payments due in the coming year are considered current.

Accounts payable are those accounts owed by the company to its creditors. Manic states its indebtedness as $3,000,000 for materials, supplies, and services. If the firm owed money to a bank or other lender that would fall due within a year, this sum would be shown under the heading "Current portion of long-term debt."

Accrued taxes, which in Manic's case come to $2,000,000, represent the sum the company estimates it owes for taxes for the past year, including federal, state, and local income taxes; personal property taxes; real estate taxes; and all others.

Accrued wages, interest, and other expense is the account showing the current balance of money owed by the company to its employees, interest on money borrowed from bondholders and banks, contributions due to the company's pension plan, and other debts that must be paid within a year. For Manic, the total in this category is $1,225,000.

Taken together, all of the debts Manic must pay within the next twelve months—the current liabilities—come to $6,225,000.

Manic has two types of bonds outstanding. First, there are *mortgage bonds,* which represent debt secured by company property. These amount to $12,000,000. The second are *debentures.* Investors buy these unsecured bonds based on the company's general credit and reputation. The company has issued debentures totaling $6,000,000. Total long-term debt, the amount due beyond the coming year, amounts to $18,000,000.

EQUITY: THE OWNERSHIP OF THE COMPANY

Next we review the shareholders' equity section of the balance sheet, which represents the ownership of the company.

Manic has issued two types of stock: preferred stock and common stock. Manic has 100,000 shares of preferred stock outstanding. Holders of these shares, which have a par value (the price at which they were sold) of $10,000,000 have prior claim over common shareholders to both dividends and assets. This means that, if the earnings of Manic are insufficient to pay anticipated dividends to both preferred and common holders, the preferred stockholders will get their due and the common holders will receive less than expected, or nothing. In the event that the company files bankruptcy, preferred stockholders get paid first and common stockholders come last—if there's enough left over for them.

Both classes—preferred and common shareholders—are owners of the company. By contrast, holders of bonds are creditors. Interest payments to the bondholders must be met before even preferred holders receive dividends; and if Manic should go out of business, all claims of the bondholders would have to be met before the shareholders would be entitled to any payment.

You can see the difference between bondholders and stockholders: When investors buy bonds in a company such as Manic, they are lending money to the company. They are paid interest and, when the bond becomes due, they will get their principal back as well. When a bond is secured by mortgages on property or by other collateral, the bond investor is reasonably sure of getting his or her money back. Debentures pay higher interest because they are unsecured—so the investor's risks are greater.

Stockholders are not lenders; they are owners of the corporation. Capital stock, whether common or preferred, represents the sum total of assets less liabilities. Preferred stockholders have priority for dividends and claims on assets, but common stock share prices are where the real action is, especially for growth companies. Together, the debt investors in the company (lenders) and the stock investors (shareholders) hold the company's total capitalization. Most companies are capitalized, or funded, by a combination of debt and equity.

In Manic's case, the outstanding 6,750,000 shares of common stock are valued on the company books at $20,000,000. This sum may have little or no relationship to the market value of the stock, or even to the amount of money the holders of the shares would receive if the company is dissolved. It's just the value that was originally assigned to the capital stock of common shares when the company was first organized.

Two types of surplus are listed by Manic. The first is *capital surplus,* which might also be called *paid-in surplus,* listed at $7,000,000. This means that the first stock was sold for $7,000,000 more than had been assigned to it in the incorporation process. In this case, the stock brought in $27,000,000 when it was sold. It had been assigned a value of $20,000,000, so the extra $7,000,000 becomes capital surplus. Adding together the stated value of the common stock and capital surplus, we obtain $27,000,000. Dividing the number of common shares—6,750,000—into this amount, we find that the company received an average of $4.00 net per share for the common stock when it was sold.

The other type of surplus is *retained earnings,* which may also be called *earned surplus.* This is the sum total of each year's net income from operations that the company has retained for the growth of the business rather than paid out to shareholders as dividends. Of course, these retained earnings belong to the shareholders whether or not they are paid out. Some corporations try to keep some (or most) of their retained earnings as working capital to fund expansion.

There are other balance sheet items you may encounter. *Prepaid expenses* or *deferred charges* refer to bills the company has paid in advance. This means some expenses were paid before they were incurred, so they cannot properly be put into the books. For example, just before the end of the year, a corporation pays $27,000 representing facilities rent for the first month of the following year. That payment should be included in next year's expenses, so it will be set up as a prepaid expense or deferred charge. These accounts are also used to amortize expenses paid in one month but applicable over a longer period. For example, a corporation pays for thirty-six months of insurance in a single payment. It sets up the payment as a prepaid expense and amortizes (or writes down to general expenses) one thirty-sixth of the payment each month.

Some companies list *intangible assets,* such as goodwill. While such assets have value, it's clearly difficult to quantify. For example, suppose a corporation purchases a competitor and, as part of the negotiation, agrees to pay $50,000 for goodwill—an admittedly arbitrary value assigned to the company's reputation and the value of name recognition. Because this is clearly an asset, it is entered as such. However, it has no physical value, so it is classified as an intangible asset.

On the liability side, take a good look at *reserves for contingencies.* It could be important to understand more about goodwill and contingencies if these are significant amounts. A contingent liability is a debt or claim that might or might not materialize. Depending on the industry, companies may set up reserves for such contingencies. For example, a company might know that a lawsuit is pending against it. In the event of a loss, or to set aside some funds for legal defense, a contingency reserve is set up and shown as a liability.

CHAPTER 4

ANALYZING THE BALANCE SHEET

*T*he balance sheet supplies you with a wealth of information about the company whose stock you are thinking of buying. But, as with anything else, you need to know what to look for.

First, let's check the *working capital* of the company, the amount of money available for use in its current operations. Working capital is derived by subtracting current liabilities from current assets; Manic Manufacturing has working capital of $27,525,000. This seems to be an amount sufficient to permit the company to stay out of financial difficulty if business falls off for a period, and enough to take advantage of any opportunities that require ready cash. Working capital is the lifeblood of the company. It's needed to make payroll; to pay and remain current on taxes, rents, notes and interest payments, and mortgages; and for the purchase of raw materials. With working capital problems, a company will not be able to sustain itself—and that means it won't make money, either.

Now we turn to the *current ratio,* or the current assets divided by the current liabilities. Manic's ratio is better than 5.4 to 1. About 2 to 1 is typical of manufacturing companies; among those whose inventories are subject to wide price fluctuations, a higher current ratio is desirable. A ratio of less than 2 to 1 is a danger sign. Such a company could run short of working capital in meeting its near-term cash requirements. However, a ratio far in excess of 2 to 1, as is true with Manic, is not necessarily a plus. This may indicate that the company is not employing its cash to full advantage in income-producing assets.

While a ratio of 2 to 1 is normal for manufacturing, utilities often operate successfully with current ratios of 1 to 1 or even less. If the company carries no inventories—for example, a nonmanufacturing concern—a current ratio of 1 to 1 is normally considered an acceptable standard.

You should track the current ratio of the company you are examining back a few years. Also, plan to keep an eye on this in the future. Look for changes in the current ratio trend to ensure that management is remaining fiscally responsible in controlling cash flow. Also, see how your candidate compares with its competitors, companies in the same industry. If the current ratio for your candidate seems out of line with those of its competitors, you might question it.

Another ratio is the acid test, also called the quick assets ratio. This is found by dividing current assets (excluding inventories) by current liabilities. The acid test more realistically evaluates the ability of some companies to meet current debts. This might be especially important for corporations that keep an inventory of high-priced items, where conversion to cash might not be readily possible, or when a company's inventory seems exceptionally high. Manic's acid test ratio stands at 1.8 to 1. Thus, we can see that about two thirds of the firm's current assets are tied up in inventories, and its ability to meet current cash needs seems reasonable.

Track the acid test ratio over a period of years and compare it with the ratios of competitive firms. A large inventory position may cause losses if materials prices drop. That would mean the company purchased its materials at a higher rate than current market value, which certainly affects its profit margin. An overly large inventory may show that the company has a considerable amount of unsalable merchandise or that it has overinvested working capital in materials.

TURNOVER

One important test of inventory position is *inventory turnover,* which is determined by dividing cost of goods sold (from the income statement, discussed in Chapter 5) by average inventory at cost. If the average inventory figure is unavailable, you can use the ending inventory figure shown on the balance sheet. You may compute an average by adding together the company's beginning and ending inventory and dividing by 2. If inventory levels are fairly consistent, this is dependable. However, if seasonal fluctuations are wide, this method could distort the true picture.

Manic has an inventory of $22,500,000; its cost of goods sold is $45,000,000 (see Chapter 5 for Manic's income statement). Thus, the inventory turnover is precisely two times. This ratio shows, on average, how many times during the period the inventory is entirely sold and replaced. In reality, of course, the warehouse isn't emptied out and restocked. Like all aspects of financial analysis, the turnover ratio is an estimate. The higher the turnover, the better. It is an indication of both quality merchandise and proper pricing. You might want to check whether the company you are analyzing is improving its inventory turnover, and how it stacks up with its competitors in this respect. Some industries, such as foods, are characterized by high turnover levels; others, such as tobacco, characteristically have low inventory turnover.

Another figure worth computing is *plant turnover,* or sales (from the income statement) divided by property, plant, and equipment. In the case of Manic, this is $67,500,000 divided by $40,000,000, so plant turnover amounts to about 1.7 times.

The higher this ratio, the better, and we would like to see it increase over time. If the company expands its plant without corresponding growth in sales, there is clearly a problem with asset utilization.

BOOK VALUE

Another useful figure is the *book value* of the common stock. To find it, add the par or stated value of common stock to retained earnings and any surplus reserves. (As noted earlier, companies occasionally earmark part of their retained earnings for contingencies or other purposes.) For Manic, we add the $20,000,000 stated value of common stock, $7,000,000 capital surplus, and $5,225,000 in retained earnings to derive a book value for the common stock of $32,225,000. We'll use this figure in a computation in the next chapter. Keep in mind that book value has no direct relationship to market value; the shares of well-regarded companies with rising sales and earnings may sell at many times their book value, while other firms with lackluster results may actually sell at a discount to book.

One other item to review is the capital structure of the company, or what proportion is represented by each component of capitalization—bonds, preferred stock, and common stock. A high proportion of bonds may make both forms of stock less attractive, while a sizable amount of preferred stock could make the common stock less appealing.

The *bond ratio* is found by dividing the face value of bonds by the total value of bonds, preferred stock, common stock, capital surplus, and retained earnings. In Manic's case, $18,000,000 divided by $60,225,000 shows that bonds constitute about 30 percent of total capitalization.

The *preferred stock ratio* results from dividing the stated value of the preferred stock by the total value of bonds, preferred and common stock, capital surplus, and retained earnings. For Manic, we divide $10,000,000 by $60,225,000 and determine that the preferred stock ratio is about 16.5 percent.

To calculate the *common stock ratio,* divide the stated value of common stock plus capital surplus and retained earnings by total capitalization, or $32,225,000 divided by $60,225,000. Common stock represents about 53.5 percent of total capitalization.

In general, an industrial company should have no more than half of its capitalization represented by *senior securities*—bonds and preferred stock. Senior securities are so called because in the event of bankruptcy, bonds and preferred stocks are senior; holders of these investments will be paid before investors in common stocks.

It is also considered desirable for no more than one quarter of total capitalization to be represented by bonds. Manic meets the senior securities test, but its bond ratio of 30 percent is a bit higher than the standard.

Utilities typically carry a much higher load of debt and preferred to total capital ratio—up to 70 or 75 percent—and can do so successfully because of their relative stability of earnings. For this reason, though, such industries are said to be interest sensitive. Because they are so heavily capitalized by debt, their earnings are adversely affected when interest rates rise.

LEVERAGE

A company with a high ratio of bonds and preferred stock is said to be highly leveraged. Leverage may or may not be an advantage to common stockholders, depending on the success of the company in utilizing other forms of securities to enhance earnings.

As an example, consider ABC Company, which has long-term debt or bonds outstanding in the amount of $50,000. The company pays interest of 5 percent, or $2,500 per year. Shareholders' equity in the company totals $100,000. The total capital structure amounts to $150,000. The interest charge on the bonds does not vary; as income increases, more money will go to the value of common stock. However, when income falls, the portion available to stockholders will drop. Here is how leverage can impact stockholders in a good year and in a bad year (Figure 4-1).

The company earned $15,000 in the good year, but just $6,500 in the bad year. In the good year, after paying bond interest of $2,500, ABC has a net profit after taxes of $12,500. The rate on long-term debt is 5 percent. The rate of return on the total capital structure is 10 percent, and the rate of return on shareholders' equity is 12.5 percent. The additional return to the stockholders through use by the company of money borrowed is 2.5 percent, or the difference between earnings on stockholder money and earnings on total capital structure.

But what about a bad year? What if net after interest payment had amounted to just $4,000? In this scenario, the rate on long-term debt remains at 5 percent. The rate of return on the total capital structure stands at 4.3 percent, but the rate of return on shareholders' equity is only 4 percent. Thus, the owners of the company would have fared better had no bonds been outstanding.

If the company you are analyzing is leveraged, check to see whether the return on equity is higher than the return on total capital structure. Look for

Figure 4-1
Impact of a Good versus a Bad Year on ABC's Leverage

Capitalization	Rate of Return	
	Good Year	Bad Year
Long-term debt $50,000 at 5% interest	$2,500 or 5%	$2,500 or 5%
Shareholders' equity $100,000	$12,500 or 12.5%	$4,000 or 4%
Capital structure $150,000	$15,000 or 10%	$6,500 or 4.3%

Debt has the effect of magnifying a company's performance and shareholder profit. In a good year, debt actually benefits the shareholder. Once the long-term debt at a rate of 5 percent is paid off, the shareholder receives a very good 12.5 percent return. However, in a bad year, the long-term debt must be paid off at the same rate of 5 percent, and the shareholder receives only a 4.3 percent return.

a trend rather than analyzing one year in isolation. If equity tends to be higher, then shareholders are benefiting. If not, the shareholders would be better off if the company had no debt.

Now that you are familiar with the essentials of the balance sheet, we will turn our attention to another key financial report: the income statement.

CHAPTER 5

ANNUAL REPORTS: THE INCOME STATEMENT

While the balance sheet depicts a company's solvency or financial position at a specific date, its income statement, also called a *profit and loss statement,* reports income, costs, expenses, and profits (or losses) over a period, usually one full year. The income statement, considered along with the balance sheet, is of crucial importance to stockholders—and to you and your club, if you are considering becoming stockholders.

INCOME STATEMENT TERMINOLOGY

The first item on Manic's income statement (Figure 5-1) is net sales of $67,500,000; this is money collected for all goods sold by the company (gross sales) minus returns and allowances. If you are studying such nonmanufacturing companies as utilities or transportation concerns, the term *revenues* corresponds to sales.

The first deduction from sales is *cost of goods sold,* also termed *cost of sales.* (A utility or insurance company might refer to this as *operating expenses.*) Subtracted here is all $45,000,000 in costs attributable to units produced by the company during the period being reported. It includes wages of production workers, costs of raw materials used in production, and expenditures for elec-

Figure 5-1
Manic Manufacturing Company Income Statement
for the Year Ending December 31, 199X

Net sales	$67,500,000
Cost of sales	45,000,000
Gross profit	$22,500,000
Selling, general, and administrative expenses	15,000,000
Operating profit	$ 7,500,000
Other income	900,000
	$ 8,400,000
Other expenses	945,000
Net income before taxes	$ 7,455,000
Provisions for federal income taxes	3,877,500
Net income after taxes	$ 3,577,500

tricity required to keep production lines moving. Another item in this cost is the change in inventory levels.

Subtracting cost of sales from sales, we arrive at Manic's gross profit of $22,500,000. Next, *selling, general, and administrative expenses,* or *nonmanufacturing costs,* of $15,000,000 are subtracted. These include executive compensation, sales commissions, and staff department outlays—including legal, rent, office supplies, advertising, and public relations expenses.

Deducting these items from gross profit results in an operating profit of $7,500,000. This is the amount Manic made from the manufacture and sale of its products.

The next line (not shown in Manic's statement) is *nonoperating income.*

OTHER INCOME

Manic's *other income* of $900,000 includes sources of income beyond the primary business. For example, here the company reports interest and dividends on securities owned, royalties on patents, profits on foreign exchange, and other such items.

The total of operating profit plus other income for Manic is $8,400,000. Next, *other expenses* are deducted. This amount is $945,000 and could include expenses such as interest paid on the company's mortgage and debenture bonds, settlements of lawsuits, and losses on foreign exchange.

Manic's *net income before taxes* is $7,455,000. After the deduction of $3,877,500 in federal taxes, net income amounts to $3,577,500. The company may declare and pay out dividends to preferred and common shareholders, and add the remainder to retained earnings.

ANALYZING THE INCOME STATEMENT

One of the most important relationships that can be determined from the income statement is *pre-tax profit margin,* arrived at by dividing profit before taxes by net sales. Manic's pre-tax profit margin is 11 percent (7,455,000/ 67,500,000).

What does this mean? If you examine the pre-tax profit margin of a company over a period of years, you can learn whether it is rising or falling. It does not have to rise consistently, but the company should be able to achieve the maximum practical pre-tax profit margin for the industry, year after year. Each industry has natural limitations on the percentage it can achieve, so it is always worthwhile to compare your target company's statements with those of its competitors. Look for a trend over many years. If the company has been able to produce consistent profits at the peak levels for the industry, that's a sign the corporation is well managed.

Do not use net (after taxes) profit margin as your basis of comparison. Taxes fluctuate for different companies from year to year, and this variation makes such a comparison less meaningful. In addition, state income taxes distort any such comparison. A company with its major operations in a state with a relatively high income tax should not be compared on an after-tax basis with a company operating in a state assessing a lower income tax.

The other important computation to be made from the income statement is *return on book value,* or *return on equity.* As you learned in examining the balance sheet, the book value of Manic common stock is $32,225,000. Dividing the company's net income of $3,577,500 by this figure, we obtain 11 percent. That means that, collectively, the stockholders earned 11 percent on their money.

Whether this result is favorable depends on Manic's trend over time; as with the pre-tax profit margin, look for consistency rather than ever-growing returns. Don't unrealistically expect that a company is a worthwhile invest-ment only if such results improve every year.

Also review how return on equity compares with that of other companies in the same industry. Any company you are considering should be at least av-erage or above in this regard with respect to similar companies in the same in-dustry, as an indication of average or superior management.

Another figure of interest is *sales per employee.* Typically, the annual report lists the number of employees. If it doesn't, call the investor relations depart-ment and ask. Then compare the productivity of the company over time with the results of other companies in the same industry. The higher the ratio be-tween sales and employees, the more efficiently the company is operating. Be aware, however, that these ratios will vary considerably by industry. An in-dustry that is more labor intensive, such as a manufacturing concern, will not be comparable to one that is less dependent on labor for its product or service.

EVALUATING MANAGEMENT

From examining the balance sheet and income statement, you already know something about the firm's management. Pre-tax profit margin and return on equity are two of the best statistical measures of managerial efficiency. What else can the annual report and other corporate publications reveal concerning management? Do not follow the example of the club member who wanted to buy a company's shares because the chief executive officer looked good! Far too many folks are overly impressed by expensively produced reports with good design and lots of color, not to mention Robert Redford look-alikes smiling at the reader. Remember that companies spend a lot of money pro-ducing annual reports. They are not going to report gloomy news or use poor-quality photographs, and they are not going to show you a picture of a depressed, unhappy president. The annual report is very much a public rela-tions document. But it also includes full financial disclosures, and that is why it is valuable to you.

Take a logical approach in studying the information available to you. If you were a professional analyst, you could get answers to specific questions and gain definite impressions about company leadership from face-to-face meetings. Although such an opportunity is likely to be closed to you, there are still conclusions to be drawn. (Incidentally, the brokerage firm your club uses probably publishes reports prepared by their own professional analysts or analytical department on companies you are interested in. Be sure to ask whether they have a report on the company you are reviewing.)

What can you ask on your own? First, what is the age composition of the top officer cadre? If ages aren't furnished, you can find them in *Standard & Poor's Register of Directors and Executives.* There should be a mix of ages, representing a combination of experience and new thinking. Too many senior citizens may mean less drive, just as an abundance of young men and women may signal insufficient seasoning in the crucible of depressed economic conditions.

Check the names of leaders, and be wary if several appear to be members of the same family. When nepotism is being practiced, make sure the management figures meet our previously mentioned tests.

What is the size of executive compensation? The corporate proxy statement should provide this information, but often it's difficult to identify with precision. The increasing complexity of executive pay options—different types, paid out at varying times—adds to the confusion. Fortunately, you can access other sources to find reasonable approximations, if not exactly accurate data. *The Wall Street Journal, Business Week,* and *Fortune* conduct surveys. A chief executive's remuneration should be in line with the size of the company and the profits attained. Check the degree of correlation between pay and performance.

What is the stock ownership of the top executive group? Here again, the proxy statement is the source of this information. A substantial number of shares in management's hands generally provides evidence of their confidence in the company's future. What about the board of directors? The board should have a majority of outsiders whose principal occupations and reputations indicate that they can make a real contribution to the company's results.

For further information on management, consult those who know the company best: its employees, suppliers, customers, stockholders, and direct competitors. Their attitudes should be factored into your decision making.

Do not overlook the notes in any annual report you review. Although customarily set in small type, these dull-appearing sentences contain important information about litigation, unusual liabilities, new pension or stock option plans, and other news you won't find elsewhere. Check the auditor's opinion to determine if there is routine approval or only a qualified endorsement. If the latter, the reason for any reservations is important, and you need to inquire further.

To summarize, always review income statement information in comparative form. How does this year look compared with last year? With five years ago? Dynamic information is always more revealing than the static profit and loss report, which is revealing only to the extent that it shows the latest entry in a trend.

You now know the essentials of annual report study. You may obtain an annual report on any publicly held company free of charge by calling the company's shareowner relations executive, listed in the Standard & Poor's or Value Line Survey corporate reports. A growing number of publicly traded companies also offer both their quarterly and annual reports to investors online through their websites. A call to the corporation will give you their location on the Internet.

CHAPTER 6

THE NAIC TOOLS FOR SMART INVESTING

*T*he stock study program of the National Association of Investors Corporation embraces five essential tools that will help you to make informed decisions about your portfolio. These tools will be explained in detail in the following seven chapters.

You will get an overview of the program in this brief introduction. You'll learn what each tool looks like, the reason for its use, what it includes, when it should be used, and when it should be updated.

In investing, you have three basic tasks:

1. To judge a company's potential value by studying its record
2. To compare several companies and select for investment the one that most nearly meets your objective
3. To stay current on stocks you own so that you can make good decisions concerning whether to purchase additional shares, hold, or sell

STOCK CHECK LIST

The simplest of NAIC's forms is the *Stock Check List.* Even the inexperienced club member can put this to good use immediately. The Stock Check List allows you to pursue the first of the three basic tasks of investing—recording and reviewing a company's sales and earnings record as well as its price history. From this data, you can decide whether the stock is a suitable candidate for purchase now or whether it might be a good choice in the future.

STOCK SELECTION GUIDE AND REPORT

The Stock Check List does not provide a thorough analysis. It is designed for use only until you have learned how to use the more sophisticated *Stock Selection Guide and Report.* Typically, you should be using this within six months of starting your investment club.

Like the Check List, the Stock Selection Guide and Report (SSG) addresses the first basic task of investing. The SSG helps you to learn facts about a company's past, take a look at how it is doing in the present, and form a judgment about its likely value in the future. The SSG ranks as the single most important guide for individual and club members. It should be completed before you purchase any security, and it should be updated annually as long as the stock is held.

The Stock Selection Guide comprises five different sections. In Section 1, *the Visual Analysis of Sales, Earnings, and Price,* you record sales, earnings, and price figures for the past ten years. This produces trend lines that show you quickly whether you have a stock worth further study. Looking at the trend lines also helps you project future earnings.

Section 2 concerns management. Management is evaluated on the basis of two factors: (1) the sales and earnings per share trend lines and (2) the pretax profit margin and return on shareholders' equity. You will remember these concepts from Chapter 5.

In Section 3 you record the last five years' high and low prices, earnings per share, high and low price/earnings ratios, dividend payout, and yield figures, which enable you to make estimates of the future.

In Section 4 you adjust these figures based on the knowledge you have developed and then estimate future price action.

In Section 5 you check whether the results you have estimated enable you to reach your goal.

STOCK COMPARISON GUIDE

The *Stock Comparison Guide* (SCG) addresses the second basic task of investing. When your club reviews several different investment opportunities, this tool helps you make an informed decision on which stock, if any, should be purchased.

The SCG lets you review quickly and easily the important differences in the same data on several companies. All of the figures needed are already available to you from the Stock Selection Guide.

There are four sections to the SCG: *Growth Comparisons, Management Comparisons, Price Comparisons,* and *Other Comparisons.* The more similar the businesses of the companies being studied, the more meaningful the SCG becomes.

PORTFOLIO MANAGEMENT GUIDE

The Portfolio Management Guide and the *Portfolio Evaluation Review Technique* (PERT) are the two NAIC forms devoted to the third basic task of investing—staying current on the stocks you already own. As your club grows older and the size of your portfolio expands, portfolio management becomes increasingly significant.

The Portfolio Management Guide is a memory jogger that requires you to record the stock's price every month. NAIC recommends that you also compare the current price with previously established price zones on a monthly basis.

Section 1 records price/earnings zones, Section 2 is devoted to price zones, and Section 3 permits you to record current price and price/earnings ratios. Section 4 lets you place the same information in a chart for easier review.

If you review each of your stocks in the Guide at each meeting, you are unlikely to miss opportunities to add to your holdings at favorable prices.

PORTFOLIO EVALUATION REVIEW TECHNIQUE

The Portfolio Evaluation Review Technique (PERT) consists of a form and two worksheets. The form allows you to record quarterly and annual change rates in earnings per share and to calculate the current price/earnings (P/E) ratio and compare it with historical P/Es. Worksheet A lets you register the percent change in earnings per share, pre-tax profit, and sales on a quarterly and an annual basis. Worksheet B is concerned with price, price/earnings ratios, and dividend and yield information on a yearly basis.

There is a PERT report to be updated and reviewed at each monthly meeting.

Is all of this overwhelming? It may look formidable to the beginner, but after a few times you and your fellow club members will be surprised at how easily and quickly the forms can be completed. Your skills at interpretation will improve rapidly.

In NAIC's 1991 survey of member clubs, 61.9 percent were found to have equaled or bettered the S&P 500 over their lifetimes (averaging nearly 10 years). In contrast, only 19 percent of the professional managers at equity mutual funds outperformed the S&P over the same time.

Regular use of NAIC tools will permit you and other members of your club to make the best possible investment decisions and significantly enhance your prospects for profitability.

The next seven chapters discuss how to go about putting the tools to use in your club.

CHAPTER 7

THE STOCK CHECK LIST

*T*he NAIC *Stock Check List* is designed to help you complete a basic stock analysis. After completing the form, you will know the recent history of sales and earnings per share and whether the stock's current price makes it a good buy.

The Check List is not meant to provide a thorough, detailed analysis. Rather, the form serves as "training wheels" for using the more detailed NAIC Stock Selection Guide and Report. Use the two tools together and, after no more than six months, you will have the experience to move beyond the Check List. After that, the NAIC Stock Selection Guide and Report can serve as your basic analytical tool.

PREPARATION

Section 1: Past Sales Record

First, let's see how to fill out the form. Information on a specific company is available at your broker's office, at your public library, or from the company itself. A call to a company's shareholder relations department can usually get you a copy of the company's annual report and a number of broker reports about the company. The major services that provide information about corporations are Standard & Poor's (S&P) and Value Line. Standard & Poor's reports prior to January 1, 1996, do not provide information for the time period needed; reports issued since that date are satisfactory. The reports of Value Line meet the NAIC investor's needs, and are widely used.

A copy of the Value Line Survey form for Motorola appears in Figure 7-1. As of this writing, reliable estimates are available for 1995, so we will use 1995 as our beginning year and work backward. Motorola's source of income is referred to as *sales.* Some businesses use the word *revenues,* and other businesses—utilities, banks, and insurance companies, for example—have other terms for their sources of income. Some have more than one source of income. The main item is usually shown on line 11 of the Value Line report. On this sheet, we see that sales for 1995 are expected to be $28.250 billion, and we record that figure on our Stock Check List at Section 1, line 1. The next year back is 1994, for which we see $22.245 billion in sales on the Value Line report. This amount goes in Section 1, line 2 on the form. (See Figure 7-2.)

In Section 1, line 3, we have added these two figures to get $50,495. The amount on line 4 is the result of dividing line 3 by 2.

To get the figure for line 5, we return to line 11 of the Value Line report and count back five years from 1995. (We count 1994 as the first year because we want to include five full years of operations.) That takes us to 1990 and the figure $10,885 for line 5. The next year back is 1989, and $9,620 goes in line 6.

Completing the calculations called for in items 7, 8, 9, and 10, we see that sales have increased 146 percent over the five years. The figure we want is the compound annual rate of growth over this five-year period. The conversion table at the end of Section 1 helps us estimate that. The table shows the percent increase on the first line and the corresponding one-year compound growth rate on the second line. We do not need an exact figure; a "ballpark" figure meets our need. We see that 146 falls between 129 and 148 on the upper line of the table and it is very close to 148. The figures corresponding to 129 and 148 are 18 and 20. Since 146 is very close to 148, we will choose 20 percent as our compound rate of growth. It would probably calculate out to 19.7 or 19.8 percent, but whole figures are good enough for these estimates.

Section 2: Earnings-Per-Share Record

Section 2 is filled in using the same procedure as for Section 1. Use the earnings-per-share figures from line 3 of the Value Line report.

Figure 7-1
Value Line Report for Motorola

Source:© 1996 by Value Line Publishing, Inc. Reprinted by permission; all rights reserved.

Figure 7-2

Stock Check List for Motorola, Page 1

NATIONAL ASSOCIATION OF INVESTORS CORPORATION **NAIC**® INVESTMENT EDUCATION FOR INDIVIDUALS AND CLUBS SINCE 1951	*Stock Check List* ® *for Beginning Investors*	Company _____ MOTOROLA INC. _____ Prepared by _____ GOM _____ Date _____ 12-11-95 _____ *See Chapter 13 of Starting and Running aProfitable Investment Club.* *While Investors are learning to use NAIC's Stock Selection Guide, it is suggested the following Check List be used for each stock considered for investment.*

1 PAST SALES RECORD

Sales for most recent year were .... (1) $ __28,250__

Sales for next most recent year were .... (2) $ __22,245__

    Total of above (1 + 2) .... (3) $ __50,495__

    Figure above divided by 2 .... (4) $ __25,248__

Sales 5 years ago were .... (5) $ __10,885__

Sales 6 years ago were .... (6) $ __9,620__

    Total of above (5 + 6) .... (7) $ __20,505__

    Figure above divided by 2 .... (8) $ __10,253__

Increase in sales in above period (8 from 4) .... (9) $ __14,995__

Percentage increase in sales (9 divided by 8) .... (10) __146__ %

CONVERSION TABLE

This % Increase in Sales Gives →	27	33	46	61	76	93	112	129	148	205	271
This % Compounded Annual Growth Rate →	5	6	8	10	12	14	16	18	20	25	30

COMPOUND ANNUAL RATE OF SALES GROWTH WAS __20__ %

Look for the percent increase that meets the objective you have set.

2 PAST EARNINGS PER SHARE RECORD

Earnings Per Share for most recent year were .... (1) $ __3.20__

Earnings Per Share for next most recent year were .... (2) $ __2.65__

    Total of above (1 + 2) .... (3) $ __5.85__

    Figure above divided by 2 .... (4) $ __2.93__

Earnings Per Share 5 years ago were .... (5) $ __0.95__

Earnings Per Share 6 years ago were .... (6) $ __1.03__

    Total of above (5 + 6) .... (7) $ __1.98__

    Figure above divided by 2 .... (8) $ __0.99__

Increase in Earnings Per Share in above period (8 from 4) .... (9) $ __1.94__

Percentage increase in earnings (9 divided by 8) .... (10) __196__ %

See **Conversion Table** above to determine ⟶ COMPOUND ANNUAL RATE OF EARNINGS PER SHARE GROWTH WAS __24__ %

Earnings Per Share have increased _____ MORE _____ than sales in this period.
                   (more)   (less)

Explain Apparent Reason for Difference in Sales and Earnings Per Share Growth: _A look at the Net Profit Margin line and Percent Earned on Total Capital on the Value Line report shows that margins increased and consequently produced more earnings per dollar of sales._

Section 3: Price Record of the Stock

The price figures needed to fill out the price table in Section 3 come from the top of the Value Line report following the words *High* and *Low.* (Data for 1995 in this section is based on updated figures from newspaper reports.) The earnings per share figures are found on line 3 of the report. The price/earnings ratios are calculated as indicated in the column headings in Section 3 (Figure 7-3).

INTERPRETING THE FIGURES

Now that we have recorded all the figures the form calls for, the question is what they tell us about Motorola. Section 1 tells us that Motorola has increased its sales by 146 percent in five years, which is 20 percent compounded annually. Our goal is 100 percent appreciation in five years, which is 14.9 percent compounded annually. Thus, Motorola more than meets our goal. The company's figures show that if it continues to grow the way it has in the past five years, it will double its sales in less than four years. Thus, Motorola has been an outstanding company in growing its sales. We probably should not expect such a high rate of growth to continue indefinitely.

Looking at Section 2, we see that earnings per share grew 196 percent in five years. That is almost twice our goal of 100 percent. The compound annual growth rate of earnings per share is 24 percent. That rate will double our money in just over three years. Clearly, we have a company with an outstanding rate of growth. This is doubly impressive when you realize that Motorola's sales are reaching $30 billion per year.

We note that Motorola's earnings per share are growing faster than its sales. We also know that earnings come from sales and therefore over an extended period cannot grow faster than sales. This suggests that we should not estimate future growth in earnings per share at a higher rate than we project sales growth. When we graduate to NAIC's Stock Selection Guide and Report, we will review the history of Motorola's pre-tax profit margins and earnings on invested capital. These figures will help us judge when we can expect further earnings growth to be limited to the sales growth rate.

Answering the questions between Sections 2 and 3 requires that we learn a little about the company. Your public library may have a folder of articles written about the company. You will want to read what Value Line, Standard and Poor's, and the company's annual report have to say. The company's share-

Figure 7-3
Stock Check List for Motorola, Page 2

Discuss Possible Reasons for Past Growth:
A new product was very successful_____ ✔ ____ .
A cyclical business that experienced recovery_____ .
A research program has produced several new products or uses for older products_____ ✔ _____ .
Purchase another company_____ .
Has taken larger share of business in its field _____ ✔ ____ .
Skill of management _____ ✔ ____ .

Will Factors Which Produced Past Growth Continue Effective
for the next five years ___ ✔ ___ yes, _____ yes, but less effective, _____ no.

3 PRICE RECORD OF THE STOCK

Present Price $___76 1/8___ . Present Earnings Per Share___3.20___ .

List Last 5 Years	High Price Each Year (A)	Low Price Each Year (B)	Earnings Per Share (C)	Price Earnings Ratio at High (A ÷ C)	at Low (B ÷ C)
1991	17.8	11.4	0.86	20.7	13.3
1992	26.6	16.1	1.08	24.6	14.9
1993	53.8	24.4	1.78	30.2	13.7
1994	61.1	42.1	2.65	23.1	15.9
1995	82.1	51.5	3.20	25.7	16.1
Totals	241.4	145.5		124.3	73.9
Averages	48.28	29.1		24.9	14.8

Average of High and Low Price Earnings Averages for the past five years.   **19.9**

Present Price is ___higher___ than high price five years ago.
(higher) (lower)

Present Price is ___328___% higher than the high price 5 years ago. Compare this figure with the percent sales increase in 1 (10) and percent earnings per share increase in 2 (10).
The price change compares with sales growth and earnings per share growth ___favorably___ .
(favorably or unfavorably)

This stock has sold as high as the current price in ___1___ of the last 5 years.
In the past five years the stock ___has___ sold at unusually ___high___ price earnings ratios.
(has) (has not) (high) (low)
The Present price earnings ratio is ___23.8___ .
In relation to past price earnings ratios the stock is currently
_____ selling at a higher ratio
___✔___ selling about the same
_____ selling lower
The average price earnings ratios of the past might be expected to continue _____ ;
or should be adjusted to ___22___ high, ___13___ low.

4 CONCLUSION

1. The past sales growth rate ___does___ meet our objective.
(does) (does not)
2. The past earnings per share growth rate ___does___ meet our objective.
(does) (does not)
3. Our conclusion has been that possible earnings per share growth rate ___will___ meet our objective in the coming five years.
(will) (will not)
4. The price of the stock is currently ___too high___ .
(acceptable) (too high)

holder relations department may send you copies of articles published about the company.

From this reading we learn that Motorola is a leader in producing chips for computers and in wireless communications research. It is also a leader in the production of various wireless communications instruments and systems. We would ascribe these superior positions to skill of management. This knowledge enables us to answer the questions concerning the reasons for Motorola's growth record.

The table in Section 3 shows us a great deal about Motorola's price. Our belief is that if a company grows in sales and earnings, the price of the stock will rise to reflect that increase in value. In 1991, Motorola earned 86 cents per share. In 1995, it earned $3.20. That is a 272 percent increase. The high price of the stock in 1991 was $17.80. In 1995, it was $82.10, according to the newspaper at the time we did our study. That is a 361 percent increase. In 1991, Motorola sold at 20.7 times earnings at its high. In 1995, it sold at 25.7 times earnings.

Now let's answer the questions in Section 3. Motorola's price is 76⅛, and five years ago it was 17.8. That is an increase of 328 percent. From the front page of the Check List we see that sales are up 146 percent and earnings per share are up 196 percent. The price increase substantially exceeds our two basic growth indicators. This suggests that a great many investors have been impressed with Motorola's growth and have been paying very good prices for it. As we look at the newspaper, we see that just this year it has sold for as high as $82.10, and as low at $51.50. We should be cautious in making a purchase.

The stock's price has been as high as it is only in the current year. In the past five years it has sold for more than 20 times earnings in each year and in one year its P/E was over 30. Currently the stock is selling at 23.8 times 1995 earnings. Value Line estimates that 1996 earnings will be $3.95 per share. That makes the P/E 19.3 at 76⅛ on next year's earnings. When we consider what the high and low price/earnings ratios of the next five years might be, we decide to be conservative and lower both from the average high of 24.9 and average low of 14.8 to 22 and 13, respectively.

The figures show that Motorola is selling at about the same P/E for the average high as it has for the past five years. The company more than meets our requirement for growth in sales and earnings, but the risk at 76⅛ is high. We should watch the stock. Its price is very volatile. We would recommend not buying it until the P/E for 1995 earnings of $3.20 is below 19.9 or until it is 14.8 or lower on estimated 1996 earnings of $3.95.

CHAPTER 8

THE NAIC STOCK SELECTION GUIDE AND REPORT: PAGE 1

*T*he most important action that any investor takes is the selection of the individual stock to put his or her money in. You as an investor never buy the stock market, no matter how much you talk about it. We repeat: You never buy the stock market. What the stock market does is always interesting, but as an investor, you buy a particular company, and the success of that company determines whether you make money.

The NAIC *Stock Selection Guide and Report* and *Stock Selection Guide* are tools to help you make that selection. We use the Stock Selection Guide with a definite objective in mind. We are looking for a company with a record of growth. We know that a record of growth does not guarantee future growth, but we believe a company is more likely to grow in the future if it has a record of growth in the past. It is growing sales and earnings per share that make a company increase in value and make its stock price go up.

If a company meets our growth objective, we next look at its pre-tax profit margin and earnings on equity. We compare these figures with those of its competitors and the standards of the industry. We want a company for which these figures are in the top half of its industry.

If a company meets these tests, we check to see whether we can buy it at a favorable price. If it is too high-priced, we postpone action until the price is right.

Recording the information needed to make these tests on the NAIC Stock Selection Guide is the subject of this chapter. It cannot be overemphasized that completion of a Stock Selection Guide in one form or another, permitting review of operating data and computation of financial ratios, should be performed for every prospective purchase.

The NAIC Stock Selection Guide and Report has been in use for five decades and has gained wide acceptance among both professional and amateur security analysts as an aid to making informed and profitable investment decisions.

Completing your first Guide may require several hours. After some experience, you will find that you need to devote no more than half an hour to the task for each company. Remember, the Stock Selection Guide contains no "magic formula" to ensure investment success. The form is only a guide to judgment, and is no more useful than the interpretation you make.

WHAT DOES *DATA* MEAN?

Many clubs are not sure how to interpret all the information captured by the Stock Selection Guide. For example, you and other members may energetically complete Guides for any number of companies, attend meetings, and make presentations summarizing each Guide. Then, however, you and your fellow members discover that nobody knows what to make of the findings.

Where does a high growth rate come from? Is it a short-term accident? Does it come from a temporary or long-term advantage of product or procedure? Is it the product of management skill and drive? If so, the growth can probably continue as long as present management is in charge. How high is a high profit margin? When is a P/E ratio high? What is the significance of book value? Is corporate debt a bad sign? Your ability to interpret the data will improve as you gain knowledge. Of course, you can always refer to this book to find the answers you are looking for.

The Guide allows you to use the past as a basis for estimating the progress of a company and the price of its stock. You have space to record ten years of history. Every decade the economy typically undergoes both up and down cycles. Using the Guide, you can review how effectively management has functioned under varying economic conditions. The Guide is really a judge of management.

It is always a good idea to look at a company's past performance and then make your prediction of where the company is moving. Of course, there is no guarantee your forecasting will prove accurate. If investing could be reduced to a formula, everyone would be a millionaire. However, in making predictions, as in interpreting the Guide, you will definitely improve.

IS THE GUIDE VALUABLE?

Is the Stock Selection Guide worthy of your time and attention? Just one example (Figure 8-1) should suffice.

A new member joined the Midwest-based First Ladies Investment Club in its eleventh year of operation. Over the initial decade, club members had paid in $19,000. Their investment was worth just $20,585. That is a return

Figure 8-1
First Ladies Investment Club

Year	Cumulative Deposits	Cumulative Withdrawals by Members	Club Value, Year End
10	$19,000	—	$ 20,585
11	20,920	—	29,229
12	22,960	—	42,381
13	25,480	—	44,672
14	28,540	—	40,615
15	31,600	—	45,658
16	34,840	$10,830	63,750
17	37,960	—	70,298
18	40,800	39,330	88,859
19	44,160	56,430	83,560
20	48,000	72,878	NA
21	51,440	86,478	84,581
22	55,320	—	88,890
23	59,880	—	108,223
24	63,860	—	113,451
25	68,420	95,478	154,769
26	74,650	105,478	159,900
27	79,450	125,478	180,569

At the end of year 27, the club had cumulative deposits of $79,450; club value was $180,569. Members had also withdrawn $125,478, a sum substantially greater than the deposits.

of less than 1 percent annually. The club members could have made several times that much simply by putting their deposits into a guaranteed bank savings account. Members were less than enthusiastic about their club's performance and were persuaded by the newcomer to join NAIC, follow NAIC principles, and use NAIC tools. Figure 8-1 shows what has happened since.

Remember, in the first decade, the First Ladies had achieved a razor-thin profit. After the introduction of NAIC principles and tools, the women earned an average return of 17.7 percent compounded annually. How many professionals could rival that result over a similar period of time? Using the NAIC Stock Selection Guide doesn't guarantee such success, but it definitely improves your odds.

Note that the NAIC Stock Selection Guide does not refer to any balance sheet items, which are used to determine the financial strength of a corporation. We are assuming that in using the Guide, you have first determined from your own analysis that the corporation is financially sound. One important factor you should not overlook is company debt. If you consider financial condition and debt structure together, you many discover threats to the company's long-term progress. If debt is sizable, you might calculate a few of the key ratios from the balance sheet, which you learned about in Chapter 4. These include working capital, current ratio, acid test, and bond ratio. And remember, as with all forms of financial analysis, be on the lookout for trends.

RECORDING INFORMATION ON THE GUIDE

First we will discuss how to enter information on the NAIC Stock Selection Guide and Report. Then we will discuss what this information means and how it helps us judge the investment potential of a stock. NAIC's Investor's Toolkit computer program makes recording information on the Guide quick and easy. When a database is used, its completion is almost instantaneous.

We will use Motorola to illustrate the use of the Guide, as we did for the NAIC Stock Check List. A copy of the Value Line report was included as Figure 7-1 on page 57. We will refer to that illustration as we discuss how to record information on the Guide. *(Note: After the Value Line report was printed, Motorola released its actual sales for 1995 as $27.050 billion, earnings per share as $2.93, and dividends as 40 cents a share. We have used these actual figures in our illustrations.)* We are doing our study in early January. Our Value Line was printed in July. We update our price information from our newspaper.

The graph in Section 1 of the Stock Selection Guide is a ratio chart or a semi-logarithmic graph. The horizontal scale is in familiar arithmetic proportion. It is used to show time. The vertical scale is based on logarithms. Equal vertical distances represent equal percentage changes, regardless of absolute values. It is designed to show compound growth rates.

There is no zero point. That's because the chart is designed to show comparisons in terms of percentage of change, and positive numbers are required for this operation. (If the semilog chart is new to you, refer to Appendix B, "How to Use the Ratio Chart and Calculator.")

With the semilog chart, a straight line represents a consistent rate of growth. The slanted guidelines on the graph beginning in the lower left corner represent compound growth rates ranging from 5 percent to 30 percent.

In analyzing companies of varying size, it makes far better sense to compare rates of growth than absolute increases in dollars. A large company might have far greater year-to-year gains, dollar-wise, than a small company; yet, on a percentage increase basis, the smaller company might have a superior record of growth.

The five vertical time lines on the right side of the heavier line of the graph are reserved for projecting results five years into the future.

The Guide was designed to analyze the figures of manufacturing, sales, and similar businesses. Banks, insurance firms, and utility companies have different names for their key operating figures. The Guide can be used for these companies also, as long as you use the figures that are pertinent for those types of companies.

For instance, four classes of revenues are shown in the Value Line report for CNA Financial, an insurance company (Figure 8-2). These are life premiums, property/casualty premiums, total investment income, and other revenues. It is always helpful to note the trend of each revenue class to see which areas are growing and which are receding. One segment may be dominant and determine the course of the business. In CNA's case, we would use the total of all four items to draw our trend line for sales and judge the growth of the company.

The loss & expense ratio is an interesting figure to use to judge insurance companies. It is a measure of underwriting profitability. The loss ratio (%) equals the sum of the millions of dollars of losses paid from premiums and reserves divided by the millions of dollars of policy premiums. The expense ratio is calculated by dividing the year's total expenses by the millions of dol-

Figure 8-2
Example of a Value Line Report for an Insurance Company

CNA FINANCIAL NYSE-CNA	RECENT PRICE **115**	P/E RATIO **11.1** (Trailing: 10.7 / Median: 14.0)	RELATIVE P/E RATIO **0.75**	DIV'D YLD **Nil**	VALUE LINE **2183**

TIMELINESS **1** Highest (Relative Price Performance Next 12 Mos.)
SAFETY **3** Average (Scale: 1 Highest to 5 Lowest)
BETA 1.15 (1.00 = Market)

High: 32.0 65.1 75.0 66.5 66.1 108.8 100.0 99.3 104.5 101.0 82.3 123.3
Low: 21.0 31.5 47.3 47.0 51.0 57.6 49.5 62.8 78.5 74.3 60.0 64.8

Target Price Range 1998 | 1999 | 2000

10.0 × Earnings p sh

1998-00 PROJECTIONS
	Price	Gain	Ann'l Total Return
High	160	(+40%)	9%
Low	110	(-5%)	-1%

Insider Decisions
	J	F	M	A	M	J	J	A	S
to Buy	0	0	0	0	0	0	0	0	0
Options	0	0	0	0	0	0	0	0	0
to Sell	0	0	0	0	0	0	0	0	0

Institutional Decisions
	4Q'94	1Q'95	2Q'95
to Buy	18	25	28
to Sell	21	13	13
Hld's(000)	60998	61103	60938

Percent shares traded 3.0 2.0 1.0

Relative Price Strength

Shaded area indicates recession

Options: ASE

1979	1980	1981	1982	1983	1984	1985	1986	1987	1988	1989	1990	1991	1992	1993	1994	1995	1996	© VALUE LINE PUB., INC.	98-00
25.02	19.88	18.48	19.35	19.29	21.64	21.75	23.70	25.78	31.89	33.58	34.03	37.08	38.51	25.77	43.30	50.95	56.60	Life Premiums per sh	67.75
36.64	29.25	32.09	31.26	27.04	31.11	39.27	61.65	71.10	80.15	87.25	101.90	107.70	102.81	114.73	105.92	156.85	169.75	Prop/Cas Premiums p sh	241.95
10.53	8.47	10.12	10.78	10.07	11.52	12.40	13.98	16.16	18.57	24.85	23.39	33.52	30.35	34.45	25.08	32.90	37.20	Investment Inc per sh	48.40
3.06	2.40	2.05	2.17	2.46	1.80	3.01	4.02	5.23	5.20	8.90	4.88	8.62	d10.79	4.26	.51	10.90	8.00	Earnings per sh ^	13.50
..	..	..	..	..	..	..	..	..	..	..	..	..	..	..	..	Nil	Nil	Div'ds Dec'l'd per sh	Nil
19.80	18.11	19.06	20.83	23.55	26.32	33.24	40.37	46.40	54.87	64.74	70.23	80.24	75.07	84.59	71.08	102.65	110.75	Book Value per sh	137.10
34.49	48.47	48.76	48.78	57.50	57.50	62.12	64.12	62.66	62.29	61.84	61.79	61.79	61.80	61.84	61.84	61.85	61.85	Common Shs Outst'g ^B	62.00
65%	90%	78%	70%	87%	99%	148%	151%	120%	106%	118%	101%	104%	119%	106%	93%	Bold figures are Value Line estimates		% Price to Book Value	100%
4.2	6.8	7.3	6.8	8.3	14.5	16.3	15.2	10.7	11.1	8.6	14.6	9.6	..	21.0	NMF			Avg Ann'l P/E Ratio	10.0
.61	.90	.89	.75	.70	1.35	1.32	1.03	.72	.92	.65	1.08	.61	..	1.24	NMF			Relative P/E Ratio	.75
..	..	..	..	..	..	..	..	..	..	..	..	..	..	..	..			Avg Ann'l Div'd Yield	Nil

CAPITAL STRUCTURE as of 9/30/95
Total Debt $3016.7 mill. Due in 5 Yrs $1300 mill.
LT Debt $3012.0 mill. LT Interest $250 mill.
(32% of Cap'l)

Pension Liability None

Pfd Stock $150.0 mill. Pfd Div'd $10.8 mill.
750 shares each of Series E and F Money
Market Cumulative Preferred (3% of Cap'l)

Common Stock 61,798,262 shs. (65% of Cap'l)
at 11/1/95

1985	1986	1987	1988	1989	1990	1991	1992	1993	1994	1995	1996		98-00
1351.4	1519.7	1615.4	1986.1	2077.0	2102.8	2291.3	2380.0	1593.8	2678.0	3150	3500	Life Premiums ($mil)	4200
2439.7	3952.8	4455.2	4992.2	5395.7	6296.6	6655.3	6353.6	7095.0	6550.2	9700	10500	Prop/Cas Prem. ($mil)	15000
770.4	896.2	1012.3	1156.5	1536.5	1445.6	2071.2	1875.6	2130.4	1551.2	2035	2300	Total Inv Inc ($mill)	3000
43.7	23.5	38.3	69.3	74.9	99.4	113.8	149.9	191.6	220.1	215	300	Other Revenues ($mill)	550
4605.2	6392.3	7121.3	8204.1	9084.0	9944.4	11132	10759	11011	11000	14800	16300	Total Revenues ($mill)	22750
-22.3%	-14.6%	-10.1%	-8.8%	-16.0%	-12.2%	-13.8%	-41.9%	-23.5%	-10.0%	-9.0%	-12.5%	Prop/Cas Und Margin	-12.0%
..	..	..	..	..	..	..	105.2	..	127.4	150	165	Insur in Force ($bill)	200
14116	16643	19563	22941	28682	31320	36604	36681	41910	44320	66500	71500	Total Assets ($mill)	85000
2064.5	2738.2	3057.6	3567.6	4153.8	4490.0	5108.6	4789.2	5381.1	4545.9	6350	6850	Net Worth ($mill)	8500
8.7%	9.5%	11.1%	9.4%	13.5%	6.9%	10.6%	NMF	5.0%	.8%	11.0%	7.0%	% Earned Net Worth	9.0%
8.7%	9.9%	11.4%	9.5%	13.8%	7.0%	10.7%	NMF	5.0%	.7%	11.0%	7.0%	% Retained to Comm Eq	9.0%
..	1%	2%	3%	2%	3%	1%	..	2%	13%	2%	4%	% All Div'ds to Net Prof	1%

For this insurance company, revenues are categorized as life premiums, property/casualty premiums, total investment income, and "other revenues." Source: © 1996 by Value Line Publishing, Inc. Reprinted by permission; all rights reserved.

lars of premiums. Both of those answers are percentages, and the two added together give the loss & expense ratio (%). A loss & expense ratio below 100% indicates that underwriting expertise is generating profits. That is a positive factor, and the further the ratio is below 100%, the better.

In the CNA example, the figure given is Property/Casualty Und (Underwriting) Margin. You will note that Property/Casualty Premiums are the major part of the business, so this figure is important.

In studying the record of a bank, we look at different figures. Banks vary greatly in the way they earn their income. Traditional banks loan money and earn interest income. Some earn a great deal from trading financial instruments. Some are like computer services and collect fees for servicing mutual funds and credit cards. You first must determine the nature of the bank's business and then note which items are the important elements in its income. First Chicago Bank in our illustration (Figure 8-3) shows two sources of revenues: net interest income and noninterest income. You should add the two together and use the sum to plot annual revenues. Percent Earned Total Assets for banks is typically below 1 percent. Over 1 percent is considered good.

Our second bank illustration is State Street Boston Corp. (Figure 8-4). This bank's loan business is small but has grown by processing shareowner accounts for mutual funds. Its noninterest income is the figure to plot.

Figure 8-3
Example of a Value Line Report for a Bank

First Chicago Bank revenues are designated net interest income and noninterest income. Source: © 1996 by Value Line Publishing, Inc. Reprinted by permission; all rights reserved.

Figure 8-4
Example of a Value Line Report for a Bank

For this bank, specializing in mutual fund accounts, revenues are classified as noninterest income.
Source: © 1996 by Value Line Publishing, Inc. Reprinted by permission; all rights reserved.

In the case of a real estate investment trust (Figure 8-5), rental income or total income is the figure to use for revenues. With an electric utility (Figure 8-6), the correct figure to use is listed as revenues in Value Line and often as operating revenues in other sources. The operating margin represents the percent of operating costs to revenues; the lower the figure, the more favorable the company's situation.

These examples should help you decide which data to use regardless of the type of business you are examining.

Figure 8-5
Example of a Value Line Report for a Real Estate Firm

| NEW PLAN REALTY NYSE-NPR | RECENT PRICE 22 | P/E RATIO 17.6 (Trailing: 18.8 / Median: NMF) | RELATIVE P/E RATIO 1.21 | DIV'D YLD 6.2% | VALUE LINE 1180 |

TIMELINESS **3** Average (Relative Price Performance Next 12 Mos.)
SAFETY **1** Highest (Scale: 1 Highest to 5 Lowest)
BETA .75 (1.00 = Market)

High: 9.2 11.9 15.3 18.4 16.8 18.8 18.6 24.5 26.1 26.4 24.4 22.6
Low: 7.3 9.2 11.0 10.8 13.3 15.3 13.8 16.1 19.6 21.5 18.8 19.6

1.50 × Dividends p sh divided by Interest Rate
3-for-2 split
2-for-1 split

1998-00 PROJECTIONS
	Price	Gain	Ann'l Total Return
High	35	(+60%)	17%
Low	25	(+15%)	9%

Insider Decisions
	A	S	O	N	D	J	F	M	A
to Buy	2	0	0	0	0	0	1	0	
Options	0	0	0	0	0	0	0	0	
to Sell	0	0	0	0	0	1	0	0	0

Institutional Decisions
	3Q'94	4Q'94	1Q'95
to Buy	21	30	20
to Sell	28	32	38
Hld's(000)	6903	6607	6386

Percent shares traded 3.0 2.0 1.0

Relative Price Strength

Target Price Range 1998 1999 2000
Shaded area indicates recession
Options: ASE

	1979	1980	1981	1982	1983	1984	1985	1986	1987	1988	1989	1990	1991	1992	1993	1994	1995	1996	©VALUE LINE PUB., INC.	98-00
	1.28	1.40	1.45	2.37	2.49	3.44	3.66	4.40	5.98	6.03	7.90	7.95	9.83	10.46	10.22	10.74	10.85	10.70	Book Value per sh A	12.50
	.30	.39	.40	.54	.59	.71	.80	.85	.84	.89	.98	1.01	1.03	.97	1.02	1.27	1.48	1.62	Funds from Ops per sh B C	2.20
	.21	.31	.31	.46	.50	.60	.70	.74	.73	.70	.87	.91	.92	.86	.87	1.04	1.20	1.30	Earnings per sh A B	1.75
	.25	.30	.34	.39	.51	.57	.65	.73	.81	.89	.97	1.05	1.13	1.21	1.28	1.32	1.37	1.41	Div'ds Decl'd per sh D ■	1.60
	2.10	1.94	2.05	1.73	2.40	2.53	2.68	3.47	2.93	3.46	3.61	4.56	3.90	6.28	7.64	11.32	14.10	16.05	Loans & Real Est per sh	21.65
	9.20	9.91	9.96	12.83	13.25	16.62	17.26	20.67	26.64	26.85	34.71	35.15	44.49	48.38	48.96	52.59	53.10	56.00	Common Shs Outst'g E	60.00
	136%	121%	166%	85%	194%	123%	163%	170%	157%	135%	104%	114%	81%	105%	131%	115%	Bold figures are Value Line estimates		Premium over Book	125%
	14.1	9.9	12.5	9.5	14.5	12.8	13.8	30.9	21.0	20.4	18.4	18.7	19.3	25.0	27.2	22.3			Avg Ann'l P/E Ratio	17.0
	10.0	7.9	9.7	8.1	12.3	10.9	12.0	14.0	18.4	16.0	15.9	16.8	17.3	22.2	23.1	18.2			Avg Ann'l P/FFO Ratio	13.0
	8.3%	9.7%	8.8%	8.9%	7.0%	7.4%	6.8%	6.2%	5.3%	6.2%	6.2%	6.1%	6.4%	5.6%	5.4%	5.7%			Avg Ann'l Div'd Yield	5.3%

CAPITAL STRUCTURE as of 4/30/95
ST Debt *Nil*
LT Debt $129.1 mill. Due in 5 Yrs $20.0 mill.
Total Interest $15.0 mill. (18% of Cap'l)
(Total interest coverage: 13.5x)

Pension Liability None

Pfd Stock None

Common Stock 53,105,634 shs. (82% of Cap'l)
as of June 2, 95

						19.7	21.9	26.2	28.5	33.8	38.0	41.4	47.6	65.3	96.4	127	160	Rental Income ($mill) A	225
						6.6	9.5	9.2	8.9	9.8	16.1	16.0	17.1	11.0	4.6	3.5	5.0	Other Income ($mill)	5.0
						67.0%	70.2%	68.7%	62.4%	69.0%	68.4%	71.4%	71.0%	67.2%	64.3%	64.5%	65.5%	Operating Margin	64.5%
						11.8	14.9	16.5	18.7	25.0	31.8	35.1	39.4	42.3	51.3	63.5	73.0	Net Profit ($mill)	105
						44.8%	46.2%	46.0%	50.1%	57.4%	58.3%	60.7%	60.9%	55.4%	50.8%	50.0%	45.5%	Net Profit Margin	47.0%
						- -	.7	1.5	2.2	2.2	3.3	4.8	10.1	.9	1.0	Nil	Nil	Capital Gains	Nil
						46.3	71.7	78.2	92.6	125.5	160.3	173.5	304.1	374.2	595.1	750	900	Loans & Real Est ($mill)	1300
						44.3	96.3	26.7	22.5	22.7	22.7	18.6	17.5	23.3	28.1	210	200	Long-Term Debt ($mill)	200
						63.1	90.9	159.4	161.9	274.2	279.5	437.2	506.3	500.6	565.5	575	650	Net Worth ($mill)	750
						81.3%	86.1%	96.7%	100.0%	98.7%	103.5%	109.7%	125.2%	125.4%	103.9%	93.5%	86.0%	% Div'ds Decl'd to FFO	73.5%
						8.0%	6.2%	5.9%	7.5%	6.6%	5.7%	4.6%	3.9%	4.7%	6.3%	6.5%	6.5%	% Expenses to Assets	6.5%
						15.1%	14.1%	11.6%	13.8%	14.5%	12.4%	11.8%	10.7%	8.6%	9.7%	9.0%	10.5%	% Earned Total Cap'l	12.5%
						19.7%	18.4%	15.2%	14.6%	15.3%	12.7%	12.0%	10.7%	8.6%	9.8%	11.0%	11.0%	% Earned Net Worth	14.0%

FUNDS FLOW ($mill.)	1992	1993	1994
Net Profit Plus			
Noncash charges	54.5	50.8	63.7
Investments Repaid	2.5	-.-	2.0
Net New Debt	-5.9	-6.2	.5
New Equity	74.8	11.7	77.0
Investments Funded	123.8	63.2	218.3
Dividends Declared	55.2	62.0	64.7

New Plan Realty Trust classifies revenues as rental income and "other income." Source: © 1996 by Value Line Publishing, Inc. Reprinted by permission; all rights reserved.

PLOTTING THE FIGURES

Now let's return to our analysis of Motorola. The first four items in the heading are self-explanatory. The place where the stock is traded is shown after the company's name at the top left part of the Value Line report. This is followed by the trading symbol. The nature of the business is described in the middle of the page following the heading "Business."

The capitalization block provides the investor with interesting information. The heading "Capital Structure" on the left side of the Value Line report shows the total debt. Motorola's capital structure is simple, being principally

Figure 8-6
Example of a Value Line Report for a Utility

Atmos Energy Corp. revenues are listed simply as "revenues," although other services use the term "operating revenues." Source: © 1996 by Value Line Publishing, Inc. Reprinted by permission; all rights reserved.

common stock and debt. Value Line says the common stock is 87% of capital, so debt is 13%. The Value Line "Business" paragraph shows that insiders own 3.5% of the stock. The Institutional Decisions box shows 374,744,000 shares currently owned by institutions, which, divided by the total of 588,573,987, is 64%.

The quarterly figures called for in the space at the upper left of the graph in the Stock Selection Guide are found at the lower left of the Value Line report. We use the latest actual figures available except when we are making a study near the end of the year. Then we are inclined to use estimated quarterly figures. The percentage change is calculated by subtracting the previous quarter value from the current quarter value, dividing that difference by the previous quarter, and multiplying by 100.

The first figures we record on the semilog graph are the sales for the past ten years. We note from the sales line on the Value Line report that Motorola's sales figure grew by one digit in the past ten years. That means we will need to use two cycles of the graph. We number the lines in the bottom cycle from 1 to 10 billion and the lines in the second cycle from 10 to 100 billion. Figure 8-7 illustrates how to plot Motorola's sales on the graph from the Value Line sheet. Plot the latest year's figures on the heavy line, the sixth vertical line from the right side. Once we have plotted a mark for each year's sales on the graph, we connect the marks with a line to get a picture of how sales have grown. A quick look suggests that our plotted data are roughly parallel to the 20 percent line on the graph. (See Figure 8-8).

To get a better picture of the historical growth rate, we draw a trend line over our plotted data.

Statisticians draw lines in several different ways. The most frequently used are the inspection or best judgment method, the midpoint method, the peak method, and the area method. In the inspection or best judgment method, you look at the plotted data and just let your eye direct you in drawing a straight line that seems to best represent the trend of the plotted data. This is also referred to as "eyeballing." After some experience, this is the method most of us settle on. (See Figure 8-9.)

The peak method calls for using the most recent peak as a fulcrum and pivoting a straight-edge down to the next peak. In Motorola's case, that takes us all the way back to our first year and does not look very representative. (See Figure 8-10.) Experience has shown that the peak method works well for a cyclical growth company. The theory is that the company's next peak year will fall somewhere along the line projected from the last two peaks.

New analysts like the midpoint method because it gives precise results with a minimum of calculation. In this method, you divide the ten-year history of sales into two five-year periods. Average the five sales figures for the first period and place the result on the line for the third year, or midpoint, of that period. Repeat the procedure for the second five-year period and then draw the trend line through the two points. When the figures show a regular rate of increase, as Motorola's do, the result tends to look much like a precisely calculated line would. But if the figures are irregular, the results can be wild. (See Figure 8-11.)

In the area method, you inspect your plotted data and attempt to draw the trend line so that the plotted data enclose equal areas of space above and

Figure 8-7
Plotting Revenues

Sales figures for Motorola are transferred from the Value Line sheet to the Visual Analysis graph.

Figure 8-8
Estimating Sales Growth

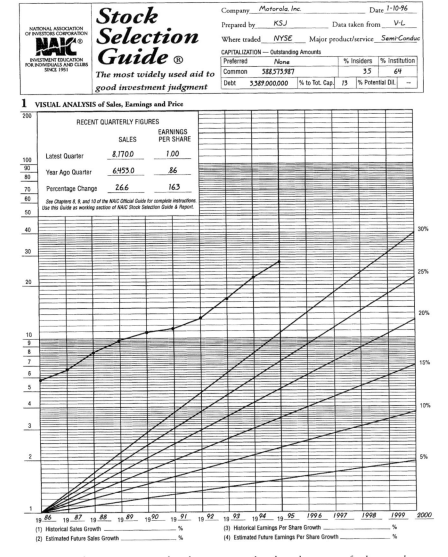

Marks representing yearly sales are connected to show the pattern of sales growth.

Figure 8-9

Best Judgment Method

The trend line for recording and projecting the rate of growth is fitted to the plotted data using the estimator's judgment.

Figure 8-10
Peak Method

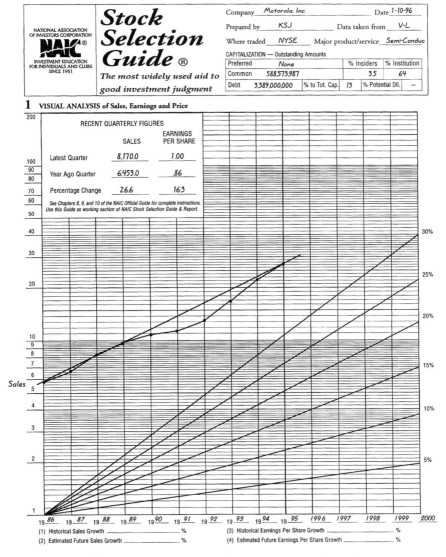

The trend line is drawn using the two most recent market peaks.

Figure 8-11

Midpoint Method

The sales history is divided into two five-year periods, sales for each period are averaged and plotted on each period's midpoint, and the trend line is drawn between the two midpoints.

below the drawn line. This will produce a line close to the one drawn in Figure 8-12.

Of course, you can calculate each year's growth and average the figures to get the average rate of growth. This is done by the computer programs available for the Guide, but such precision is not necessary. We are just looking for ballpark figures.

If we decide that the inspection method gives an adequate picture of the past rate of growth, how do we determine what rate of growth it represents? We compare it with the trend lines drawn on the graph. First we go to the left side of the graph and measure the distance from where our trend line intersects the line for 1986 down to the corner where the guidelines start. Then we take a ruler and measure down that same distance from the trend line at the heavy vertical line (1995) of the graph. This point falls about midway between the 15 percent and the 20 percent growth guidelines, or about 17.5 percent. (See Figure 8-13.) Using NAIC's Investor's Toolkit, the computer-calculated rate is 17.9 percent. As we said earlier, exact rates are not important. Approximate figures are an adequate guide.

Our next step is to record earnings per share on the graph. We find these figures on line 3 of the Value Line report. Again, we see that earnings start at two digits in 1986 and increase to three digits in 1995. We will therefore need two cycles of the graph to record them. The lines in the bottom cycle will stand for cents and those in the second cycle from the bottom for dollars. Once we have recorded the earnings-per-share figures on the year lines, we connect them with a dotted line to distinguish them from the sales. (See Figure 8-14.)

The final step in completing the graph is to record the high and low prices for each year on the vertical year lines. We find these prices at the top of the Value Line report across from the words "High" and "Low." We connect the high and low marks with a straight line so that the high and low prices look like bars on the graph. (See Figure 8-15.)

Figure 8-12
Area Method

The trend line is drawn so that equal areas are encompassed by the plot above and below the trend line.

Figure 8-13
Determining Sales Growth Rate

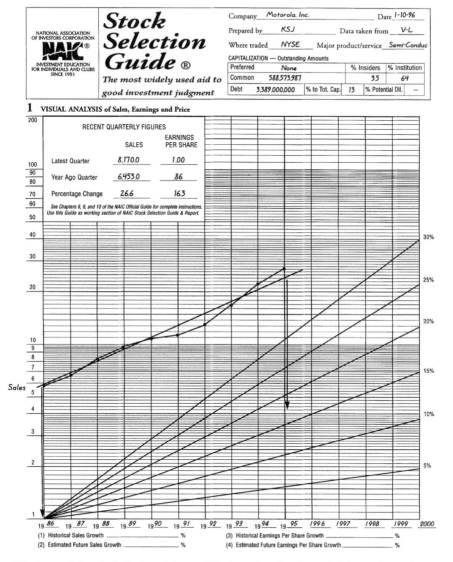

The distance below the beginning of the trend line is used on the other end of the graph to estimate the percentage of sales growth.

Figure 8-14

Plotting Earnings per Share

Earnings-per-share figures are taken from the Value Line report and plotted along with the sales figures for Motorola.

Figure 8-15
Plotting High and Low Prices

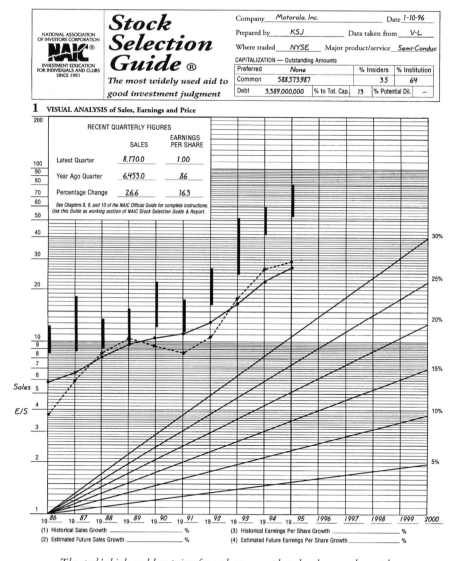

The stock's high and low prices for each year are plotted as bars on the graph.

CHAPTER 9

THE NAIC STOCK SELECTION GUIDE AND REPORT: PAGE 2

*P*age 2 of the Stock Selection Guide contains Sections 2 through 5.

The figures for Section 2, "Evaluating Management," are calculated for you in some reports; in other cases, you will have to calculate them yourself. Line A, "Percent Pre-Tax Profit on Sales," is figured by dividing net income before taxes by sales and expressing the result as a percentage. Value Line does not give you net income before taxes, but it does have figures that permit you to calculate it. First take the income tax rate, 37 percent for 1995, and express it as a decimal, 0.37. Subtract that figure from 1.00 (1.00 − 0.37 = 0.63). Value Line shows net profit as $1.935 billion for 1995. Dividing that by 0.63 gives us $3.071 billion. Dividing this by sales of $27.050 billion (*Note: We are using actual sales instead of the estimate shown in the Value Line Report*), we get 11.35 or 11.4, corrected to the first place. We repeat that process for each year. Figure 9-1 shows the completed section.

Value Line calls equity "net worth" and has calculated that figure for us. Place those yearly figures in the correct columns in line B of Section 2. You will find that these figures may vary between different services and the company's annual report. That is because different accountants make different adjustments to the earnings figures before they make their final calculations for pre-tax profits. Accountants also calculate earnings on equity in different ways. For instance, some base it on beginning equity and others on ending equity. Some

Figure 9-1

Evaluating Management

2 EVALUATING MANAGEMENT	Company _Motorola Inc._												
		19_86_	19_87_	19_88_	19_89_	19_90_	19_91_	19_92_	19_93_	19_94_	19_95_	LAST 5 YEAR AVG.	TREND UP / DOWN
A	% Pre-tax Profit on Sales (Net Before Taxes ÷ Sales)	4.5	6.2	7.4	7.4	6.1	5.4	6.0	9.0	11.0	11.4	8.6	↑
B	% Earned on Equity (E/S ÷ Book Value)	7.0	10.2	13.2	14.0	11.7	9.8	11.2	15.9	17.2	17.5	14.3	↑

base it on the average of beginning and ending equity. The differences are not usually important, but it makes good sense to take all of your figures from the same source to make sure they have all been subjected to the same treatment.

For Section 3, you can get the present and past years' high and low prices from the newspaper. The other figures can be taken from the Value Line report or are calculated. The first line is for figures five years ago, and each succeeding line is for the next year. The high and low prices are the same ones we used to plot the price bars in Section 1. Earnings per share values come from line 3 of the Value Line table of figures.

The high and low price/earnings ratios are not given by Value Line but are easily computed by doing the calculations indicated in the column heading. Dividends per share are shown on line 4 of the Value Line table. Percent payout can be calculated based on the directions in the column heading, or you can use the figures in the Value Line table under the heading "% All Dividends to Net Profit." The differences will normally be minor.

In columns B, D, E, and G we add up the figures for the five years and put the totals on line 6. We divide these totals by 5 to give us five-year averages. Line 8, average price/earnings ratio, is used to enter the average of the high and low averages on line 7 in columns D and E. The current P/E (line 9) is found by dividing the current price by the last twelve months' earnings per share. If we are doing our study in the latter half of the company's fiscal year, it is helpful to base the current P/E on the coming year's estimated earnings as shown in the Value Line report. As we were writing this book Motorola's actual figures for 1995 became available, and, as shown in Figure 9-2, we have used the actual figures in place of Value Line's estimates.

In Section 4, part A, the average high P/E is taken from Section 3, line 7, column D, unless we decide to adjust it, which we have done and will explain later (see page 96, P/E History). The estimated high earnings per share for five years in the future can be determined in two ways. One is by looking

Figure 9-2
Price/Earnings History

3 PRICE-EARNINGS HISTORY as an indicator of the future

This shows how stock prices have fluctuated with earnings and dividends. It is a building block for translating earnings into future stock prices.

PRESENT PRICE ____56 1/4____ HIGH THIS YEAR ____82.500____ LOW THIS YEAR ____51.500____

Year	A PRICE	B PRICE	C Earnings Per Share	D Price Earnings Ratio	E	F Dividend Per Share	G % Payout F ÷ C X 100	H % High Yield F ÷ B X 100
	HIGH	LOW		HIGH A ÷ C	LOW B ÷ C			
1 1991	17.8	11.4	0.86	20.7	13.3	.19	22.1	1.7
2 1992	26.6	16.1	1.08	24.6	14.9	.20	18.5	1.2
3 1993	53.8	24.4	1.78	30.2	13.7	.22	12.4	0.9
4 1994	61.1	42.1	2.65	23.1	15.9	.31	11.7	0.7
5 1995	82.5	51.5	2.93	28.2	17.6	.40	13.7	0.8
6 TOTAL		145.5		126.8	75.4		78.4	
7 AVERAGE		29.1		25.4	15.1		15.7	
8 AVERAGE PRICE EARNINGS RATIO		20.3	9 CURRENT PRICE EARNINGS RATIO				19.2	

(Est. 56 1/4/3.68=15.3)

at where the trend line for earnings per share five years in the future crosses our year 2000 line. We read that on the graph in Section 1 as $6.10. (See Figure 10-1 in the next chapter).

The other method for estimating earnings per share five years into the future is called the preferred procedure. It starts with estimated sales rather than earnings per share. It is assumed that sales estimates are ordinarily more reliable than earnings per share estimates. Also, the analyst, based on reasons he or she has selected, determines the other elements in the procedure, tax rate and profit margin. The calculations are shown in the upper right corner of the graph in Section 1 (see Figure 10-1 for the completed Stock Selection Guide). Reading estimated sales on the graph from our sales trend line at the year 2000, we get $55.5 billion. For our pre-tax profit margin, we go to line A of Section 2. The pre-tax profit margin has been on an upswing for the past ten years. We are looking for a time in the future when favorable conditions prevail; therefore, we pick 10 percent as the possible pre-tax profit margin at the next peak for this company. That is over the 8.6 percent average for the last five years but under the 11 percent that has been attained in the last two years. That 10 percent of the $55.5 billion in estimated sales amounts to $5.55 billion. Value Line is estimating the tax rate at 37 percent, which means that 63 percent (100 − 37 = 63) of 5.55 billion will be after-tax income. That figure, divided by the 588,573,987 shares we have recorded at the top of the page, gives us $5.94 for our estimated earnings per share five years in the future. These figures, $5.94 and $6.10, are close enough to give us confidence that our estimates under both procedures are reasonable.

We can use either one as we proceed. The use of the lower figure will, of course, be more conservative. If the company you are studying has convertible stock or substantial options outstanding, you would make a corresponding adjustment in the pre-tax earnings figure to cover the additional shares that might be issued.

The average low price for the next five years can be estimated in five different ways. We will discuss how to choose among them later. The first procedure is to multiply the average low P/E for the last five years by the current year's earnings per share. The theory is that a growing company will be increasing its earnings each year and probably will not sell at a lower P/E than it has in the past. The average low P/E for the last five years comes from column E, line 7.

The recent severe market low price is not necessarily the lowest price in the last five years, although we should consider that as a possibility. Here we look at the events of the past five years and ask ourselves, "Was there one year in particular when negative stock market forces were very strong and knocked most stock market prices down, or was there one year in which this particular company faced severe problems?" If we were working in 1988, we would remember that 1987 was a bad year for the stock market and would consequently use the low of that year for part B, line (c). If there were no such year, we would use the low of the five-year period. To calculate line (d), we divide the current annual dividend by the *highest* yield figure in Section 3, column H.

To set our price zones, we take the high we projected in Section 4, part A, 119 (118.8 rounded to the nearest full number), and subtract the possible low we chose in part B, 44. Subtracting 44 from 119 gives us 75, the range over which we expect the stock will sell. We divide that by 3 and get 25. That enables us to produce three zones, which we name the *buy, maybe,* and *sell zones.*

The upside/downside ratio is calculated by measuring the distance from the price at which we can buy the stock at this time, 56¼, to our estimated high, 119 (119 − 56¼ = 62.8). These 62.8 points are our upside potential. The risk on the downside (56¼ down to our low of 44) is 12.3 points. Dividing the upside points (62.8) by the downside points (12.3) suggests that our upside potential is 5.1 times the downside.

We expect our gain in the stock to come in two ways: from possible appreciation and from dividends. Part E of Section 4 is an indication of our possible gain from price appreciation. The source of the figures and the computations to be performed are precisely indicated. Figure 9-3 shows this section completed.

Section 5 is designed to show us the percent annual return the stock will produce for us if all of the estimates we have made actually develop. In part A, we divide the actual reported dividend, $0.40 (.10 × 4), by the current price to get 0.007. Multiplying that figure by 100 to convert it to a percentage gives us 0.7 percent.

We expect a growing company to increase its dividend each year as its earnings grow. We calculate the average dividend yield per year expected over the next five years by following the extended earnings per share trend line to the mid-year line of the five-year period, or 1998. That point is $4.60 (see Figure 10-1, EPS trend line for 1998). Section 3, column G, line 7, shows us that the company historically pays out 15.7 percent of earnings in dividends. Multiplying $4.60 by 15.7 percent suggests that the average dividend will be 72 cents. That figure divided by $56¼, the current price, indicates that this stock's average dividend yield over the next five years will be 1.3 percent.

In Section 4, part E, we calculated that we could enjoy as much as 112 percent appreciation in the stock's price over the next five years. In part C of

Figure 9-3
Evaluating Risk and Reward

4 EVALUATING RISK and REWARD over the next 5 years

Assuming one recession and one business boom every 5 years, calculations are made of how **high** and how **low** the stock might sell. The upside-downside ratio is the key to evaluating risk and rev

A HIGH PRICE — NEXT 5 YEARS
Avg. High P/E ___20___ (3D7 as adj.) X Estimate High Earnings/Share ___5.94___ = Forecast High Price $ ___118.8___ (4A1)

B LOW PRICE — NEXT 5 YEARS
(a) Avg. Low P/E ___15.1___ (3E7 as adj.) X Estimated Low Earnings/Share ___2.93___ = $ ___44.2___
(b) Avg. Low Price of Last 5 Years = ___29.1___ (3B7)
(c) Recent Severe Market Low Price = ___24.4___
(d) Price Dividend Will Support Present Divd. = ___.40___ = ___24___
                                High Yield (H)   ___.017___
Selected Estimated Low Price = $ ___44.2___ (4B1)

C ZONING
___119___ (4A1) High Forecast Price Minus ___44___ (4B1) Low Forecast Price Equals ___75___ (C) Range. 1/3 of Range = ___25___ (4CD)
(4C2) Lower 1/3 = (4B1) ___44___ to ___69___ (Buy)
(4C3) Middle 1/3 = ___69___ to ___94___ (Maybe)
(4C4) Upper 1/3 = ___94___ to ___119___ (4A1) (Sell)
Present Market Price of ___56 1/4___ is in the ___Buy___ (4C5) Range

D UP-SIDE DOWN-SIDE RATIO (Potential Gain vs. Risk of Loss)
High Price (4A1) ___119___ Minus Present Price ___56 1/4___ = ___62.8___ = ___5.1___ To 1
Present Price ___56 1/4___ Minus Low Price (4B1) ___44___   ___12.3___   (4D) interest terms.)

E PRICE TARGET (Note: Simple interest calculation is not at compounded rate.)
High Price (4A1) ___119___ = (___2.12___) X 100 = (___212___) – 100 = ___112___ % Appreciation
Present Market Price ___56 1/4___   (4E)

Figure 9-4
Five-Year Potential

5 5-YEAR POTENTIAL This combines price appreciation with dividend yield to get an estimate of total return. It provides a standard for comparing income and growth stocks.

A Present Full Year's Dividend $ __40__

Present Price of Stock $ __56.25__ = __.007__ X 100 = __.7__ (5A) Present Yield or % Returned on Purchase Price

Note: Results are expressed as a simple rate; use the table below to convert to a compound rate.

B AVERAGE YIELD OVER NEXT 5 YEARS

Avg. Earnings Per Share Next 5 Years __4.60__ X Avg. % Payout (3G7) __.157__ = __.722__ = __1.3__ %

Present Price $ __56.25__ (5B)

C ESTIMATED AVERAGE ANNUAL RETURN OVER NEXT FIVE YEARS

5 Year Appreciation Potential (4E) __112__ / 5 = __22.4__ %

Average Yield (5B) . . . . __1.3__ %

Average Total Annual Return Over the Next 5 Years (5C) __23.7__ %

Table to Convert From Simple to Compound Rate

Simple Rate 2 4 6 8 10 12 14 16 18 20 22 24 26 28 30 32 34 36 38 40

Compound Rate 2 4 6 8 10 12 14 16 18 20 22 24

Section 5 we divide that figure by 5 to get the percent yearly average appreciation, 22.4 percent. Adding the yearly expected appreciation, 22.4 percent, to the expected yearly dividend income, 1.3 percent, we get an anticipated 23.7 percent. This is referred to as *total return.* See Figure 9-4 for a summary of the figures in this section. The total return of 23.7 percent in arithmetic or simple interest terms converts, according to the table, to roughly 16½ percent compounded annually.

Next, let's discuss what the figures we have calculated tell us about this stock.

CHAPTER 10

WHAT THE NAIC STOCK SELECTION GUIDE AND REPORT TELLS US

VISUAL ANALYSIS

*T*he Capitalization box at the top of page 1 of the Stock Selection Guide and Report requires us to look at the company's capital structure. Is there an unusual amount of debt or potential dilution that should be noted here? As we gather this information by consulting a service or the company's 10K or annual report, other items may come to our attention. For Motorola, Value Line shows us that while there is $3.4 billion of debt, that is only 13 percent of the company's total capitalization, and all of the balance is common stock. Furthermore, the service indicates that the company is earning enough money each year to pay the interest on its debt fifteen times. Some of the debt is convertible into common stock, but the dilution does not look like it would be substantial. Our conclusion from these facts is that Motorola has a capital structure that should be favorable to the common shareowner. The completed Stock Selection Guide for Motorola appears in Figure 10-1.

We classify Motorola as a major company in a major industry. Ordinarily, we would expect a company its size to have a growth rate of 5 to 7 percent. Companies with sales in the billions have more difficulty producing growth at a rate above that than smaller companies. A look at the trend line we have drawn through Motorola's sales figures for the past ten years gets our attention for two reasons. One is the rapid rate of growth for a company its size.

Figure 10-1

Stock Selection Guide ®

The most widely used aid to good investment judgment

NATIONAL ASSOCIATION OF INVESTORS CORPORATION

NAIC ®

INVESTMENT EDUCATION FOR INDIVIDUALS AND CLUBS SINCE 1951

Company __Motorola, Inc.__ Date __1-10-96__
Prepared by __KSJ__ Data taken from __V-L__
Where traded __NYSE__ Major product/service __Semi-Conduc__

CAPITALIZATION — Outstanding Amounts

			% Insiders	% Institution
Preferred	None			
Common	588,573,987		3.5	64
Debt	3,389,000,000	% to Tot. Cap. 13	% Potential Dil.	—

1 VISUAL ANALYSIS of Sales, Earnings and Price

Figure 10-1 (Continued)

2 EVALUATING MANAGEMENT Company _Motorola Inc._

		19 86	1987	19 88	19 89	19 90	19 91	19 92	1993	19 94	19 95	LAST 5 YEAR AVG.	TREND UP	DOWN
A	% Pre-tax Profit on Sales (Net Before Taxes ÷ Sales)	4.5	6.2	7.4	7.4	6.1	5.4	6.0	9.0	11.0	11.4	8.6	↑	
B	% Earned on Equity (E/S ÷ Book Value)	7.0	10.2	13.2	14.0	11.7	9.8	11.2	15.9	17.2	17.5	14.3	↑	

3 PRICE-EARNINGS HISTORY as an indicator of the future

This shows how stock prices have fluctuated with earnings and dividends. It is a building block for translating earnings into future stock prices.

PRESENT PRICE **56 1/4** HIGH THIS YEAR **82.500** LOW THIS YEAR **51.500**

		A PRICE HIGH	B PRICE LOW	C Earnings Per Share	D Price Earnings Ratio HIGH A ÷ C	E Price Earnings Ratio LOW B ÷ C	F Dividend Per Share	G % Payout F ÷ C X 100	H % High Yield F ÷ B X 100
1	1991	17.8	11.4	0.86	20.7	13.3	.19	22.1	1.7
2	1992	26.6	16.1	1.08	24.6	14.9	.20	18.5	1.2
3	1993	53.8	24.4	1.78	30.2	13.7	.22	12.4	0.9
4	1994	61.1	42.1	2.65	23.1	15.9	.31	11.7	0.7
5	1995	82.5	51.5	2.93	28.2	17.6	.40	13.7	0.8
6	TOTAL		145.5		126.8	75.4		78.4	
7	AVERAGE		29.1		25.4	15.1		15.7	
8	AVERAGE PRICE EARNINGS RATIO			20.3	9	CURRENT PRICE EARNINGS RATIO		19.2	

4 EVALUATING RISK and REWARD over the next 5 years

(Est. 56 1/4/3.68=15.3)

Assuming one recession and one business boom every 5 years, calculations are made of how high and how low the stock might sell. The upside-downside ratio is the key to evaluating risk and rew.

A HIGH PRICE — NEXT 5 YEARS
Avg. High P/E _20_ (3G7 as adj.) X Estimate High Earnings/Share _5.94_ = Forecast High Price $ _118.8_ (4A1)

B LOW PRICE — NEXT 5 YEARS _15.1_
(a) Avg. Low P/E (3G7 as adj.) X Estimated Low Earnings/Share _2.93_ = $ _44.2_
(b) Avg. Low Price of Last 5 Years = _29.1_ (3B7)
(c) Recent Severe Market Low Price = _24.4_
(d) Price Dividend Will Support Present Divd. = _.40_ = _24_
High Yield (H) .017
Selected Estimated Low Price = $ _44.2_ (4B1)

C ZONING
_119_ High Forecast Price Minus _44_ Low Forecast Price Equals _75_ Range. 1/3 of Range = _25_
(4A1) (4B1) (C) (4CD)
(4C2) Lower 1/3 = (4B1) _44_ to _69_ (Buy)
(4C3) Middle 1/3 = _69_ to _94_ (Maybe)
(4C4) Upper 1/3 = _94_ to _119_ (4A1) (Sell)
Present Market Price of _56 1/4_ is in the **Buy** (4C5) Range

D UP-SIDE DOWN-SIDE RATIO (Potential Gain vs. Risk of Loss)
High Price (4A1) _119_ Minus Present Price _56 1/4_ = _62.8_ = _5.1_ To 1
Present Price _56 1/4_ Minus Low Price (4B1) _44_ = 12.3 (4D)

E PRICE TARGET (Note: Simple Interest calculation is not at compounded rate.) Interest terms.)
High Price (4A1) _119_ = (_2.12_) X 100 = (_212_) − 100 = _112_ % Appreciation
Present Market Price _56 1/4_ (4E)

5 5-YEAR POTENTIAL This combines price appreciation with dividend yield to get an estimate of total return. It provides a standard for comparing income and growth stocks

Note: Results are expressed as a simple rate; use the table below to convert to a compound rate.

A Present Full Year's Dividend $ _.40_ = _.007_ X 100 = _.7_ Present Yield or % Returned on Purchase Price
Present Price of Stock $ _56.25_ (5A)

B AVERAGE YIELD OVER NEXT 5 YEARS
Avg. Earnings Per Share Next 5 Years _4.60_ X Avg. % Payout (3G7) _.157_ = _.722_ = 1.3 %
Present Price $ _56.25_ (5B)

C ESTIMATED AVERAGE ANNUAL RETURN OVER NEXT FIVE YEARS
5 Year Appreciation Potential (4E) _112_ = 22.4 %
5
Average Yield (5B) . . . . 1.3 %
Average Total Annual Return Over the Next 5 Years (5C) 23.7 %

Table to Convert From Simple to Compound Rate

Simple Rate 2 4 6 8 10 12 14 16 18 20 22 24 26 28 30 32 34 36 40
Compound Rate 2 4 6 8 10 12 14 16 18 20 22 24

The second is the relative steadiness of the line for a business that is inclined to be quite cyclical.

What is the rate of growth for Motorola's sales? We plotted lines using four different methods. Refer back to pages 73 through 79 in Chapter 8. The best judgment method line we have drawn shows a growth rate of about 18 percent, and the others range from approximately 16 to 19 percent. NAIC's Investor's Toolkit software program for the Guide computes the growth rate exactly and comes up with 17.9 percent. The historical growth rate—the rate at which we estimated the company has grown in the past ten years—is recorded at the bottom of the graph. Some members of the club may estimate 17 percent; others may go as high as 20 percent. The exact figure is not important. What we are deciding at this point is: has the company grown fast enough in the past ten years to make it a candidate for further study? Earlier, when we were looking for a large company for our portfolio, we said we would be happy with a company that had grown 5 to 7 percent. This company, at 18 percent, has a growth rate higher than we would hope to find for a small company. Motorola seems to give us the growth of a small company along with the greater strength and stability of a giant company. Motorola more than meets our test for rate of sales growth.

Next, we check the earnings-per-share growth rate line. Since we are buying shares in this company and have found its sales growth rate to be satisfactory, we want to see whether management is translating that growth into a similar rate of growth in earnings per share. The dotted line on the graph shows earnings-per-share growth, which has exceeded sales growth for the past five years. The slope of the line makes that very clear.

It is always a good idea to check whether the growth rate in earnings per share for the last five years has been the same as or better than the rate for the first five years of our study. It is clear that growth over the last five years has been very vigorous. It is difficult for a company to sustain a rate of growth as great as that which Motorola shows from 1992 through 1994. Our Toolkit program calculates the historical growth rate at 22.3 percent. Our best judgment method estimate for the latest five years would be 25 percent or better. Obviously, Motorola meets our second test of advancing earnings per share at a rate at least as high as sales growth.

At this point, we should make a judgment as to how Motorola's sales and earnings might grow over the coming five years. Experience has shown that a compounded growth rate above 15 percent a year is very difficult for a company to maintain. It is usually advisable not to project growth at a higher rate, though there are exceptions to that rule. Investors saw Wal-Mart grow at a rate in excess of 20 percent for many years. NAIC members have owned large numbers of shares in AFLAC, McDonald's and RPM and watched them produce extraordinary rates of growth year after year. RPM has now had forty-nine straight years of increased sales and earnings per share. Nevertheless, experience dictates that we forecast a little under the rate of the past five years, especially if that rate is above 15 percent.

At this point, it is a good idea to try to develop as good an understanding of the business as possible. You can do this by reading what the investment services say about the company. Your business library may have a folder of clippings of articles about the company. Your broker may have issued research reports on the company or have copies of reports others have issued. You can also call the shareholder relations department of the company; Value Line and Standard & Poor's will have the phone number in their report on the company. That department will mail you copies of the company's latest releases, its annual report, and copies of brokers' articles about it.

From these materials we learn that Motorola is a leader in the communications industry, particularly in the wireless area—cellular phones, pagers, and two-way radios. The whole world is its market, and many experts believe its growth could continue for many years.

We know there is never a guarantee that such growth will take place, but we decide to project Motorola's sales and earnings for the next five years at a compound annual rate of growth of 15 percent. There is always the question of from where we make that projection. The figures in Section 2 have some influence on that decision. However, with Motorola's record of increasing pretax profit margin and its current good though not excessive margin, we decide to project based on the most recent year's earnings per share. If we thought the company's present margin was too high and would not be maintained over the next five years, we might project from slightly below the earnings of the latest year. If we had good reason to believe they would be better, we would project above.

PRE-TAX AND EQUITY MARGINS

The pre-tax profit margin is the amount of profit that a company makes on each dollar of sales before taxes. The profit margin on Motorola's products before taxes over the past ten years has ranged from 4½ percent to 11 percent. Compared with drug companies and a number of other businesses, this is a very modest figure. The margins in different industries vary greatly, and in time the investor learns the rate common to a particular industry and consequently recognizes margins that are outstanding. In the manufacturing industry the margins cover a wide range, 10 to 20 percent being common. In banking an operating margin above 1 percent is considered exceptional.

The interesting thing about Motorola's pre-tax profit margin is that it has increased steadily over the past ten years. That indicates management's successful attention to controlling costs and increasing margins. At the same time, Motorola's margin does not seem excessive for its seemingly dominant position in the industry. Without knowing much detail about the operations, we would think that Motorola has room to maintain or increase its pre-tax margin.

Motorola's earnings on equity have followed the same pattern as its pre-tax profit margin. Earnings have been steadily increasing over the years, but are not at a level that seems impossible to sustain. If management is able to increase both sales and margins, Motorola's profit could be remarkable. The investor usually finds the greatest opportunity in companies where the percent earned on equity is above 20 percent. That is a very significant indicator of the rate at which shareowner value is increasing.

PRICE/EARNINGS HISTORY

Section 3, a record of the price/earnings history of the stock, is very important. NAIC's experience with thousands of investors shows that the great majority does a very good job of identifying high-growth companies. The most frequent error they make is paying too high a price for the stock.

The figures in Section 3 are all precise. While we emphasize that the figures in the Stock Selection Guide and Report should be adjusted to reflect changes we expect to take place, many people accept the figures as they are and make no changes. The important figures to look at in this section are the price/earnings ratios. These ratios change tremendously over a business cycle. Look at Figure I-5 on pages 8 and 9 of this book. In the seventy years spanned by that table, the average price/earnings ratio on the Dow Jones Industrials has been as low as 6.8 and as high as 25.1. When market optimism is very low, P/E ratios decline. When market optimism is high, they soar.

The first thing the investor should ask when studying a P/E is where are we now in the long-term stock market cycle. We have enjoyed an upward-moving stock market since 1983 (at the time of this writing, it is 1996). History tells us that a severe break in the upward market trend is due. Yet, many factors in the world economy suggest that we could still have a number of years of market buoyancy. While the stock market is high by past standards, the excessive speculation that usually occurs before a major long-term break in the market does not seem to be present. The average price/earnings ratio on the S&P 500 is currently around 15. Although ratios are above the average for the past twenty years, they are not excessively high. No one ever knows what the market will do, but a good case can be made at this time that we are in a period of market enthusiasm in which average P/E ratios of 15 to 21 may prevail for some time. A number of thoughtful analysts believe that a long-term decline in the market will not occur for a number of years.

For our prediction five years into the future, our conclusion at this time is that prevailing P/E ratios are likely to continue. If we were in a period where average high ratios for the past ten years had been around 7 to 10, we would believe that an increase of 4 or 5 points would be reasonable five years forward, and would consider adjusting our projected average high P/E upward. If we judged that we were really in a period of excessive speculation and that a long-term change in the direction of the market was at hand, we would consider changing the current average high P/E to a lower figure five years out.

The P/E of a company can be affected by investor attitude toward its industry. Companies in a growth industry usually enjoy P/E ratios above the average. Also, the higher the rate of growth the company has had and the longer it has produced that growth, the higher its P/E is likely to be. Value Line periodically publishes the average P/E ratios that have prevailed in various industry classifications.

Some companies are entering a period of declining growth. When that happens, the P/E for the company will decline. A classic illustration is Wal-Mart. For many years management pushed Wal-Mart's annual sales and earnings per share ahead at 25 percent or better, and the P/E ran between 25 and 35. Then the rate of growth began to slow, and the P/E gradually dropped. The result has been that while the company is still experiencing excellent growth, its lower growth rate has led to a lower P/E and the price of the stock has changed little in several years, in spite of sizable increases in sales and earnings per share.

As we look at the P/E record of Motorola, we conclude that the company's average high P/E has been well above the market average. This, we would judge, is due to the high growth rate of sales and earnings produced by the company's management for at least the past ten years. The reports we read from management and security analysts suggest that they believe Motorola's growth is likely to continue at a high rate for at least the next five years. Our decision is to use 20, which is just below the last five years' average of the average high and low P/E ratios, as shown in Section 3, line 8, to make our five-year projection of earnings per share.

EVALUATING RISK AND REWARD

We have two estimates of what Motorola will be earning per share five years in the future. One we obtained by projecting our earnings per share trend line five years into the future at 15 percent, compounded annually, as we explained earlier. This gave us a figure of $6.10 as Motorola's potential earnings per share for the year 2000.

We obtained another estimate using what we call the preferred procedure, which is based on a projection of sales rather than earnings and the application of our estimated tax rates and profit margins. Analysts generally believe that sales can be more accurately projected than can earnings per share. Also, the separate application of a chosen tax rate and pre-tax profit margin gives you more control over your estimate. By projecting sales at 15 percent to the year 2000, we derive a sales projection of $55.5 billion. Section 2, part A shows us that the pre-tax profit margin has been increasing steadily and has been above 11 percent for the last two years. We are making an optimistic projection and so decide to use 10 percent rather than the average of the last five years, 8.6 percent. This gives us a pre-tax profit of $5.55 billion.

Value Line estimates the future tax rate at 37 percent. Since we have no ideas of our own concerning the future tax rate, we go along with Value Line. If 37 percent of profit is going to go out in taxes, we will have a balance of 63 percent left ($100\% - 37\% = 63\%$) as after-tax income. That gives us $3.496 billion, which, divided by the 588,573,987 shares outstanding, leaves us $5.94 per share according to the preferred method (see Figure 10-1). That is fairly close to the $6.10 we obtained by projecting our earnings per share trend line. We could use either one to project our high price for the year 2000.

There is no guarantee that the stock will sell that high in 2000. But our judgment is that if the company grows at 15 percent, which is below the rate of 17.9 percent at which it has grown for the last ten years, and if it sells at a P/E of 20, it will reach that price.

We know that in a five-year period stocks will both go up and go down. We have estimated a possible high for our stock. The next question is how low is this stock likely to go in the next five years. A look at the high and low prices of the past five years shows that the price has been very volatile. NAIC suggests five different ways of estimating the possible low price. Four of these are shown in Section 4, part B of the Guide. The fifth is useful only at a certain period in the market cycle.

The first method, shown on line (a), is the same as we used in estimating the high price. We take the average low P/E for the past five years and multiply it by earnings per share for the latest year in our study. The theory is that in a growing company, earnings will advance each year. The current year should show the lowest earnings of the coming five years, and, multiplied by the average low P/E, should determine the lowest price the stock will sell at. The second method for judging the potential low price is to use the average low price for the last five years found in Section 3, column B, line 7. The third method uses the recent severe market low, and the fourth method uses the price the dividend will support. A fifth possible low price is calculated by taking the recent high price of 82.50 and reducing it by 25 percent, which would result in 61.8.

The method of line (a) is probably the most appropriate for Motorola. This is generally the most reliable procedure for a growing company. Methods (b) and (c) are better guides for cyclical companies, where the movement up and down is dictated more by general economic conditions than by growth in the company. Method (d) is best used when the company you are looking at is bought more for yield than for growth. The idea here is that buyers looking for yield watch the price of a stock, and when it comes down to the point where the yield is as high as it has been at past low periods they come into the market and buy the stock. Their buying reverses the downward trend of the stock.

The fifth procedure is often used when the market is starting upward after a long downward trend. For instance, in the 1970s stock prices and price/earnings ratios moved downward for a long period. The upward trend started in the 1980s. Stocks were moving to new highs and lows and moving higher each year. Working with five years of downward-moving prices at a time when prices were moving upward resulted in forecast lows that kept investors from buying good stocks. In such periods, corrections in the market seldom exceeded 25 percent. Calculating a possible low in this manner and comparing it with the others can be useful under such market conditions. This method is not useful in other market conditions, however. Note that in Motorola's case the correction from high to low has been as much as 50 percent in one year and over 30 percent in the other years.

We chose 44 as our possible low price for Motorola—44.2 rounded to the nearest whole number.

The purpose of the zoning section, part C, is to estimate the price ranges over which we should question whether to buy, hold, or sell the stock. Our goal is to double our money in the coming five years. If we buy Motorola at the current price and it reaches our projected high of 119, we will have attained that goal. Dividing the price range between our projected high and low into thirds shows us the area in which we could buy the stock and the area where we could sell and approximate our goal.

The upside/downside ratio, part D, is another way to check whether we can currently buy the stock at a price that is favorable. Here the idea is that we want our potential on the upside to be three times our risk on the downside. This means we would like the figure in this section to be 3 to 1 or better. Again, we should keep in mind that we are working with possibilities or probabilities and not events that will precisely match our figures. In Motorola's case our upside/downside ratio at a price of 56¼ is 5.1 to 1. This suggests that the odds on the upside are better than those on the downside by 5 to 1. A buy in the present price range does not appear to be risky. This is a very-high growth stock; it is a leader in its field, and our study shows that we could double our money. We would buy. If the price were at its recent high of 82½, we would conclude that the risk is high and that a purchase should be postponed.

If we buy the stock and its price moves up into the sell zone, we should consider whether to sell. Based on the experience of NAIC investors, when you own a stock with a growth rate as high as this stock has, it is dangerous to sell it. You should consider a sale only if the growth rate comes down and there is no apparent reason to expect it to go back up in the foreseeable future. Or speculation may drive the stock to an unreasonable high. For instance, if

Motorola's price suddenly moved up to 225, that would represent a P/E of 70, almost three times its normal high P/E of 25.4. Common sense suggests that price is not likely to be maintained because it is so far out of line with earnings. In such a case, we might sell, say, 25 percent of our holdings and look for another outstanding growth company for a new opportunity.

If the price of the stock declines, it may be that we have realized enough profit from our stock and should review the prospects of our remaining shares. If the company is still judged a well-managed company with good growth prospects, we will continue to hold our shares.

Part E of Section 4 calculates the percent appreciation we may attain from this stock if the sales and earnings growth and price action we have estimated for this stock work out as calculated. Since our goal is a 100 percent gain in five years, we are satisfied that Motorola's 112 percent meets our goal.

FIVE-YEAR POTENTIAL

Section 5 provides a further check that the combination of dividend income and appreciation projected for this stock will enable us to achieve our goal of doubling value in the coming five years. Part A is the calculation of our yield at the time of purchase. Part B is the calculation of the average annual dividend return estimated over the next five years. In part C we add these together and see that if all goes according to our estimates, we will enjoy an annual return of 23.7 percent. We need 20 percent a year to double our value. These figures are based on an arithmetic calculation. Using compounded annual figures, the total needed to double the stock's value would be 14.9 percent per year. For Motorola, using the conversion table, we have approximately 16½ percent compounded annual growth.

REACHING A FINAL DECISION

The final set of eight questions in the Stock Selection Guide and Report is designed to help us reach a decision based on the results we have calculated as to whether this company is the kind of investment we are looking for.

For Question 1 we review the sales and earnings per share record and conclude that both are growing at a rate sufficient to double our values in five years. Our decision is that this growth is likely to continue for the next five years. The company's growth seems to be based on superior research producing a superior product. We summarize our conclusions in the space provided.

Question 2 covers the three most important tests of management: Is it producing the desired rate of sales growth? Does it meet our standards for earnings growth? If so, is it earning a good rate on equity? If those answers are positive, we must answer the additional question: can we buy those good things at a reasonable price?

Question 3 directs us to check the P/E ratios and price zones. We conclude that Motorola's high growth rate has been recognized by the market as reflected in a high P/E. The price is currently in the middle of our buy zone.

It is a good idea to look at the three tests of safety concerning the price. That is what Question 4 guides us to do. If the stock has sold for a price as high as we are going to pay for it in several of the past five years, that is an indication that we can get out if something unforeseen turns up about the company suggesting that we have made a mistake and should sell it. Motorola has sold at a price as high as we are going to have to pay in two of the past five years. This is favorable. Second, Motorola's upside/downside ratio is 5 to 1, which is also favorable. However, due to the business cycle which has been very long on the upside, we will select average. The third test indicates that we could more than double our investment in five years. All three tests suggest that a buy at 56¼ is favorable at this time.

It is important to consider the market characteristics of the stock. This is the focus of Question 5. If the stock is not well known and valued by the market, its good qualities may not be recognized for a long time, and the investor will not benefit. Value Line has a sixteen-year record on Motorola. The company is older than that, but the record of the last sixteen years shows it has been an important business for all those years. It operates worldwide. Its products are sold to government, businesses, and consumers. It is a leader in its industry. It is well known to both institutional and individual investors. Its stock is listed on the New York Stock Exchange. All of these things tell us that its investment characteristics are favorable.

If the company's investment characteristics are good, we next examine the characteristics of its main industry. Question 6 prompts us in this area. Motorola is in both the electronics and communications industries, two of the biggest and fastest-growing in the world. Continued growth will come from population (supplying the many still lightly industrialized nations), product development, scientific advances, and international growth. Al-

Figure 10-1 (Continued)

GOALS IN SELECTING A STOCK

You want to look ahead five years by **judging** Management capability and **evaluating** the Price you should pay for a stock. You should also look at **Other Considerations** and reach a **Conclusion**. Your findings are registered in the table at the right and your Conclusion below.

Novice and professional investors to varying degrees may act hastily on new products, tips, technical clues and short term factors rather than being methodical in their decisions. Thirty years of experience with this type of report tends to show that there is a RULE OF FIVE, which is this: If five companies are analyzed for their five year future, one may have unforeseeable trouble, three may be on target, and one may have unpredictable good fortune.

CONCLUSION: _____*Motorola has a sales and earnings*_____

_____*per share growth record that more than meets*_____

_____*our goal. Its margins are good but not super.*_____

_____*Its price is a little high. Buy on dips.*_____

(1) Our goal is to find a company with **able** MANAGEMENT; and (2) to buy a stock at a **good** PRICE.

	Page	Good	Average	Poor
Judging Management				
Driving Force	3	✔		
Earned on Sales	3	✔		
Earned on Equity	3	✔		
Evaluating Price				
High in 5 Years	4	✔		
Low in 5 Years	4	✔		
Upside-Downside Ratio	4		✔	
Yield Current	4			✔
Total Return	4	✔		
Other Considerations				
Industry Potentials	4	✔		
State of Business Cycle	4		✔	
Stock Price Trends	4		✔	
Quality of Stock	4	✔		
Capitalization and Finance	2	✔		

METHOD-DATA-INSTRUCTIONS

This report organizes data presentation in a concise professional manner, avoiding among other things the agony of deciding what factors to cover. Because writing is a chore, the cross-out-method lets you report your judgments with ease. The data used comes from Value Line and Standard and Poor's Reports that are available on many listed and unlisted companies. You may wish to check your 5 year "high estimate" with Value Line's estimated Target Price Range for 3 to 5 years

hence. Instructions for completing pages 3 and 4 of this report are in the NAIC Official Guide obtainable from the National Association of Investors Corporation, P.O. Box 220, Royal Oak, Michigan 48068. Other sources of data are annual and quarterly reports from companies, brokers reports and visits to company annual meetings. You may learn by yourself, or with several friends, or by actually investing $20 or $50 a month through an investment club you have formed with friends.

1 WHAT DOES THE VISUAL ANALYSIS SHOW?

The trend of (sales) (~~revenues~~) is (up) (~~down~~) (~~sideways~~).

The trend of earnings per share is (up) (~~down~~) (~~sideways~~).

The price trend of the stock is (up) (~~down~~) (~~sideways~~).

If sales trend is up, the increase seems to have come from (taking a greater share of the market) (~~mergers and acquisitions~~) (new products or new product applications produced by research).

In my opinion, the stock should be (investigated) (~~discarded~~) because the trend of sales is (favorable) (~~neutral~~) (~~unfavorable~~); the trend of earnings per share is (favorable) (~~neutral~~) (~~unfavorable~~); the price is (~~favorable~~) (neutral) (~~unfavorable~~).

Also for other reasons as follows: *The company's*

_____*products seem to be tops. The company*_____

_____*is very strong in Asia and Pacific Rim*_____

_____*countries and its margins have been*_____

_____*growing.*_____

2 DOES THE COMPANY PASS THE THREE MANAGEMENT TESTS?

Investors lose money because of failing to test for good management. Instead they rely on outlook for the industry, new products, or a plausible story for protection and often lose.

TEST I: DRIVING FORCE OF MANAGEMENT
Management as indicated by the past record has the necessary ability to expand sales (yes) (~~no~~). The rate of sales expansion on the VISUAL ANALYSIS looks like ___*17.9*___ % annually. The rate of sales expansion is likely to be (~~better~~) (same) (~~worse~~) in the next five years.

TEST II: EARNED ON SALES
Management seems to have the ability to (~~maintain~~) (increase) profit margins (see 2A, Evaluating Management on page 2 at left). It shows the Pre-Tax Profit Margins for each of the last five years as follows in

chronological order:
___*5.4*___ %, ___*6.0*___ %, ___*9.0*___ %, ___*11.0*___ %, ___*10.9*___ %.

TEST III: EARNED ON EQUITY
The company has earned on invested capital from ___*7.1*___ % to ___*17.1*___ %. See 2B, Evaluating Management on page 2 at left. Earnings on equity are (above) (~~below~~) 10%.

I conclude from these three tests that the company has (good) (~~average~~) (~~poor~~) management and will be (stronger) (~~same~~) (~~weaker~~) in five years.

Over a period of five years, a well-managed company will generally gain ground while a poor one loses its earning power. Remember this in making your decision.

continued . . .

Figure 10-1 (Continued)

3 WHAT IS THE PRICE RANGE LIKELY TO BE FOR THE NEXT FIVE YEARS?

Complete Section 3 of the Stock Selection Guide & Report (page 2). Two considerations are important: (1) It is usually better to project sales and apply profit margins and taxes than to project earnings per share on the chart because profit margins tend to have definite upside limits; and (2) it is well to pay less attention to, or discard the much higher price-earnings ratios existing in years of low earnings. Also, avoid being misled by sales increases in early years of a new product or attributable to government or other types of contracts that may not be renewed or are due entirely to the upswing of a business cycle.

Have price-earnings (P/E) ratios for the past five years been trending ~~(downward)~~ ~~(level)~~ (upward)? Is the P/E ratio (higher) ~~(same)~~ ~~(lower)~~ than its competitors? Have the average price earnings ratios of the

past five years been influenced by years when the ratio was (unusually high) ~~(unusually low)~~?

Over the next five years, the stock might be expected to reach a high price of __119__ and also a low of __44__ when the next depression comes. It now sells at __56 1/4__ , indicating ~~(little)~~ (average) ~~(great)~~ risk. Its suggested buy prices should range from __44__ to __69__ , hold from __69__ to __94__ , and sell from __94__ to __119__ .

These are the zones calculated in the Stock Selection Guide & Report (Section 4C, page 2). Be a careful buyer.

4 HOW DOES THE STOCK MEET THE THREE SAFETY TESTS OF PRICE?

Unsuccessful investment clubs and investors make two mistakes; (1) selection of poorly managed companies, (2) pay too much for stocks. The second mistake is by far the most prevalent and most damaging, and is easily corrected. Big losses have been taken in high grade stocks because they were bought mainly, "because they were moving" or sold "because they went down"—not because of price. The best results have been obtained by investors that buy carefully.

TEST I: SHOWS PROBABILITY OF GETTING OUT EVEN
The stock under review has sold at its present price in (__two__)* ~~(none)~~ of the last five years. The risk of loss seems ~~(small)~~ (average) ~~(considerable)~~ at the present price on the basis of price history.

* *Three of five is a good standard.*

TEST II: STACK THE ODDS IN THE INVESTORS FAVOR
The upside-downside ratio from Section 4D, page 2 of the Stock Selection Guide & Report is __5.1__ to 1. This is ~~(favorable)~~ (average) ~~(unfavorable)~~, indicating that we need to pay attention to past price history (considerably) ~~(some)~~ ~~(not much)~~.

TEST III: THESE STANDARDS HELP INVESTORS AVOID LOSS
The pay-off test is whether at least 100% appreciation is possible in five years—or in the case of cyclical stocks, 20% a year for the number of years held. Analysis shows a high price of __119__ is reasonable in __5__ years, equal to __22.4__ % a year.

In the case of cyclical stocks, comment should include the number of months the cycle has advanced and the dangers on this account.

5 WHAT ARE THE INVESTMENT CHARACTERISTICS OF THE COMPANY?

The Company is (well established) ~~(new)~~ and operates (internationally) ~~(nationally)~~ ~~(regionally)~~. The product line or service is (diversified) ~~(narrow)~~ and sold to (consumers) (manufacturers) (government). The business cycle affects sales and earnings ~~(not much)~~ ~~(severely)~~ (average). The company is ~~(largest)~~ (in top four) ~~(a smaller factor)~~ in its industry. The company and products are (well known) ~~(average)~~

~~(not known)~~ to the investing public. Its common stock is listed on (New York) ~~(American)~~ ~~(other exchange)~~ ~~(unlisted)~~ and has price records covering (five years) ~~(only ____ years)~~. It has a (continuous dividend record dating from __16 +__) ~~(a spotty dividend record)~~ ~~(no dividend record)~~. Investment characteristics are (good) ~~(average)~~ ~~(poor)~~.

6 WHAT ARE THE CHARACTERISTICS OF THE COMPANY'S MAJOR INDUSTRY?

The __electronics__ industry is (established) ~~(new)~~ and has (exceptional) ~~(average)~~ ~~(below average)~~ potential. The potential is based on (population) (product development) (science) (international expansion). Sales, profit margins and earnings per share fluctuate with the business cycle ~~(widely—like the steel industry)~~ ~~(narrowly—like food)~~ (average—like oil). Capital investment per dollar of sales in the industry is (high—like chemicals) ~~(low—like clothing manufacture)~~ ~~(aver-~~

~~age—like metal products manufacturing)~~, making it ~~(easy)~~ (difficult) for new competition to enter the business. Price competition between companies is ~~(no problem)~~ ~~(severe)~~ (average).

In my opinion, the major industry, everything considered, is (favorable) ~~(average)~~ ~~(unfavorable)~~. The company being analyzed will be (aided by the trend of the industry) or ~~(will have to take business from competitors to grow)~~.

7 WHAT ABOUT THE BUSINESS CYCLE?

About 33 months is an average business cycle, though variations from this norm are wide.

A well-managed company gains on marginal competitors in a depression or inflation as a general rule. In a period of business recovery, high grade stocks advance first, second grade stocks next, and marginal stocks last, as a general rule. Also, non-growth cyclical stocks are good purchases when business

turns up and should be sold in the later stages of the cycle because of exposure to substantial drops in price, earnings, and sometimes dividends.

The trend of business has been (up) ~~(down)~~ for __144 +__ months. The current stage of the business cycle tends to ~~(help)~~ (not affect) ~~(hurt)~~ profits of the company. The present stage of the business cycle suggests ~~(no concern)~~ (caution) ~~(daring)~~ for the stock under review.

8 WHAT ABOUT THE STOCK MARKET AND YIELDS ON BONDS?

The price the stock is selling at is __56 1/4__ and the Dow Jones Averages are at: Industrials __4802.45__ , Transportation __1916.17__ and Utilities __217.94__ . This provides a reference in case of review of this stock in the future.

From the Value Line, it is seen that the stock under review has performed, as compared relatively (better) ~~(same)~~ ~~(below)~~.

You may also want to comment on the behavior of bond yields and Treasury Bill rates. Yields tend to rise in the later stages of a business cycle (attracting money from the stock market) and fall when business slows and investors want safety.

Bond yields may ~~(attract)~~ (not affect) ~~(discourage)~~ investment in this stock currently though it is a growth business, Motorola is still affected by the business cycle. While entrepreneurs may come up with competing products, the capital needed to produce them will slow the competition. Nevertheless, competition is strong in the industry. Our conclusion is that the company is in a good industry.

For Question 7, we make an effort to determine where we are in the business and stock market cycle. Stock prices have been going up since 1983 without a lengthy major setback. That is unusual and suggests that we should not be surprised if a correction occurs. Prices could drop 25 percent or more. We would hope that they would not stay down for a lengthy period, but there have been times when a downtrend has continued for ten years or more. That suggests that our purchases should have a strong upside potential.

A long downward trend is a period of exceptional opportunity for the investor. During such periods practically every stock is an exceptional buy. But for investors such times are very difficult psychologically. The climate tends to be very pessimistic. The media features all the bad possibilities. The end of the world seems more likely than a recovery in business and the stock market. However, once the investor has gone through a down period and enjoyed the subsequent recovery, investing during a down period is much easier.

The standard Wall Street wisdom advises the investor to move out of the stock market at the peak and wait for the bottom to come back. Such logic is beyond question. The problem is that few possess the ability to pick those spots. A number of studies have been made in recent years comparing the records of individuals who try to move out of the market at peaks and back in at bottoms with the records of those who invest in good-quality stocks and move only when they decide to change one stock for another. Professors Jess H. Chua and Richard S. Woodward of the University of Calgary found that the individual who made an effort to get in and out in response to market moves had to catch 80 percent of the moves to equal the record of the individuals who stayed in the market.

A major reason that investors are not successful in moving in and out of the market is that the major part of an up or down move ordinarily takes place in just a few days. The person out of the market misses a good part of the move while waiting to get back in, as does the individual planning on getting out. One study points out that the market from 1982 to the break in 1987 contained 1,276 trading days. If you were fully invested during all that time, your annual return would have been 26.3 percent. If you were out during the twenty days with the largest gains, your return would have been 13.1 percent. If you missed the forty days with the biggest gains, your return would have been only 4.3 percent.

Less than 4 percent of the trading days generated 80 percent of the return. The individual trying to get in and out of the market at the most profitable times faces a formidable task. It has been said that the greatest risk is not being in the market but being out of the market.

As we make a study of a company using the NAIC Stock Selection Guide and Report, it is good to keep in mind that although every stock we select has prospects of meeting our goal, not all of them will do so. Some will approximate our goal. Some will do much better, and some will be a disaster. One of NAIC's founders, and the man who developed NAIC's Stock Study Procedures, referred to the likely results as the rule of five. Out of every five stocks the investor carefully selects, one is likely to have unexpected trouble, three are likely to meet expectations, and one is likely to have unpredictable good fortune. We obtain our goal with the average.

The computerized version of the Stock Selection Guide does not include the questions contained in the Stock Selection Guide and Report. It is a good idea to ask them and verify that the answers are what you want. We want the company to pass the management and price tests posed by the Guide. Has management produced the sales and earnings-per-share growth we seek? Has management produced the pre-tax profit margins and earnings on equity that meet or surpass its competitors? Do the stock's price figures indicate it can meet our goals and the safety tests we have established? Also, do we know enough about the company and its position in its industry to make informed decisions?

ONE LAST WORD

The NAIC Stock Selection Guide focuses on two important areas—management and price. The management tests are sales and earnings per share growth, the percentage of pre-tax profit on sales (profit margin), and the percent earned on equity. Weighing the record of these investment factors and then adding judgment as to the future potential will give the investor a good feeling for the management of the company. If these items suggest you have a company producing sales, earnings, and margins capable of making the company more valuable in the future, you would then proceed to determine whether the stock appears to be attractive at its current price level.

The second part of the NAIC Stock Selection Guide deals with price. While some companies may meet all of the management tests, the price of the stock is all-important. Possible judgments are required that might effect the stock in the next five years, such as looking at the price earnings ratio and this current multiple in relation to the possible future growth of the company.

The NAIC Stock Selection Guide is not an all-inclusive tool, but the factors included in the Guide cover about 80% of what determines the potential of the stock.

Investors will find many other investment factors mentioned by writers and security analysts. In NAIC's experience, these other items are interesting and add to the investor's knowledge and understanding of the company, as well as the investment process, but are generally of considerably less significance and value in determining the investment's future value than the basic factors in the Guide. The computer has made the calculation of many items quick and easy and investors should not hesitate to look at every item, but it is vital to keep one's emphasis on the factors that have major influence and not give undue weight to items of interest, but of lesser value.

CHAPTER 11

THE STOCK COMPARISON GUIDE

*I*nvariably, in every club, one or two people emerge who are able to sway their colleagues regardless of the merits of their case. To help your club buy the best stock, rather than voting on the best sales job, turn to the NAIC Stock Comparison Guide. This form should be produced during the meeting as reports are given. A giant version of the Guide that everyone can see is ideal.

To keep preconceived prejudices out of the picture, some clubs label their alternative investment opportunities not by name but by the letters A, B, and C. This strategy focuses attention exclusively on the data presented on the form.

Putting the Stock Comparison Guide to use is simple once Stock Selection Guides have been completed on the candidate companies. Arrangement of data generally follows the same order in which findings appear in the Stock Selection Guide. One person in the club should be assigned at each meeting to prepare the Guide. This can be done as members give their reports on individual companies. After the last report is given, the club turns its attention to the Stock Comparison Guide.

Findings based on the Stock Comparison Guide will prove more meaningful if the companies under review are in similar industries. However, the comparisons made are basic to the investment potential of any stock, and as long as members keep the differences between companies in mind, the comparisons will be profitable. NAIC's software provides a quick and easy way to prepare this form. All of NAIC's stock evaluation software includes the Stock Comparison Guide.

DESIRABLE CHARACTERISTICS

As individual members make reports to the group, evaluate the data to decide whether they reflect true growth. Is growth the result of management, an accident of the industry, patent advantage, or a special skill? Keep in mind these desirable characteristics:

1. A consistent record of growth in sales and earnings per share (the more consistent this record is, the more reliable it is as an indicator of the future).

2. A high pre-tax profit margin, reflecting management skill in operating efficiently, in securing a special advantage in the industry, in developing patent advantage, or in some other special area. Understanding the nature of the advantage helps you to project its likely longevity.

3. High return on stockholders' equity—this is another indicator of management skill and shows the rate at which share value is increasing.

4. A high rate of earnings plowback, permitting expansion financing without dilution of present stockholders' interests.

5. Established products or services of superior quality with further potential.

6. Alert, aggressive management capable of developing new products or services to broaden markets.

7. Relative independence from the business cycle and other external influences such as government regulation.

As a matter of sound practice, we recommend that all reports be heard before discussion by the membership takes place. The reports should be limited in time to permit ample time for questions and comments by the audience.

The sample Guide in Figure 11-1 features three leading companies in the electronic connector industry: AMP, Molex, and Thomas & Betts.

We first check for the company with the highest projected growth rate in sales and earnings per share. These figures are taken from the ratio chart of the corresponding Stock Selection Guides (see Figures 11-2, 11-3, and 11-4). Keep in mind that we are looking first at the historical rate of growth and then at the rate projected out five years. If we are right in our projection, it will be the most important of the two indicators. On our Stock Comparison Guide, we draw circles around the figures that are highest. The leader in both instances is Molex.

Figure 11-1

Completed Stock Comparison Guide with Data for AMP, Molex, and Thomas & Betts

NATIONAL ASSOCIATION OF INVESTORS CORPORATION **NAIC ®** INVESTMENT EDUCATION FOR INDIVIDUALS AND CLUBS SINCE 1951	*Stock Comparison Guide* ®	Prepared by _____ Date 8-31-95 _____ See Chapter 11 of the NAIC Official Guide for complete instructions. **NAME OF COMPANY**

GROWTH COMPARISONS (From Section 1 of the NAIC Stock Selection Guide)	AMP	Molex	Thomas & Betts		
(1) Historical % of Sales Growth	10.7	(17.2)	14.4		
(2) Projected % of Sales Growth	11	(18)	12		
(3) Historical % of Earnings Per Share Growth	11.7	(17.2)	7		
(4) Projected % of Earnings Per Share Growth	12	(18)	10		

MANAGEMENT COMPARISONS
(From Section 2 of the NAIC Stock Selection Guide)

(5) % Profit Margin Before Taxes (Average for last 5 years) (2A) Trend	16.5	(19.3)	16.7		
(6) % Earned on Equity (Average for last 5 years) (2B) Trend	(16.5)	13.9	16.4		
(7) % of Common Owned by Management	----	47% com / 100%B	---		

PRICE COMPARISONS
(See Sections 3-5 of the NAIC Stock Selection Guide)

(8) Estimated Total Earnings Per Share For Next 5 Years	18.18	10.45	22.05		
(9) Price Range Over Last 5 Years High (3A) Low (3B)	71.50 - 26.12	28.25 - 11.3	67.75 - 33.50		
(10) Present Price	42	20 1/2	54 1/4		
Price Earnings Ratio Range Last 5 Years (11) Highest (3D)	31	28.1	23.5		
(12) Average High (3D7)	25	22.5	19.8		
(13) Average (3-8)	20.5	17.3	17.2		
(14) Average Low (3E7)	16	12.1	14.6		
(15) Lowest (3E)	13.7	10.7	13.1		
(16) Current Price Earnings Ratio (3-9)	15	(14.3)	16.3		
Estimated Price Zones (17) Lower-Buy (4C2)	34 1/8 - 52 3/4	15 - 25 3/4	45 3/8 - 65 1/2		
(18) Middle-Maybe (4C3)	52 3/4 - 71 1/2	25 3/4 - 36 3/4	65 1/2 - 85 3/4		
(19) Upper-Sell (4C4)	71 1/2 - 90	36 3/4 - 47 1/2	85 3/4 - 106		
(20) Present Price Range (4C5)	BUY	BUY	BUY		
(21) Upside Downside Ratio (4D)	(6.1)	4.9	5.8		
(22) Current Yield (5A)	2.9	0.1	(3.9)		
(23) Combined Estimated Yield (5C)	25.9	(26.5)	23.8		

OTHER COMPARISONS

(24) Number of Common Shares Outstanding	106.5 Mil	23.7 Mil 25.7 Mil A	17 Mil		
(25) Potential Dilution from Debentures, Warrants, Options		94.2 TN B 25 Mil PFD			
(26) Percent Payout (3G7)	35	1.4	59		
(27)					
(28)					
(29) Date of Source Material	6-30-95	6-30-95	6-30-95		
(30) Where Traded	NYSE	OTC	NYSE		

Figure 11-2

Stock Selection Guide for AMP, Inc.

Figure 11-2 (Continued)
Stock Selection Guide for AMP, Inc.

2 EVALUATING MANAGEMENT   Company _____ AMP Inc.

		19 85	19 86	19 87	19 88	19 89	19 90	19 91	19 92	19 93	19 94	LAST 5 YEAR AVG.	TREND UP	TREND DOWN
A	% Pre-tax Profit on Sales (Net Before Taxes ÷ Sales)	20.0	19.5	17.2	19.3	20.0	11.8	15.2	18.6	19.8	17.0	16.5	✓	
B	% Earned on Equity (E/S ÷ Book Value)	22.7	20.4	16.6	20.4	21.8	10.8	14.5	18.5	21.0	17.5	16.5	✓	

3 PRICE-EARNINGS HISTORY as an indicator of the future

This shows how stock prices have fluctuated with earnings and dividends. It is a building block for translating earnings into future stock prices.

PRESENT PRICE _42_   HIGH THIS YEAR _48 3/4_   LOW THIS YEAR _40_

	Year	A PRICE HIGH	B PRICE LOW	C Earnings Per Share	D Price Earnings Ratio HIGH A ÷ C	E Price Earnings Ratio LOW B ÷ C	F Dividend Per Share	G % Payout F ÷ C X 100	H % High Yield F ÷ B X 100
1	1990	39 1/2	26 1/8	1.87	21.1	14.0	0.64	34.2	2.5
2	1991	37 7/8	27 1/2	1.00	(37.9)	(27.5)	0.72	(72.0)	2.6
3	1992	45	32 7/8	1.52	29.6	21.6	0.74	(48.7)	2.3
4	1993	71 1/2	34 1/8	2.31	31.0	14.8	0.85	36.8	2.5
5	1994	54 1/4	40 1/2	2.96	18.3	13.7	1.00	33.8	2.5
6	TOTAL		161 1/8		100.0	64.1		104.8	
7	AVERAGE		32 1/4		25.0	16.0		34.9	
8	AVERAGE PRICE EARNINGS RATIO	20.5		9	CURRENT PRICE EARNINGS RATIO	15 (42/2.80)			

4 EVALUATING RISK and REWARD over the next 5 years

Assuming one recession and one business boom every 5 years, calculations are made of how **high** and how **low** the stock might sell. The upside-downside ratio is the key to evaluating risk and reward

A HIGH PRICE — NEXT 5 YEARS
Avg. High P/E _20.5_ (3D7 as adj.) X Estimate High Earnings/Share _4.40_ = Forecast High Price $ _90_ (4A1)

B LOW PRICE — NEXT 5 YEARS
(a) Avg. Low P/E _16_ (3E7 as adj.) X Estimated Low Earnings/Share _2.60_ = $ _41 5/8_
(b) Avg. Low Price of Last 5 Years = _32 1/4_
(c) Recent Severe Market Low Price = _34 1/8_ (3B7)
(d) Price Dividend Will Support   Present Divd. / High Yield (H) = _1.20 / .026_ = _46 1/8_
Selected Estimated Low Price = $ _34 1/8_ (4B1)

C ZONING
_90_ (4A1) High Forecast Price Minus _34 1/8_ (4B1) Low Forecast Price Equals _55 7/8_ (C) Range. 1/3 of Range = _18 5/8_ (4CD)
(4C2) Lower 1/3 = (4B1) _34 1/8_ to _52 3/4_ (Buy)
(4C3) Middle 1/3 = _52 3/4_ to _71 1/2_ (Maybe)
(4C4) Upper 1/3 = _71 1/2_ to _90_ (4A1) (Sell)
Present Market Price of _42_ is in the _BUY_ (4C5) Range

D UP-SIDE DOWN-SIDE RATIO (Potential Gain vs. Risk of Loss)
High Price (4A1) _90_ Minus Present Price _42_ / Present Price _42_ Minus Low Price (4B1) _34 1/8_ = _48 / 7 7/8_ = _6.1_ (4D) To 1

E PRICE TARGET (Note: This shows the potential market price appreciation over the next five years in simple interest terms.)
High Price (4A1) _90_ / Present Market Price _42_ = (_2.14_) X 100 = (_214_) − 100 = _114_ (4E) % Appreciation

5 5-YEAR POTENTIAL   This combines price appreciation with dividend yield to get an estimate of total return. It provides a standard for comparing income and growth stocks.

A Present Full Year's Dividend $ _1.20_ / Present Price of Stock $ _42_ = _.029_ X 100 = _2.9_ (5A) Present Yield or % Returned on Purchase Price

Note: Results are expressed as a simple rate; use the table below to convert to a compound rate.

B AVERAGE YIELD OVER NEXT 5 YEARS
Avg. Earnings Per Share Next 5 Years _3.75_ X Avg. % Payout (3G7) _.349_ = _1.30875_ / Present Price $ _42_ = _3.1_ (5B) %

C ESTIMATED AVERAGE ANNUAL RETURN OVER NEXT FIVE YEARS
5 Year Appreciation Potential (4E) _114_ / 5 = _22.8_ %
Average Yield (5B) .... _3.1_ %
Average Total Annual Return Over the Next 5 Years (5C) _25.9_ %

Table to Convert From Simple to Compound Rate

Simple Rate	2	4	6	8	10	12	14	16	18	20	22	24	26	28	30	32	34	36	38	40
Compound Rate	2	4	6	8	10	12	14	16	18	20	22	24								

Figure 11-3

Stock Selection Guide for Molex, Inc.

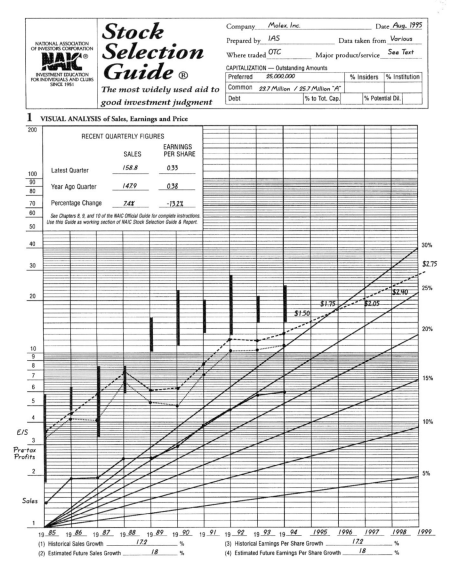

Figure 11-3 (Continued)
Stock Selection Guide for Molex, Inc.

2 EVALUATING MANAGEMENT

Company _____ Molex, Inc. _____

		19 85	19 86	19 87	19 88	19 89	19 90	19 91	19 92	19 93	19 94	LAST 5 YEAR AVG.	TREND UP	TREND DOWN
A	% Pre-tax Profit on Sales (Net Before Taxes ÷ Sales)	23.7	25.4	23.8	27.8	21.0	18.4	19.6	21.1	18.3	19.3	19.3	✓	
B	% Earned on Equity (E/S ÷ Book Value)	20.0	22.0	18.6	24.3	16.6	12.6	13.7	15.2	14.9	13.0	13.9		✓

3 PRICE-EARNINGS HISTORY as an indicator of the future

This shows how stock prices have fluctuated with earnings and dividends. It is a building block for translating earnings into future stock prices.

PRESENT PRICE _20 1/2_   HIGH THIS YEAR _24_   LOW THIS YEAR _16 5/8_

	Year	A PRICE HIGH	B PRICE LOW	C Earnings Per Share	D Price Earnings Ratio HIGH A÷C	E Price Earnings Ratio LOW B÷C	F Dividend Per Share	G % Payout F÷C X 100	H % High Yield F÷B X 100
1	1990	22.4	11.3	0.64	(35.0)	(17.7)	0.01	1.6	0.1
2	1991	19 1/8	12.95	0.86	28.1	(19.0)	0.015	1.7	0.1
3	1992	28 1/4	12 1/2	1.17	24.1	10.7	0.015	1.3	0.1
4	1993	20 7/8	15 1/8	1.14	18.3	13.3	0.015	1.3	0.1
5	1994	23 7/8	15 3/8	1.24	19.3	12.4	0.015	1.2	0.1
6	TOTAL		67 1/4		89.8	36.4		7.1	
7	AVERAGE		13.45		22.5	12.1		1.4	
8	AVERAGE PRICE EARNINGS RATIO			17.3		9 CURRENT PRICE EARNINGS RATIO		14.3 (20 1/2 / 1.43)	

4 EVALUATING RISK and REWARD over the next 5 years

Assuming one recession and one business boom every 5 years, calculations are made of how high and how low the stock might sell. The upside-downside ratio is the key to evaluating risk and reward.

A HIGH PRICE — NEXT 5 YEARS
Avg. High P/E _17.3_ (3D7 as adj.)   X Estimate High Earnings/Share _2.75_   = Forecast High Price $ _47 1/2_ (4A1)

B LOW PRICE — NEXT 5 YEARS
(a) Avg. Low P/E _12.1_ (3E7 as adj.)   X Estimated Low Earnings/Share _1.24_   = $ _15_
(b) Avg. Low Price of Last 5 Years = _13.45_
(c) Recent Severe Market Low Price = _15[3B]/8_
(d) Price Dividend Will Support   Present Divd. / High Yield (H) = _.02_ = _Not applicable_
Selected Estimated Low Price = $ _15_ (4B1)

C ZONING
_47 1/2_ (4A1) High Forecast Price Minus _15_ (4B1) Low Forecast Price Equals _32 1/2_ (C) Range. 1/3 of Range = _10.83_ (4CD)

(4C2) Lower 1/3 = (4B1) _15_ to _25 3/4_ (Buy)
(4C3) Middle 1/3 = _25 3/4_ to _36 3/4_ (Maybe)
(4C4) Upper 1/3 = _36 3/4_ to _47 1/2_ (4A1) (Sell)

Present Market Price of _____ is in the _BUY_ (4C5) Range

D UP-SIDE DOWN-SIDE RATIO (Potential Gain vs. Risk of Loss)

$$\frac{\text{High Price (4A1) } 47 1/2 \text{ Minus Present Price } 20 1/2}{\text{Present Price } 20 1/2 \text{ Minus Low Price (4B1) } 15} = \frac{27}{5 1/2} = 4.9 \text{ To 1 (4D)}$$

E PRICE TARGET (Note: This shows the potential market price appreciation over the next five years in simple interest terms.)

$$\frac{\text{High Price (4A1) } 47 1/2}{\text{Present Market Price } 20 1/2} = (2.32) \text{ X } 100 = (232) - 100 = 132 \text{ (4E) \% Appreciation}$$

5 5-YEAR POTENTIAL

This combines price appreciation with dividend yield to get an estimate of total return. It provides a standard for comparing income and growth stocks.

A Note: Results are expressed as a simple rate; use the table below to convert to a compound rate.

$$\frac{\text{Present Full Year's Dividend \$ } 0.02}{\text{Present Price of Stock \$ } 20 1/2} = 0.0009756 \text{ X } 100 = 0.1 \text{ (5A) Present Yield or \% Returned on Purchase Price}$$

B AVERAGE YIELD OVER NEXT 5 YEARS

$$\frac{\text{Avg. Earnings Per Share Next 5 Years } 2.05 \text{ X Avg. \% Payout (3G7) } .014}{\text{Present Price \$ } 20 1/2} = \frac{.029}{} = .14 \text{ (5B) \%}$$

C ESTIMATED AVERAGE ANNUAL RETURN OVER NEXT FIVE YEARS

$$\frac{\text{5 Year Appreciation Potential (4E) } 132}{5} = 26.4 \%$$

Average Yield (5B) .... _.1_ %
Average Total Annual Return Over the Next 5 Years (5C) _26.5_ %

Table to Convert From Simple to Compound Rate

Simple Rate 2 4 6 8 10 12 14 16 18 20 22 24 26 28 30 32 34 36 38 40
Compound Rate 2 4 6 8 10 12 14 16 18 20 22 24

Figure 11-4
Stock Selection Guide for Thomas & Betts

Figure 11-4 (Continued)
Stock Selection Guide for Thomas & Betts

2 EVALUATING MANAGEMENT Company _Thomas & Betts (TNB)_

		19 85	19 86	19 87	19 88	19 89	19 90	19 91	19 92	19 93	19 94	LAST 5 YEAR AVG.	TREND UP	TREND DOWN
A	% Pre-tax Profit on Sales (Net Before Taxes ÷ Sales)	23.0	21.5	15.3	16.4	19.9	16.7	18.2	17.3	17.0	14.5	16.7	✓	
B	% Earned on Equity (E/S ÷ Book Value)	20.3	18.8	12.8	13.9	17.9	14.8	15.5	16.8	18.6	16.5	16.4	✓	

3 PRICE-EARNINGS HISTORY as an indicator of the future

This shows how stock prices have fluctuated with earnings and dividends. It is a building block for translating earnings into future stock prices.

PRESENT PRICE _54 1/4_   HIGH THIS YEAR _57 3/8_   LOW THIS YEAR _47 1/8_

	Year	A PRICE HIGH	B PRICE LOW	C Earnings Per Share	D Price Earnings Ratio HIGH A÷C	E Price Earnings Ratio LOW B÷C	F Dividend Per Share	G % Payout F÷C X 100	H % High Yield F÷B X 100
1	1990	43 1/4	33 1/2	2.15	20.1	15.6	1.33	61.9	4.0
2	1991	49 3/4	37	2.44	20.4	15.2	1.48	60.7	4.0
3	1992	67 3/4	41 1/2	2.88	23.5	14.4	1.64	56.9	4.0
4	1993	60 3/4	45 3/8	3.46	17.6	13.1	1.80	52.0	4.0
5	1994	55 3/4	46	3.16	17.6	14.6	1.96	62.0	4.3
6	TOTAL		203 3/8		99.2	72.9		293.5	
7	AVERAGE		40 5/8		19.8	14.6		58.7	
8	AVERAGE PRICE EARNINGS RATIO _17.2_			9 CURRENT PRICE EARNINGS RATIO				16.3 (54 1/4/3.33)	

4 EVALUATING RISK and REWARD over the next 5 years

Assuming one recession and one business boom every 5 years, calculations are made of how high and how low the stock might sell. The upside-downside ratio is the key to evaluating risk and reward

A HIGH PRICE — NEXT 5 YEARS
Avg. High P/E _19.8_ (3D7 as adj.) X Estimate High Earnings/Share _5.35_ = Forecast High Price $ _106_ (4A1)

B LOW PRICE — NEXT 5 YEARS
(a) Avg. Low P/E _14.6_ (3E7 as adj.) X Estimated Low Earnings/Share _3.16_ = $ _46_
(b) Avg. Low Price of Last 5 Years = _40 5/8_ (3B7)
(c) Recent Severe Market Low Price = _45 3/8_
(d) Price Dividend Will Support $\frac{\text{Present Divd.}}{\text{High Yield (H)}}$ = $\frac{2.12}{.043}$ = _49 1/4_
Selected Estimated Low Price = $ _45 3/8_ (4B1)

C ZONING
_106_ (4A1) High Forecast Price Minus _45 3/8_ (4B1) Low Forecast Price Equals _60 5/8_ (C) Range. 1/3 of Range = _20.2_ (4CD)
(4C2) Lower 1/3 = (4B1) _45 3/8_ to _65 1/2_ (Buy)
(4C3) Middle 1/3 = _65 1/2_ to _85 3/4_ (Maybe)
(4C4) Upper 1/3 = _85 3/4_ to _106_ (4A1) (Sell)
Present Market Price of _54 1/4_ is in the _BUY_ (4C5) Range

D UP-SIDE DOWN-SIDE RATIO (Potential Gain vs. Risk of Loss)
$\frac{\text{High Price (4A1)} \quad 106 \quad \text{Minus Present Price} \quad 54 1/4}{\text{Present Price} \quad 54 1/4 \quad \text{Minus Low Price (4B1)} \quad 45 3/8}$ = $\frac{51 3/4}{8 7/8}$ = _5.8_ (4D) To 1

E PRICE TARGET (Note: This shows the potential market price appreciation over the next five years in simple interest terms.)
$\frac{\text{High Price (4A1)} \quad 106}{\text{Present Market Price} \quad 54 1/4}$ = (_1.95_) X 100 = (_195_) − 100 = _95_ (4E) % Appreciation

5 5-YEAR POTENTIAL This combines price appreciation with dividend yield to get an estimate of total return. It provides a standard for comparing income and growth stocks.

Note: Results are expressed as a simple rate; use the table below to convert to a compound rate.

A Present Full Year's Dividend $ _2.12_ / Present Price of Stock $ _54 1/4_ = _0.039_ X 100 = _3.9_ (5A) Present Yield or % Returned on Purchase Price

B AVERAGE YIELD OVER NEXT 5 YEARS
Avg. Earnings Per Share Next 5 Years _4.40_ X Avg. % Payout (3G7) _.587_ = $\frac{2.583}{\text{Present Price } \$ \quad 54 1/4}$ = _4.8_ (5B) %

C ESTIMATED AVERAGE ANNUAL RETURN OVER NEXT FIVE YEARS
5 Year Appreciation Potential (4E) _95_ / 5 = _19.0_ %
Average Yield (5B) .... _4.8_ %
Average Total Annual Return Over the Next 5 Years (5C) _23.8_ %

Table to Convert From Simple to Compound Rate

Simple Rate 2 4 6 8 10 12 14 16 18 20 22 24 26 28 30 32 34 36 38 40
Compound Rate 2 4 6 8 10 12 14 16 18 20 22 24

Management's ability to earn a high return on sales and on stockholders' equity are key tests. Molex boasts the best profit margin, while AMP and Thomas & Betts rank virtually even in return on equity, ahead of Molex. Molex management owns nearly half of the common shares outstanding.

OBTAINING FIVE-YEAR ESTIMATED EARNINGS

The figure for item 8 of the Stock Comparison Guide, "Estimated Total Earnings per Share for the Next Five Years," comes from Section 1 of the Stock Selection Guide. (See Figure 11-3). Looking at the earnings-per-share trend line, add together the five figures where the projected earnings trend line intersects the time lines. The result is total estimated EPS for the next five years. The closer the current stock price is to this total, the more favorable is the price. Buying a stock for the sum of the next five years' earnings is equivalent to investing at 20 percent a year. Such a price may be difficult to find, and in some market periods probably cannot be found, but you should always keep this figure in mind. Although none of the companies approaches the target, the Molex price is most favorable in terms of the price/earnings ratio. Price/earnings ratio comparisons should be made between companies on both a current and a historical basis. P/E ratios tend to move up and down as stock prices move in major cycles.

Some stocks with a record of consistent growth tend to sell at a higher-than-average P/E ratio. If a stock is currently selling at a higher P/E than other companies in the same industry, compare it now with its own P/E five years ago and the general level of P/Es at that time. If the P/E ratios today and five years ago are comparable, the stock may still be a good long-term purchase. But keep in mind that any stock selling at an unusually high multiple is likely to suffer a sizable adjustment in a weak market if its results fail to meet the expectations of the investment community.

All of the three companies under study are at lower multiples today compared with the average for the last five years. This is shown by a comparison of the figures on line 13 with those on line 16. Molex offers the lowest current P/E, but those of the two competitors are comparable. All three stocks are in the "buy" range.

Item 23, "Combined Estimated Yield," comprises two figures. One is the estimated average appreciation, and the other is the average dividend yield for the next five years. The combined value is obtained from Section 5C

(Average Annual Total Return) of the Stock Selection Guide. AMP and Molex offer the highest combined estimated yields, although all three companies more than meet our goal in this respect.

The *payout,* or percent of earnings paid out as dividends, may indicate management's growth philosophy. Growth takes capital. When management retains a large share of earnings, financing expansion becomes easier. Growth financed with retained earnings usually accrues to the benefit of the shareholders. If, however, growth is financed by issuing additional stock, present holders' equity in the company will be diluted. Molex's payout is substantially lower than that of either AMP or Thomas & Betts.

Items that investors may find helpful to add to the "Other Comparisons" section are the percentage of debt to capitalization and the percent of stock held by institutions.

Some investors are interested in a stock's *beta.* Beta is a mathematical notation that measures a stock's volatility in comparison with the market as a whole. A beta rating of 1 indicates that the stock tends to move with the market, both up and down. Higher betas indicate greater volatility, and lower betas indicate that the stock is not influenced by overall trends as much as other issues. High betas are produced by high sales and earnings growth rates and excellent profit margins, items the investor has already covered in his or her Guide study.

INDUSTRY BACKGROUND

Now let's take a look at how these facts and figures relate to this particular industry as a whole.*

The connector manufacturing industry is large but highly fragmented, with some 600 contenders. Connector demand varies widely from quarter to quarter, putting continuing pressure on management to maximize production and distribution efficiency. Computer systems account for more than a third of connector use worldwide, with telecommunications representing another fifth. The remainder is divided among military/aerospace (15%), industrial (15%), automotive (10%), and consumer applications (5%). Of all the connector markets, only military/aerospace has a disappointing outlook.

---

* This industry background is based on material published by David L. Babson & Co. The Stock Selection Guides were prepared by NAIC's Investor Advisory Service.

The average selling price for connectors has declined by 3 to 5 percent a year since 1985. About 100 companies have failed. The larger competitors, as exemplified by our three entries, have responded to greater competition by improving quality and service. AMP, with about a fifth of the worldwide market, is five times larger than its nearest competitor. Since its incorporation in 1941, AMP has increased sales 100 times for an annual growth rate of 9.7 percent, comfortably outpacing gross domestic product. AMP produces more than 100,000 different products. Foreign customers account for 60 percent of sales. The company spends more than $260 million a year on product development and improvement of its production processes.

Molex ranks second in the industry. In recent years, Molex has been the most rapidly growing. Seventy percent of its sales are foreign, and half of its revenues come from the expanding Far East market.

Thomas & Betts has been building its position in electronic connectors, historically having focused on more slowly growing electric connectors. Only 40 percent of the firm's business comes from abroad.

The companies are selling at lower multiples now because of the recession and concern over whether they can regain former growth rates. However, the strongest companies should continue to do well.

With this knowledge of the industry and the data provided on the three firms, which if any would you buy? Every investor is entitled to his or her own opinion. But remember, experience suggests that, on average, the companies with the most favorable figures are likely to do best. Our selection at this time would be Molex, because its historical and projected sales growth rates and earnings per share growth rates are the highest. Also, its pre-tax profit margin is the highest. Its P/E ratio is the lowest of the three.

CHAPTER 12

THE PORTFOLIO MANAGEMENT GUIDE

As your club's portfolio grows with time, portfolio management becomes more important. The value of current deposits being invested in a new stock will pale in comparison with the total amounts invested over the years.

Many new investment club members feel that their only challenge is making a sound decision when contemplating the initial purchase of a security. The error lies in overlooking the vital importance of managing a security once it is bought. As famed financier Bernard Baruch said, "There ain't no such animal as a permanent investment." In other words, the stock you bought yesterday is not the one you hold today, because circumstances have surely changed—for better or worse.

The successful investment club reviews its portfolio at least once a year. Each stock should have the potential of reaching your goal of doubling in the next bull market. Use the Challenge Tree procedure explained in Chapter 14 to check the potential of a current holding against a possible replacement.

One strategy for investing successfully dictates that you put all of your funds into a single stock that is destined to outperform all others. The trouble with this idea is, which stock is it? No one can say for certain. Hindsight is always 20/20.

NAIC's experience suggests that for the average individual, adequate portfolio management amounts to reviewing each stock annually to confirm that it has the potential of doubling in value over the next five years (or what-ever your goal for it is) and ensuring that there is good diversification both by industry and by size of company.

DIVERSIFY BY SIZE

Your club should be sure to diversify its holdings, because diversification is an important way to reduce risk. For most investors, diversification means buy-ing stocks in a range of different industries. Investment club members have found that diversification by company size is also important. However, don't carry diversification too far. Know your club's limits, and hold only as many stocks as you can watch carefully.

Your club should organize its portfolio management program so that each holding becomes the responsibility of a single member. You may choose to have portfolio management reviews of individual stocks on an ongoing basis so that all stocks are covered once a year. It is advisable to look at your portfolio as a whole once a year and check (1) industry diversification, (2) size diversification, and (3) the ability of the total portfolio to double in value by the next market peak.

The Stock Selection Guide helps you determine the selling zone for a stock. A comparison of current price with established zones should be part of the club meeting whether the stock is in the "buy" or "sell" zone. It is un-likely that a stock with a high rate of growth would be sold unless it is sub-stantially overpriced. Even then, only a part of the holding might be sold. Stocks with a good growth rate that are in the buy zone should be added to the club's list of buy candidates at that meeting.

FILLING IN THE FORM

Some of the figures in Section 1 of the Portfolio Management Guide, "Price/Earnings Zone," come from other sources. The figures in columns 2 and 3 are taken from line 7, columns D and E of Section 3 of the Stock Selec-tion Guide. Column 2 represents the average high P/E for the past five years, and column 3 is the average low P/E. The headings of columns 4, 5, and 6 show how these figures are arrived at. The only logic behind the calculation of the figures in columns 5 and 6 is that experience has shown these figures to be reasonable guides. It is always important to consider the market and economic conditions that existed when those figures were developed and how they compare with current conditions.

In Section 2, "Price Zones," column 1 indicates the top of the buy zone. You can obtain this number from Section 4C2 of the SSG. Column 2 is used to specify the bottom of the sell zone, item 4C4 on the Stock Selection Guide.

Section 3 is devoted to recording earnings, prices, and price/earnings ratio computations. Column 1 lists quarterly earnings periods, and column 2 gives the earnings per share for each. You may obtain this information from the company's quarterly report or from other published reports. (See the lower left corner of the Value Line sheet under the heading "Earnings per Share.") Column 3 gives the cumulative earnings figure for the most recent four quarters. That is the sum for the quarter on this line and those on the three preceding lines. Column 4 records the specific day on which the price is recorded in column 5.

Column 6 shows the result of dividing price (column 5) by the latest four quarters' earnings (column 3). Columns 7 through 12 present similar data calculated for the second and third months of the same quarter.

The Portfolio Management Guide not only disciplines club members to examine a stock's price on a regular basis, but depicts the crucial relationship over time of price to P/E ratio. NAIC's software provides a quick and easy way to prepare this form.

PRICE/EARNINGS JUDGMENT FACTORS

A word of caution: The Portfolio Management Guide can be dangerous to the creation of maximum profits in certain cases. In using price/earnings ratios, it is important to use judgment when analyzing the figures. Keep in mind that these ratios move up and down in long cycles just like stock prices. When there are long periods of severely depressed prices and very low stock market optimism, the price/earnings ratios on the Dow Jones averages may fall to the area of 5 to 7. This also happens during periods of very high inflation. As the market moves out of a depressed period, P/E ratios start moving up and will reach 18 to 21 on the Dow Jones averages. When you are studying a company, it is important to judge where in the cycle the economy and market are now, and estimate where they might be at the end of five years.

P/E ratios will also vary for individual companies. Generally, the higher the rate of sales and earnings per share growth rate, the higher the P/E ratios the company will command in the market. The length of time over which a company has maintained a good growth rate will also affect its P/E ratio. A company that has a reputation for high-quality management, a special product, or market advantage will surely be rated higher than its competitors.

Cyclical companies often sell at low P/Es when their earnings are at a peak because investors know a big dip is likely in the future. Since investors also know such companies will probably weather a recession and recover to higher earnings, the prices of such companies usually do not decline as much as earnings. As a result, such companies, as opposed to growth companies, are likely to sell at the highest P/Es when they are experiencing the greatest difficulty. The auto companies are notable for their cyclical nature.

As you gain experience and your club goes through down markets and the following recovery, your ability to recognize and judge these various factors will grow.

AN ILLUSTRATION

The accompanying Portfolio Management Guide (Figure 12-1) on Abbott Laboratories illustrates how the P/E ratio advances for a company with a high rate of growth and continuing bright prospects. Examine the "Chart of Market Prices and P/E Ratios" (Section 4). You'll see that in the four-year span under study, the market price, except for year three, has almost always been well within the buy zone. The P/E ratios are another story. Over nearly the entire period under discussion, the P/Es have remained in the "hold" zone, with more of the remainder in the sell zone than in the buy zone.

Any investor selling in the second year, when the P/E first flashed "sell," would not have shared in the company's continued growth. It is often a good idea, for a current year, to consider estimated earnings, since that will give you a P/E ratio for the current year closer to its historical level.

We advise buying stocks with the expectation of seeing their value double within five years. However, you should recognize that a stock's doubling in value is not a sell indicator. Reevaluate the situation when your goal is reached. Are future gains likely? If so, then continue to hold. Is upside potential limited in comparison with downside risk? If this seems to be the case, consider selling. At that point, go through the same evaluation as you would for a new prospective company.

Figure 12-1

Completed Portfolio Management Guide for Abbott Laboratories

NATIONAL ASSOCIATION OF INVESTORS CORPORATION **NAIC** ® INVESTMENT EDUCATION FOR INDIVIDUALS AND CLUBS SINCE 1951	*Portfolio Management Guide* ®	See Chapter 12 of the NAIC Official Guide for instructions on the use of this guide.

Company ___Abbott Laboratories___   Prepared by _____

1 PRICE EARNINGS ZONES   Refer to Section 3, columns D and E, line 7, of your Stock Selection Guide study of this company for the information in columns 2 and 3 below.

1	2	3	4	5	6
YEAR	Average Price Earnings Ratios for Previous Five Years		Sum of Cols. 2 and 3	Column 4 divided by 2	Column 5 Multiplied by 1 1/2
	High	Low		Low P/E Guide Line	High P/E Guide Line
1990	17.2	11.4	28.6	14.3	21.5
1991	18.8	11.8	30.6	15.3	23.0
1992	20.0	12.4	32.4	16.2	24.3
1993	19.6	12.4	32	16.0	24.0

2 PRICE ZONES   See Section 4C of the Stock Selection Guide. 1 below is top of Buy Zone. 2 below is bottom of Sell Zone

YEAR	1. Consider Buying Below	2. Consider Selling Above
1990	22	41
1991	26	48
1992	29	49
1993	33	55

3 CUMULATIVE EARNINGS AND CURRENT PRICE-EARNINGS RATIO COMPUTATIONS

1	2	3	4	5	6	7	8	9	10	11	12
3 Months Ending	Earnings Per Share	Total Earnings for Last 4 Quarters	Date	Price	P/E Ratio at Time of Meeting	Date	Price	P/E Ratio at Time of Meeting	Date	Price	P/E Ratio at Time of Meeting
3/89	.183										
6/89	.207										
9/89	.19										
12/89	.26	.84	1/26	12 1/2	14.9	2/27	13	15.5	3/25	14 1/2	17.3
3/90	.22	.88	4/27	13 1/8	14.9	5/27	13 3/8	15.2	6/26	13 5/8	15.5
6/90	.24	.91	7/26	14 7/8	16.3	8/27	15	16.5	9/26	14 7/8	16.3
9/90	.22	.94	10/27	15	16.0	11/26	15 1/4	16.2	12/27	16 1/4	17.3
12/90	.29	.97	1/27	17	17.5	2/26	17	17.5	3/27	17	17.5
3/91	.26	1.01	4/28	20	19.8	5/27	21	20.8	6/26	27	26.7
6/91	.285	1.06	7/27	27	25.5	8/27	26	24.5	9/26	24 3/4	23.3
9/91	.265	1.10	10/28	22 1/8	20.1	11/26	25	22.7	12/28	25 1/2	23.2
12/91	.35	1.16	1/27	28	24.1	2/26	31 1/8	26.8	3/27	33 1/4	28.7
3/92	.31	1.21	4/27	32 1/4	26.7	5/28	30 1/4	25.0	6/25	33	27.3
6/92	.34	1.27	7/28	32	25.2	8/28	33	26.0	9/26	32 5/8	25.7
9/92	.32	1.32	10/28	30 1/2	23.1	11/27	25	18.9	12/29	24 1/8	18.3
12/92	.42	1.39	1/28	25	18.0	2/26	26 1/4	18.9	3/29	26 1/8	18.8
3/'93	.38	1.46	4/27	25	17.1	5/27	23 1/8	15.8	6/27	24 3/4	17.0
6/93	.41	1.53	7/29	23	15.0	8/28	23 1/8	15.1	9/27	23 7/8	15.6
9/93	.38	1.59	10/28	23 7/8	15.0	11/27	23 1/2	14.8	12/29	23	14.5
12/93	.50	1.67	1/28	23 1/4	13.9	2/26	26	15.6	3/28	27 1/2	16.5

Figure 12-1 (Continued)
Completed Portfolio Management Guide for Abbott Laboratories

4 CHART OF MARKET PRICES AND PRICE-EARNINGS RATIO

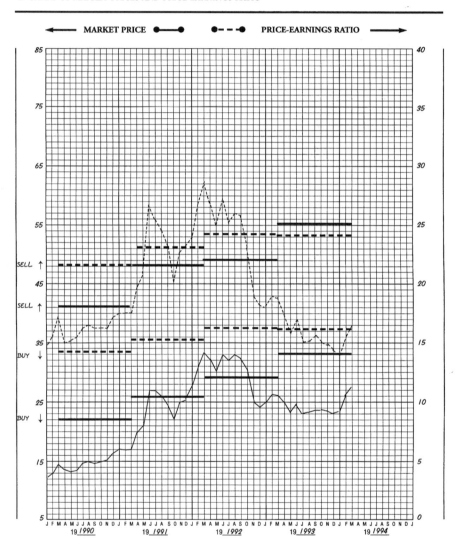

Remember that many, many companies advance significantly in price. Media General Financial Services identified the 100 stocks that achieved the greatest price appreciation in the decade of the 1980s. The advances ranged from 9,637 percent for the leader to 1,184 percent for the bottom entry.

We advocate that you buy and hold high-growth stocks and make additional purchases when the price dips. Whenever the growth rate of the company under scrutiny is 12 percent or higher, use the Portfolio Management Guide for deciding whether to purchase on dips, not whether to sell on peaks. We counsel against selling at apparent peaks and buying back after a decline in price. Very few investors can profit from such speculation, especially for high-growth stocks.

NAIC suggests that investors look at the portfolio as a total entity once a year. The club's total portfolio should be displayed, showing the current price, the estimated five-year low, and the estimated five-year high for each stock, and with columns showing each stock's size and industry classification. Such a display might look like the one in Figure 12-2.

The purpose of the review is threefold: (1) to check the diversification of the portfolio by industry, (2) to check the diversification by size, and (3) to confirm growth potential. In one set of columns in Figure 12-2 we have listed the annual revenues of each company (M is millions, B is billions) and then classified it L for very large, M for medium, and S for small.

This division comes out as follows:

L		M		S	
Abbott Labs	$14,218	Becton-Dick.	$10,462	ALLIED Group	$15,975
Amoco	16,937	Century Tel.	13,281	Kuhlman	7,647
Colgate-Palm.	12,818	Dynatech	14,875	Linear Tech.	4,525
		Synovus Fin.	13,050	Medic Comp.	8,000
	$43,973		$51,668		$36,147

A first look at the above table suggests that we are well off our rough goal of $33,500 each in L and S and $67,000 in M (one quarter, one quarter, and one half of total value, respectively). S at $36,147 is OK, but we are high on L. However, the wide difference in the size of companies between the bottom end of L and the upper end of M suggests that this is not of concern. We believe our holdings at the small aggressive end are about right.

In the right column of Figure 12-2 we list the business of each company as described on the Value Line sheet. We have no industry in mind that we want to concentrate on, and we believe we have a good spread between different industries.

Figure 12-2
Example of Club Portfolio Display

Stock	Shares	No. of Current Price	Value	5-Year High Price	Value	5-Year Low Price	Value	Sales	Size	Industry
Abbott Labs	350	40.625	14,218	60	21,000	26	9,100	10.0 B	L	Health care
ALLIED Group	450	35.500	15,975	75	33,750	22	9,900	300.0 M	S	Insurance
Amoco	250	67.75	16,937	83	20,750	56	14,000	27.0 B	L	Petro—largest
Becton–Dick.	150	69.75	10,462	95	14,250	51	7,650	2.7 B	M	Medical mfg.
Century Tele.	425	31.25	13,281	78	33,150	22	9,350	500.0 M	M	Telecom.
Colgate-Palm.	175	73.25	12,818	125	21,875	53	9,275	7.5 B	L	Household
Dynatech	1,000	14.875	14,875	46	46,000	12	12,000	470.0 M	M	Comm.
Kuhlman	665	11.5	7,647	26	17,290	9	5,985	240.0 M	S	Elect. mfg.
Linear Tech.	100	45.25	4,525	114	11,400	27	2,700	200.0 M	S	Comp. prod.
Medic Comp.	125	64	8,000	128	16,000	27	3,375	10.7 M	S	Mgt. system
Synovus Fin.	450	29	13,050	78	35,100	21	9,450	6.0 B	M	Fin. service
Cash			2,152		2,152		2,152			
Total			$133,940		$272,717		$94,937			

L, Large company; M, Medium-sized company; S, Small company.

Our more detailed study comes when we look at the columns for the five-year high and low. Our current value is $133,940, and our estimated high at the next market peak is $272,717. That shows we should be able to meet our goal of doubling; our portfolio doesn't need adjustment for that purpose. Our risk on the downside is $39,000 or 29 percent. When we look at individual stocks, we are pretty well satisfied with our group L stocks. As giants they have a better-than-average growth rate and should add stability in a recessionary period.

In group B we have some disagreement in the club about continuing to hold Becton-Dickinson since our study does not indicate that the upside potential we would like is there. Some members argue that our Stock Selection Guide study of this holding should provide for a higher growth rate and P/E ratio and consequently argue to hold it. Others feel that the high we have on record is accurate and that we should sell the stock. The club's decision is to restudy the stock over the next couple of meetings. We also have members who feel the estimated high for Dynatech is unrealistic, and our decision is to restudy it also.

Members should update the information in Figure 12-2 and bring it to the meeting regularly over the following year.

STAY IN THE MARKET

Getting in and out of the stock market is very dangerous. Studies have shown that individuals who invest in good-quality stocks of companies with a fairly steady increase in sales and earnings levels do better than investors who move from one group of stocks to another and in and out of stocks. There are very few investors who are willing to jeopardize all that they have earned for such speculation. One of the reasons that the "switcher" has difficulty succeeding is that when the market changes directions and starts up, the upward movement takes place so quickly that many investors miss the opportunity.

For instance, a study by Delaware Funds showed that in the ten up markets following 1970, 39 percent to 75 percent of the increases came within a two-week period.

John J. Curran, writing in *Fortune,* pointed out that while stocks provided a return of 17.6 percent through the decade of the 1980s, the greater part of the gain took place on just 40 of the 2,528 days the stock market was open during that period. If you were out of the market on those days, your average gain would have been only 4 percent a year.

CHAPTER 13

PORTFOLIO EVALUATION REVIEW TECHNIQUE*

WHAT IS PERT?

NAIC stresses the importance of long-term investment, emphasizing the fact that one should "buy the company rather than the stock" and should do this with the intention of doubling the value in five years.

PERT stands for *Portfolio Evaluation Review Technique.* It is a method for systematically following up on stocks and a portfolio in terms of fundamentals. These are the same fundamentals used in the NAIC Stock Selection Guide that influence the investor to buy the stock in the first place, namely earnings-per-share growth, sales growth, pre-tax profit growth, pre-tax profit margin, tax rate, current P/E ratio compared to historical P/E ratios, upside-downside ratio, and percent dividend yield.

PERT is an organized procedure for regularly verifying that the company you have invested in is meeting the goals your Stock Selection Guide indicated it was likely to do. It is strongly recommended that the investor first become familiar with the manual versions of the NAIC stock study tools including the Stock Selection Guide and PERT. The NAIC stock study tools are applicable to growth stocks—those stocks the investor seeks to double in value in five years. Like the other NAIC stock study tools, PERT is an aid to judgment, a guide for judgment, but not a substitute for judgment.

* This lesson was prepared by Ralph L. Seger, Jr.

131

WHY PERT?

The expected future growth rate of a company that can be financed from internal sources of capital is shown by the following formula:

$$\% \text{ Return on Equity} \times (1 - \text{Dividend Payout Ratio})$$

One minus the dividend payout ratio is expressed as a decimal. For example, if the dividend payout ratio is 35 percent, then $1 - 0.35$ is 0.65. If the percent return on equity is 20 percent, then:

$$20\% \times 0.65 = 13\% = \text{limit on growth rate}$$

The 13 percent is the rate of growth that can be financed by the earnings retained by the company.

Of course, other factors enter the picture, such as the amount of debt being used, the number of shares outstanding, and the amount of competition the company faces in manufacturing and/or selling its products and services. The calculation of percent return on equity (% ROE) can be broken down into three main components: profit margin, asset turnover, and leveraging of the equity base. Each component can contribute to a company's overall level of profitability as expressed by its % ROE, and understanding what each component represents can be a big help in understanding how a company is generating its profits.

Mathematically, the calculation is expressed as:

$$\% \text{ ROE} = \frac{\text{Pre-Tax Profits} \times (1 - \text{Tax Rate})}{\text{Sales}} \times \frac{\text{Sales}}{\text{Assets}} \times \frac{\text{Assets}}{\text{Equity}} \times 100$$

Where:

$$\frac{\text{Pre-Tax Profits} \times (1 - \text{Tax Rate})}{\text{Sales}} = \text{Net Profit Margin}$$

$$\frac{\text{Sales}}{\text{Assets}} = \text{Asset Turnover}$$

$$\frac{\text{Assets}}{\text{Equity}} = \text{Balance Sheet Leverage}$$

Net profit margin is the amount of profit generated for every dollar of sales. This is probably the most important component of profitability for any company, sometimes referred to as "the hard way of making money." That is because it is based on the amount of pre-tax income a company can generate from doing business, which includes producing products and services that are in demand and can be sold at a competitive price, as well as how well a company can manage and control its costs. Sometimes a change in tax rate can influence net margins, so investors should always begin their research with pre-tax margins before using the tax rate to compute after-tax margins.

Asset turnover is the amount of sales generated for every dollar of assets. The greater the turnover, the greater the profit contribution from this component of ROE. Some industries have high turnover rates (like discount stores and groceries), but typically these same companies also face stiff price competition and therefore have relatively lower profit margins (first component above). Conversely, companies and industries that can command higher profit margins (like drug and precision instrument companies) frequently have lower turnover rates. This component is often known by another name as well: *asset utilization,* or to what degree a company is generating sales from a given level of assets. If two companies in the same business have the same amount of assets, the company generating more sales is doing a better job with this component of ROE.

Balance sheet leverage is how much a company is using borrowed funds and other liabilities to help support its business and operations. Obviously, the more debt that is used, the bigger the company can get in terms of total assets and the greater the contribution to profitability from this component of ROE. Keep in mind, however, that there is a trade-off as more and more borrowed funds are used to support a business, and that trade-off is increased risk. The greater the use of balance sheet leverage, the greater the risk a company is assuming in order to achieve a given level of ROE. Two companies in the same industry may have the same ROE, but the one that achieves it through higher margins rather than higher leverage is likely to be valued more by investors.

Thus, overall profitability depends on how much profit a company can make on every dollar of sales (which deals with fundamentals like pre-tax margins, profit growth, and tax rate), and how well a company can use its equity base, borrowed funds, and all its assets to support sales growth. These are the key factors that help to determine earnings growth.

The future price action of a stock, in the long term, is primarily dependent on two factors: earnings per share and price/earnings ratios. PERT Worksheet A is a systematic method of collecting quarterly operating data about a company. The accompanying illustration of PERT Worksheet A (Figure 13-1) shows the various headings for entering data. All data is entered on a quarterly basis and for the last 12 months.

The quarterly data to be inserted for each quarter are earnings per share, pre-tax profit, and sales. The analyst must also compute a percent change compared to the same quarter a year ago for earnings per share, pre-tax profit, and sales in addition to calculations for quarterly pre-tax profit as a percent of sales and the quarterly tax rate as a percent of pre-tax profits.

For the last 12 months, data is the sum of the last four quarters for earnings per share, pre-tax profit percent change, pre-tax profit as a percentage of sales, sales, income tax, and the income tax rate as a percent of pre-tax profits. Calculations must be done for the percentage change of earnings per share, pre-tax profits, and sales.

INTERPRETATION OF DATA

There are three ways of looking at the data. One method involves examining the calculations and trend of the data shown. A second is to chart the twelve months' trailing data on a Stock Selection Guide and examine the actual results and trends compared to expectations at the time you bought the stock. The third method is the PERT report, including PERT Worksheets A and B.

Two fundamental factors drive the price of a stock up and down. One is growth or lack of growth of earnings per share, while the second is the price/earnings ratio. The time to make the decision as to whether to continue to hold, sell, or switch is probably when it becomes apparent that the growth characteristics have changed.

If you find the profit margin declining and/or the rate of growth of sales declining from the level you anticipated at the time you bought the stock, chances are you are going to be disappointed in the price performance. The question is always what is causing the change. Is it short-term or long-term? A short-term change probably represents a buy opportunity. A long-term change suggests a sell.

Figure 13-1
PERT Worksheet A for Abbott Laboratories

NATIONAL ASSOCIATION OF INVESTORS CORPORATION

INVESTMENT EDUCATION FOR INDIVIDUALS AND CLUBS SINCE 1951

PERT Worksheet—A

Company _Abbott Labs_

PERIOD	QUARTERLY DATA — EPS $	EPS % CHANGE	PRE-TAX PROFIT $ MIL	PRE-TAX PROFIT % SALES	PRE-TAX PROFIT % CHANGE	SALES $ MIL	SALES % CHANGE	INCOME TAX RATE	LAST 12 MONTHS — EPS $	PRE-TAX PROFIT $ MIL	PRE-TAX PROFIT % SALES	SALES MIL	INCOME TAX $ MIL	INCOME TAX % RATE	% CHANGE EPS	% CHANGE PRE-TAX PROFIT	% CHANGE SALES
03/1990	0.26		315	21.9		1438		28.5	1.01	1234	22.3	5523					
06/1990	0.28		336	22.4		1503		28.5	1.05	1275	22.3	5707					
09/1990	0.26		309	20.5		1507		28.5	1.09	1311	22.2	5904					
12/1990	0.33		391	22.9		1710		28.5	1.13	1351	21.9	6159					
03/1991	0.30	15.4	360	21.8	14.3	1654	15.0	29.5	1.17	1396	21.9	6374	402	28.8	15.8	13.1	15.4
06/1991	0.31	10.7	381	22.6	13.4	1683	12.0	29.5	1.20	1441	22.0	6554	418	29.0	14.3	13.0	14.8
09/1991	0.30	15.4	357	21.6	15.5	1654	9.8	30.4	1.24	1489	22.2	6701	439	29.5	13.8	13.6	13.5
12/1991	0.36	9.1	446	23.6	14.1	1886	10.3	28.8	1.27	1544	22.5	6877	455	29.5	12.4	14.3	11.7
03/1992	0.35	16.7	409	21.8	13.6	1878	13.5	28.0	1.32	1593	22.4	7101	464	29.1	12.8	14.1	11.4
06/1992	0.37	19.4	458	24.0	20.2	1909	13.4	30.8	1.38	1670	22.8	7327	493	29.5	15.0	15.9	11.8
09/1992	0.33	10.0	387	19.7	8.4	1969	19.0	28.0	1.41	1700	22.2	7642	493	29.0	13.7	14.2	14.0
12/1992	0.42	16.7	485	23.1	8.7	2097	11.2	28.0	1.47	1739	22.1	7853	499	28.7	15.7	12.6	14.2
03/1993	0.41	17.1	480	23.5	17.4	2046	8.9	28.0	1.53	1810	22.6	8021	519	28.7	15.9	13.6	13.0
06/1993	0.42	13.5	481	23.2	5.0	2074	8.6	28.0	1.58	1833	22.4	8186	513	28.0	14.5	9.8	11.7
09/1993	0.38	15.2	439	21.3	13.4	2060	4.6	28.0	1.63	1885	22.8	8277	528	28.0	15.6	10.9	8.3
12/1993	0.48	14.3	543	24.4	12.0	2228	6.2	28.0	1.69	1943	23.1	8408	544	28.0	15.0	11.7	7.1
03/1994	0.45	9.8	523	23.6	9.0	2215	8.3	30.0	1.73	1986	23.2	8577	566	28.5	13.1	9.7	6.9
06/1994	0.46	9.5	538	24.4	11.9	2204	6.3	30.0	1.77	2043	23.5	8707	592	29.0	12.0	11.5	6.4
09/1994	0.49	13.2	502	22.3	14.4	2255	9.5	30.0	1.82	2106	23.7	8902	621	29.5	11.7	11.7	7.6
12/1994	0.53	10.4	604	24.3	11.2	2482	11.4	30.0	1.87	2167	23.7	9156	650	30.0	10.7	11.5	8.9
03/1995	0.52	15.6	592	23.5	13.2	2524	14.0	29.5	1.94	2236	23.6	9465	669	29.9	12.1	12.6	10.4
06/1995	0.53	15.2	605	24.2	12.5	2500	13.4	29.8	2.01	2303	23.6	9761	684	29.7	13.6	12.7	12.1
09/1995	0.48	11.6	542	22.7	8.0	2391	6.0	29.5	2.06	2343	23.7	9897	694	29.6	13.2	11.3	11.2
12/1995	0.59	11.3	660	25.4	9.3	2597	4.6	29.5	2.12	2399	24.0	10012	708	29.5	13.4	10.7	9.3
03/1996	0.61	17.3	681	25.5	15.0	2672	5.9	29.5	2.21	2488	24.5	10160	734	29.5	13.9	11.3	7.3
06/1996	0.60	13.2	667	24.7	10.2	2699	8.0	29.5	2.28	2550	24.6	10359	752	29.5	13.4	10.7	6.1
09/1996	0.54	12.5	597	22.6	10.1	2646	10.7	29.5	2.34	2605	24.5	10614	768	29.5	13.6	11.2	7.2
A	C	D	E	F	G	H	I	J / K	L	M	N	O	P	Q	R	S	T

Abbott Laboratories Consolidated Statement of Earnings, 1996 and 1995

	First Quarter—March		Second Quarter—June		Third Quarter—September	
	1996	1995	1996	1995	1996	1995
Net sales	$2,672,177,000	$2,524,397,000	$2,699,240,000	$2,500,310,000	$2,646,194,000	$2,390,753,000
Cost of products sold	1,156,217,000	1,088,911,000	1,143,947,000	1,086,023,000	1,177,247,000	1,070,253,000
Research and development	268,616,000	247,175,000	304,846,000	287,360,000	278,970,000	255,829,000
Selling, general, and administrative	572,346,000	598,832,000	598,866,000	532,277,000	615,269,000	521,754,000
Total operating cost and expenses	1,997,179,000	1,934,918,000	2,047,659,000	1,905,660,000	2,071,486,000	1,847,836,000
Operating earnings	674,998,000	589,479,000	651,581,000	594,650,000	574,708,000	542,917,000
Interest (income) expense, net	7,117,000	2,942,000	12,042,000	4,650,000	17,265,000	5,247,000
Other (income) expense, net	(13,124,000)	(5,313,000)	(27,728,000)	(14,461,000)	(39,560,000)	(4,246,000)
Earnings before taxes	681,005,000	591,850,000	667,267,000	604,461,000	597,003,000	541,916,000
Taxes on earnings	200,896,000	174,596,000	196,844,000	180,431,000	176,116,000	159,965,000
Net earnings	$480,109,000	$417,254,000	$470,423,000	$424,030,000	$420,887,000	$382,051,000
Net earnings per common share	0.61	0.52	0.60	0.53	0.54	0.48
Average shares outstanding	785,826,000	801,262,000	783,404,000	797,229,000	779,665,000	793,385,000
Tax rate	29.5%	29.5%	29.5%	29.8%	29.5%	29.5%

For Abbott Laboratories we have included a Consolidated Statement of Earnings, or income statement, for the quarters of March, June, and September 1996 and 1995. On PERT Worksheet A (Figure 13-1) we have inserted for each respective quarter data from the income statement, followed by calculations of quarterly data and last twelve months' data. For example, for March 1996, information taken directly from the income statement was earnings per share of $0.61, earnings before taxes or pre-tax profit of $681 million, sales of $2,672 million, and a tax rate of 29.5 percent. The calculations made are:

Present earnings per share change compared to a year earlier—
$0.61 − $0.52 = 0.09 / 0.52 = .173 or 17.3%

Pre-tax profit percent change compared to a year earlier—
681 million − 592 million = 89 million / 592 million = .15 or 15%

Pre-tax profit as a percent of sales—
681 million / 2,672 million × 100 = 25.5%

Percent change in sales compared to a year earlier—
2,672 million − 2,524 million = 148 million / 2,524 million = 5.9%

If the tax rate is not supplied, it can be computed by taking the dollar amount of taxes paid of 200.9 million and dividing by the pre-tax profits of 681 million for a percentage of 29.5 percent.

The data for the last 12 months, on the right side of PERT Worksheet A, is the sum of the last four quarters. To calculate the last 12 months' earnings per share, we would add the quarterly earnings figures of:

6/95	0.53
9/95	0.48
12/95	0.59
3/96	0.61
	2.21 Last 12 Months' EPS

The percent change over a 12-month period is shown in the three columns at the right. For example: the change in EPS—$2.21 for the 12 months ended 3/96 compared to $1.94 for the 12 months ended 3/95—is an increase of 13.9 percent.

Clubs and individual investors should consider adding more shares to their existing holdings when deciding what to buy. PERT Worksheet A with the calculation of growth and percent profit margin is one of the tools to use to aid your decision. If growth and profit margins are about as you expected when you bought the stock, further investment in the issue is attractive. Of course, the decision to buy more or not depends on the value of the stock. PERT Worksheet B (Figure 13-2), like the back of the Stock Selection Guide, shows the history of prices, earnings per share, P/E ratios, average P/E ratios, dividends, dividend payout, and high yield.

It may not be practical for all the members of a club to review all the PERT Worksheets A for every stock in the portfolio. The PERT report compiles on one sheet of paper many of the investment characteristics revealed in the Stock Selection Guide and PERT Worksheet A.

Growth Characteristics

Quarterly earnings per share

Quarterly sales

Figure 13-2
PERT Worksheet B for Abbott Laboratories

NATIONAL ASSOCIATION
OF INVESTORS CORPORATION
INVESTMENT EDUCATION
FOR INDIVIDUALS AND CLUBS
SINCE 1951

PERT Worksheet—B

Company __Abbott Laboratories__   Symbol _____

YEAR	EPS	PRICE RANGE HIGH	PRICE RANGE LOW	P/E RATIO HIGH	P/E RATIO LOW	5 YEAR AVERAGE P/E RATIO HIGH	5 YEAR AVERAGE P/E RATIO AVG	5 YEAR AVERAGE P/E RATIO LOW	DIV/ SHARE	% PAYOUT THIS YEAR	% PAYOUT 5 YEAR AVERAGE	% HIGH YIELD
1986	0.58	13.8	7.9	23.8	13.6				0.21	36.2		2.7
1987	0.70	16.8	10.0	24.0	14.3				0.25	35.7		2.5
1988	0.83	13.1	10.7	15.8	12.9				0.30	36.1		2.8
1989	0.96	17.6	11.6	18.3	12.1				0.35	36.5		3.0
1990	1.13	23.2	15.6	20.5	13.8	20.5	16.9	13.3	0.42	37.2	36.3	2.7
1991	1.27	34.9	19.6	27.5	15.4	21.2	17.5	13.7	0.50	39.4	37.1	2.6
1992	1.47	34.1	26.1	23.2	17.8	21.1	17.8	14.4	0.58	39.5	37.9	2.2
1993	1.69	30.9	22.6	18.3	13.4	21.6	18.1	14.5	0.66	39.1	38.4	2.9
1994	1.87	34.0	25.4	18.2	13.6	21.6	18.2	14.8	0.76	40.6	39.3	3.0
1995	2.12	44.8	30.6	21.1	14.4	21.7	18.3	14.9	0.82	38.7	39.4	2.7
A	B	C	D	E	F	G	H	I	J	K	L	M

Quarterly pre-tax profits

Trailing 12 months' earnings per share

Profitability

Quarterly pre-tax profit margins

Valuation

Relative value—the current P/E ratio as a percent of the five-year average P/E ratio

Current P/E ratio as a percent of the growth rate

Upside-downside ratio

Potential percent annual total return

Other

Percent dividend yield

From our PERT Worksheet A we derive our quarterly and latest 12 months'

Earnings per share

Sales

Pre-tax profits and pre-tax profit margins

From the completed Stock Selection Guide we copy

Name

Estimated earnings per share in 12 months

Annual indicated dividend

Estimated growth rate

Estimated low price—users are advised to use their judgment and insert high and low prices from a recent Guide

From the PERT Worksheet B files added

Average low P/E ratio

Average P/E ratio

Average high P/E ratio

Figure 13-3 represents a PERT report for a portfolio valued as of November 11, 1996. For a potential buy, we would look for all of the following:

EPS growth meeting our expectations

Pre-tax profit margin growth meeting our expectations

Pre-tax profit margins meeting our expectations and being reasonably maintained at a satisfactory level

Last twelve months' earnings per share growing to meet our expectations

Upside-downside ratio of 3 to 1 or greater

Relative value of 100 or less—preferably less

For a potential sell, we would look for both a current P/E ratio equal to or higher than the average high P/E ratio and an upside-downside ratio of 1 to 1 or less.

In reviewing the PERT report for Abbott Laboratories, we note that the earnings per share and pre-tax profit margins, in the double digits, continue to meet our objectives. Management has been able to maintain a constant and favorable level for pre-tax profit margins. However, as we continue our review, the upside-downside ratio is 2.1 to 1, suggesting that the stock is currently selling at the high end of the buy range. This is further supported by a relative value figure of 116 percent. We would support watching Abbott Labs and waiting for a more favorable price action before purchasing additional shares.

Note that your current P/E ratio is calculated on your estimate of earnings per share about 12 months in the future. Sources of estimated earnings per share are:

Zacks Analyst Watch 1-800-399-6659

Standard & Poor's Earnings Guide 1-800-221-5277

Nelson's Earnings Outlook 1-800-333-6357

You can interpolate between the forecast for the current year and the following year depending how many months have gone by the current year.

The sources of the data for PERT Worksheet A are company quarterly reports and quarterly financial public relations releases. Get on the mailing list. Newspaper reports of earnings do not include pre-tax profits or taxes. Use

Figure 13-3
Sample PERT Report

National Association of Investors Corporation ®
Investment Education for Individuals and Clubs Since 1951

Portfolio Evaluation Review Technique

PERT ®

Date November 12, 1996

DIV	COMPANY	% YLD	EST EPS	QTR END	EPS $	% CHG	SALES MIL $	SALES % CHG	PRE-TAX MILL $	% SALES	% CHG	TRAILING 12 MOS EPS $	% CHG	CUR P/E	PRICE	RV	5YR HI	AVG	LOW	EST GROWTH RATE EPS	P/E AS % OF GROWTH RATE	US/DS	% COMPD ANNUAL RATE OF RETURN	EST LOW PRICE	EST HIGH PRICE	
0.96	Abbott Labs	1.8	2.51	9/96	.54	12.5	2646	10.7	597	22.6	10.1	2.34	13.6	21.2	53.3	116	21.7	18.3	14.9	13.0	163	2.1	15	36	89	
				9/95	.48		2391		542	22.7		2.06															
0.52	Brady W.H.	2.3	1.50	10/96	.29	16.0	97	22.8	11	11.3	22.2	1.27	2.4	15.3	23.0	94	18.9	16.2	13.5	18.0	85	7.4	27	19	55	
				10/95	.25		79		9	11.4		1.24															
0.12	Dallas Semi.	0.6	1.72	9/96	.28	-17.6	72	18.0	12	16.7	-14.3	1.36	9.7	12.2	21.0	78	19.7	15.7	11.6	15.0	81	12.3	30	18	59	
				9/95	.34		61		14	23.0		1.24															
0.48	First USA	0.8	4.20	9/96	1.06	27.7	358	46.7	116	32.4	33.3	3.92	30.7	14.6	61.5	107	17.2	13.7	10.1	20.0	73	4.1	26	40	150	
				9/95	.83		244		87	35.7		3.00															
0.0	Healthcare Com.	0.0	2.42	6/96	.55	17.0	62	17.0	32	51.6	14.3	2.08	23.8	18.4	44.5	97	26.2	18.9	11.7	20.0	92	4.8	31	26	131	
				6/95	.47		53		28	52.8		1.68															
0.48	Hewlett Pack.	1.0	3.42	7/96	.40	-27.3	9105	17.7	616	6.8	-29.0	2.49	16.4	14.0	47.9	90	19.7	15.5	11.3	17.0	82	2.3	28	14	126	
				7/95	.55		7739		867	11.2		2.14															
0.20	Linear Tech.	0.5	1.80	10/96	.40	2.6	90	3.4	48	53.3	2.1	1.73	37.3	22.9	41.3	96	30.7	23.8	16.8	17.0	135	3.4	26	23	103	
				10/95	.39		87		47	54.0		1.26															
0.64	Nordson	1.2	3.57	7/96	.65	-18.8	147	-5.2	18	12.2	-21.7	2.79	1.5	15.3	54.5	70	25.4	21.8	18.2	16.0	95	12.9	33	46	16	
				7/95	.80		155		23	14.8		2.75															
0.56	Newell	1.9	1.76	9/96	.47	14.6	762	17.1	123	16.1	12.8	1.53	10.9	16.7	29.4	90	22.2	18.5	14.7	13.0	128	6.6	23	24	64	
				9/95	.41		651		109	16.7		1.38															
0.40	PepsiCo	1.3	1.53	9/96	.09	-76.9	7867	2.3	442	5.6	-50.9	1.05	-13.9	20.5	31.4	114	21.3	18.0	14.7	14.0	146	1.9	16	19	55	
				9/95	.39		7693		901	11.7		1.22															
0.49	Pall Corp	1.9	1.40	7/96	.44	10.0	282	11.0	72	25.5	14.3	1.20	15.4	18.6	26.1	85	26.1	21.8	17.4	14.0	133	10.1	26	23	62	
				7/95	.40		254		63	24.8		1.04															
0.52	Sysco Corp.	1.5	1.67	9/96	.41	13.9	3679	11.8	120	3.3	10.1	1.57	10.6	20.9	34.9	95	25.0	22.1	19.2	10.0	209	3.2	17	27	61	
				9/95	.36		3292		109	3.3		1.42															
B	C	D	E	F	G	H	I	J	K	L	M	N	O	P	Q	R	S	T	U	V	W	X	Y	AA	AB

141

these sources for data before the quarterly report or financial public relations release is received.

For PERT Worksheet B as well as the Guide, you must use the fiscal year price range. Source data is the company's annual report for the last two years. Further back, use price chart or prior annual reports. *Barron's* and *The Wall Street Journal* are sources of high and low price for the past 52 weeks. Pick the publication issue closest to the end of the fiscal year. Value Line or Standard & Poor's data can be used to start to build a PERT A data file for several years of quarters, but does not include pre-tax profits.

SUMMARY

PERT is a good way to keep track of the fundamental performance of your stocks. It supplements the Stock Selection Guide. It helps your portfolio management efforts in terms of the same criteria you used to buy the stock, that is, growth, profitability, and value. It helps to provide you with factual data to assist in a judgment to buy, hold, or sell. PERT helps an investor manage a portfolio.

The investor readily discovers that PERT requires a considerable number of calculations. Two computer programs are available through NAIC that support PERT. One is called STB Stock Analyst; the second, Investor's Toolkit Complete, has a PERT module included. These programs are a great convenience for the investor.

CHAPTER 14

THE CHALLENGE TREE

*T*he Challenge Tree is a systematic approach to improving the performance of your portfolio. It shows you how to compare the merits of one stock against another. Even if you are a relatively inexperienced investor, you can use Challenge Tree guidelines to avoid some of the hazards of buying and selling stocks.

The Challenge Tree utilizes a five-year estimate of a stock's future price range—long enough to include the business cycle extremes of boom (bull market) and recession (bear market). The Challenge Tree guides you to companies with good management that should earn more and be worth more in the coming five years. It also guides you in comparing the prices of stocks and directing your attention to possible substantial price appreciation opportunities.

The Rule of Five is an investment theory for intelligent portfolio management. The rule holds that of every five stocks owned over a five-year period, one will encounter difficulty unforeseen by the investor, three will perform more or less according to expectations, and one will far exceed the standard set for it. With the Challenge Tree, you will be able to upgrade your portfolio as any disappointing results become apparent.

The Challenge Tree uses the five-year upside/downside ratio and quality considerations to enhance your portfolio's defensive strength. The two major indicators for purchase are:

1. A stock selling in the lowest third of its estimated five-year price range and showing potential for 100 percent appreciation during that time.

2. A stock offering sound reasons to expect substantial price appreciation in the next six to eighteen months.

These indicators help you to focus clearly on goals and enable you to turn aside "story" stocks and other speculative hazards in favor of solid information.

ASSEMBLING DATA

First, the NAIC Stock Selection Guide should be completed for the two stocks being considered for purchase or sale (Figures 14-1 and 14-2). If you already have NAIC Portfolio Management Guide or PERT records on the companies, all the better.

Next, transfer your information to the Challenge Tree Comparative Form (Figure 14-3). The gain to five-year high and loss to five-year low are calculated for each stock as follows:

$$\% \text{ Gains} = \frac{\text{Five-Year High Price} - \text{Present Price}}{\text{Present Price}}$$

$$\% \text{ Loss} = \frac{\text{Present Price} - \text{Five-Year Low Price}}{\text{Present Price}}$$

Questions in Figure 14-3 under the "6 to 18 Month Upside Action" heading should be answered using single words. However, there is room for brief comments if necessary.

MAKING DECISIONS

The challenger stock must be of equal or higher quality. Both *Standard & Poor's Stock Guide* and Value Line are reliable sources of quality ratings. The Challenge Tree form (Figure 14-3) calls for the S&P rating. If another service is used, indicate that on the form.

Here's the Challenge Tree reasoning: Suppose you purchased a stock based on the estimate that its value would double in five years. It is now in the middle third of its range, having posted a 33 to 66 percent gain. This stock appears to have realized 50 percent of its potential gain in the past six to eighteen months. Its upside/downside ratio has dropped from 3 to 1 when you purchased it to 1 to 1. The upside gain, because of the stock's rise, has deteriorated from 100 percent to 50 percent.

Figure 14-1
Stock Selection Guide for Weis Markets

Figure 14-1 (Continued)
Stock Selection Guide for Weis Markets

2 EVALUATING MANAGEMENT

Company __Weis Markets__

	19 86	19 87	19 88	19 89	19 90	19 91	19 92	19 93	19 94	19 95	LAST 5 YEAR AVG.	TREND UP	TREND DOWN
A % Pre-tax Profit on Sales (Net Before Taxes ÷ Sales)	9.5	10.2	10.8	10.7	10.9	11.1	11.6	10.9	10.8	10.4	11.0		✔
B % Earned on Equity (E/S ÷ Book Value)	19.2	18.9	18.9	18.2	17.5	16.9	17.7	17.2	16.1	14.8	16.5		✔

3 PRICE-EARNINGS HISTORY as an indicator of the future

This shows how stock prices have fluctuated with earnings and dividends. It is a building block for translating earnings into future stock prices.

PRESENT PRICE __29__   HIGH THIS YEAR __34 3/8__   LOW THIS YEAR __24 1/4__

	Year	A PRICE HIGH	B PRICE LOW	C Earnings Per Share	D Price Earnings Ratio HIGH A÷C	E Price Earnings Ratio LOW B÷C	F Dividend Per Share	G % Payout F÷C X 100	H % High Yield F÷B X 100
1	1991	27 7/8	22 1/8	1.42	20	16	.36	25	1.6
2	1992	41 5/8	23 7/8	1.66	25	14	.434	26	1.8
3	1993	37	27	1.82	20	15	.500	27	1.9
4	1994	37 1/2	28 1/8	1.91	20	15	.560	29	2.0
5	1995	34 3/8	24 1/4	1.93	18	13	.600	31	2.5
6	TOTAL		125.375		103	73	.64	138	
7	AVERAGE		25		20.6	14.6		27.6	
8	AVERAGE PRICE EARNINGS RATIO __17.6__			9	CURRENT PRICE EARNINGS RATIO __15__				

4 EVALUATING RISK and REWARD over the next 5 years

Assuming one recession and one business boom every 5 years, calculations are made of how **high** and how **low** the stock might sell. The upside-downside ratio is the key to evaluating risk and reward.

A HIGH PRICE — NEXT 5 YEARS
Avg. High P/E __17.6__ (3D7 as adj.) X Estimate High Earnings/Share __2.30__ = Forecast High Price $ __40.50__ (4A1)

B LOW PRICE — NEXT 5 YEARS
(a) Avg. Low P/E __14.6__ (3E7 as adj.) X Estimated Low Earnings/Share __1.93__ = $ __28__
(b) Avg. Low Price of Last 5 Years = __25__
(c) Recent Severe Market Low Price = __24 1/4__ (3B7)
(d) Price Dividend Will Support $\frac{\text{Present Divd.}}{\text{High Yield (H)}}$ = $\frac{.64}{.025}$ = __25.6__
Selected Estimated Low Price = $ __24 1/4__ (4B1)

C ZONING
__40.50__ (4A1) High Forecast Price Minus __24.25__ (4B1) Low Forecast Price Equals __16.25__ (C) Range. 1/3 of Range = __5.50__ (4CD)
(4C2) Lower 1/3 = __24.25__ (4B1) to __29.75__ (Buy)
(4C3) Middle 1/3 = __29.75__ to __35.25__ (Maybe)
(4C4) Upper 1/3 = __35.25__ to __40.50__ (4A1) (Sell)
Present Market Price of __29__ is in the __BUY__ (4C5) Range

D UP-SIDE DOWN-SIDE RATIO (Potential Gain vs. Risk of Loss)
$\frac{\text{High Price (4A1)} \quad 40.50 \quad \text{Minus Present Price} \quad 29}{\text{Present Price} \quad 29 \quad \text{Minus Low Price (4B1)} \quad 24.25}$ = $\frac{11.50}{4.75}$ = __2.4__ (4D) To 1

E PRICE TARGET (Note: This shows the potential market price appreciation over the next five years in simple interest terms.)
$\frac{\text{High Price (4A1)} \quad 40.50}{\text{Present Market Price} \quad 29}$ = (__1.40__) X 100 = (__140__) − 100 = __40__ (4E) % Appreciation

5 5-YEAR POTENTIAL

This combines price appreciation with dividend yield to get an estimate of total return. It provides a standard for comparing income and growth stocks.

A $\frac{\text{Present Full Year's Dividend \$} \quad .64}{\text{Present Price of Stock \$} \quad 29}$ = __.022__ X 100 = __2.2__ (5A) Present Yield or % Returned on Purchase Price

Note: Results are expressed as a simple rate; use the table below to convert to a compound rate.

B AVERAGE YIELD OVER NEXT 5 YEARS
$\frac{\text{Avg. Earnings Per Share Next 5 Years} \quad 2.18 \quad \text{X Avg. \% Payout (3G7)} \quad .276}{\text{Present Price \$} \quad 29}$ = __.60__ = __2.1__ (5B) %

C ESTIMATED AVERAGE ANNUAL RETURN OVER NEXT FIVE YEARS
$\frac{\text{5 Year Appreciation Potential (4E)} \quad 40}{5}$ = __8__ %
Average Yield (5B) .... __2.1__ %
Average Total Annual Return Over the Next 5 Years (5C) __10.1__ %

Table to Convert From Simple to Compound Rate
Simple Rate 2 4 6 8 10 12 14 16 18 20 22 24 26 28 30 32 34 36 38 40
Compound Rate 2 4 6 8 10 12 14 16 18 20 22 24

Figure 14-2

Stock Selection Guide for First Financial Management Corporation

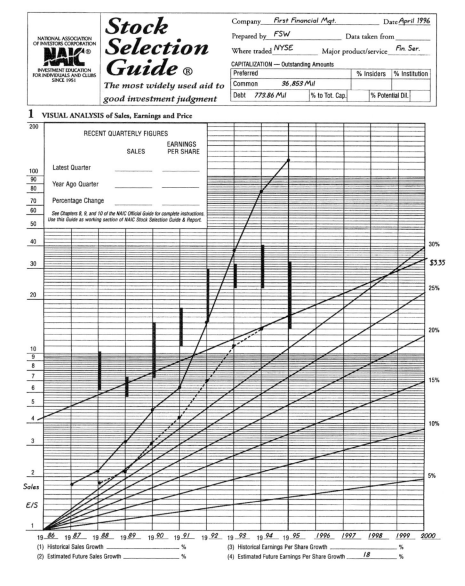

Stock Selection Guide ®

NATIONAL ASSOCIATION OF INVESTORS CORPORATION

NAIC ®

INVESTMENT EDUCATION FOR INDIVIDUALS AND CLUBS
SINCE 1951

The most widely used aid to good investment judgment

Company	First Financial Mgt.		Date	April 1996
Prepared by	FSW		Data taken from	
Where traded	NYSE	Major product/service	Fin. Ser.	

CAPITALIZATION — Outstanding Amounts

			% Insiders	% Institution
Preferred				
Common	36,853 Mil			
Debt	773.86 Mil	% to Tot. Cap.		% Potential Dil.

1 VISUAL ANALYSIS of Sales, Earnings and Price

RECENT QUARTERLY FIGURES

	SALES	EARNINGS PER SHARE
Latest Quarter		
Year Ago Quarter		
Percentage Change		

See Chapters 8, 9, and 10 of the NAIC Official Guide for complete instructions. Use this Guide as working section of NAIC Stock Selection Guide & Report.

(1) Historical Sales Growth _____ %
(2) Estimated Future Sales Growth _____ %
(3) Historical Earnings Per Share Growth _____ %
(4) Estimated Future Earnings Per Share Growth _____18_____ %

Figure 14-2 (Continued)
Stock Selection Guide for First Financial Management Corporation

2 EVALUATING MANAGEMENT　　Company __First Financial Mgmt. Corp.__

		19 _86_	19 _87_	19 _88_	19 _89_	19 _90_	19 _91_	19 _92_	19 _93_	19 _94_	19 _95_	LAST 5 YEAR AVG.	TREND UP	DOWN
A	% Pre-tax Profit on Sales (Net Before Taxes ÷ Sales)			13.0	11.4	11.5	13.2	11.0	11.8	10.7	9.4	11.2	✓	
B	% Earned on Equity (E/S ÷ Book Value)			13.5	16.4	10.3	14.1	5.2	10.5	10.8	11.7	10.5	✓	

3 PRICE-EARNINGS HISTORY as an indicator of the future

This shows how stock prices have fluctuated with earnings and dividends. It is a building block for translating earnings into future stock prices.

PRESENT PRICE __21__　　　HIGH THIS YEAR __33 3/4__　　　LOW THIS YEAR __14 1/4__

	Year	A PRICE HIGH	B PRICE LOW	C Earnings Per Share	D Price Earnings Ratio HIGH A÷C	E Price Earnings Ratio LOW B÷C	F Dividend Per Share	G % Payout F÷C X 100	H % High Yield F÷B X 100
1	1991	17 5/8	11	.44	40	25			
2	1992	30 1/4	15	.74	41	20			
3	1993	31 7/8	23 1/8	1.15	28	20			
4	1994	39	23 3/8	1.43	27	16	.098	7	
5	1995	33 3/4	14 1/8	1.67	20	8	.10	6	
6	TOTAL		86.625						
7	AVERAGE		17.33						
8	AVERAGE PRICE EARNINGS RATIO				9	CURRENT PRICE EARNINGS RATIO			

4 EVALUATING RISK and REWARD over the next 5 years

Assuming one recession and one business boom every 5 years, calculations are made of how **high** and how **low** the stock might sell. The upside-downside ratio is the key to evaluating risk and reward.

A HIGH PRICE — NEXT 5 YEARS
Avg. High P/E __18__ (3G7 as adj.)　X Estimate High Earnings/Share __3.35__　= Forecast High Price $ __60__ (4A1)

B LOW PRICE — NEXT 5 YEARS
(a) Avg. Low P/E __10__ (3E7 as adj.)　X Estimated Low Earnings/Share __1.67__　= $ __17__

(b) Avg. Low Price of Last 5 Years = __17 3/8__ (3B7)

(c) Recent Severe Market Low Price = __14 1/8__

(d) Price Dividend Will Support Present Divd. / High Yield (H) = _____ = __--__

Selected Estimated Low Price = $ __14 1/8__ (4B1)

C ZONING
__60__ (4A1) High Forecast Price Minus __14 1/8__ (4B1) Low Forecast Price Equals __45 7/8__ (C) Range. 1/3 of Range = __15 1/4__ (4CD)

(4C2) Lower 1/3 = (4B1) __14 1/8__ to __29 3/8__ (Buy)
(4C3) Middle 1/3 = __29 3/8__ to __44 5/8__ (Maybe)
(4C4) Upper 1/3 = __44 5/8__ to __60__ (4A1) (Sell)

Present Market Price of __21__ is in the __BUY__ (4C5) Range

D UP-SIDE DOWN-SIDE RATIO (Potential Gain vs. Risk of Loss)
High Price (4A1) __60__ Minus Present Price __21__ = __39__ = __5.7__ To 1
Present Price __21__ Minus Low Price (4B1) __14 1/8__ = __6 7/8__ = (4D)

E PRICE TARGET (Note: This shows the potential market price appreciation over the next five years in simple interest terms.)
High Price (4A1) __60__ / Present Market Price __21__ = (__2.86__) X 100 = (__286__) − 100 = __186__ (4E) % Appreciation

5 5-YEAR POTENTIAL　This combines price appreciation with dividend yield to get an estimate of total return. It provides a standard for comparing income and growth stocks.

A Present Full Year's Dividend $ __--__ / Present Price of Stock $ __--__ = __--__ X 100 = __--__ (5A) Present Yield or % Returned on Purchase Price

Note: Results are expressed as a simple rate; use the table below to convert to a compound rate.

B AVERAGE YIELD OVER NEXT 5 YEARS
Avg. Earnings Per Share Next 5 Years __--__ X Avg. % Payout (3G7) __--__ = __--__ / Present Price $ __--__ = __--__ % (5B)

C ESTIMATED AVERAGE ANNUAL RETURN OVER NEXT FIVE YEARS
5 Year Appreciation Potential (4E) __186__ / 5 = __37.2__ %
Average Yield (5B) .... __--__ %
Average Total Annual Return Over the Next 5 Years (5C) __37.2__ %

Table to Convert From Simple to Compound Rate

Simple Rate 2 4 6 8 10 12 14 16 18 20 22 24 26 28 30 32 34 36 38 40

Compound Rate 2 4 6 8 10 12 14 16 18 20 22 24

Figure 14-3

Challenge Tree Form Comparing Weis Markets and First Financial
Management Corporation

Challenge Tree
Comparative Form ®

Date _____ April 10, 1996 _____

	COMPANY HELD	CHALLENGING COMPANY
	Weis Markets	First Financial Mgt. Co.
Current Price	29	21
Estimated 5 Year High	40.50	60
Estimated 5 Year Low	24.25	14.125
Gain to 5 Year High	11.50 - 40%	39 - 186%
Loss to 5 Year Low	4.75 - 16%	6 7/8 - 33%
5 Year Upside-Downside Ratio	2.4	5.7
Lower Price Range	24.25 - 29.75	14 1/8 - 29 3/8
Middle Price Range	29.75 - 35.25	29 3/8 - 44 5/8
Upper Price Range	35.25 - 40.50	44 5/8 - 60
S & P Quality Rating	A+	B+
Value Line Timeliness Rating	4	3
6 to 18 Months Upside Action	Neutral	Good
Earnings Advancing	Down Likely	Yes
Business Cycle Upswing	Down to Neutral	Neutral
Industry Outlook	Very Competitive	Good
Upside-Downside Outlook	Fair	Good
Growth Stock Potential	Poor	Very Good
New Products Coming In	More Competition	Purchases

JUDGING MANAGEMENT	Good	Average	Poor	Good	Average	Poor
Driving Force:						
Rate of Sales Gain			✔	✔		
Rate of Earnings Per Share Gain			✔	✔		
Earned on Sales		✔		✔		
Earned on Equity		✔			✔	
Evaluating Price:						
High in 5 Years		✔		✔		
Low in 5 Years		✔		✔		
Upside-Downside Ratio			✔	✔		
Current Yield		✔				✔
Total Return			✔	✔		
Other Considerations:						
Industry Potentials			✔	✔		
State of Business Cycle		✔		✔		
Stock Price Trends			✔		✔	
Quality of Stock	✔				✔	
Capitalization and Finance	✔				✔	

NATIONAL ASSOCIATION
OF INVESTORS CORPORATION

NAIC ®

INVESTMENT EDUCATION
FOR INDIVIDUALS AND CLUBS
SINCE 1951

If you can identify a replacement stock of equal or higher quality, a 3 to 1 upside/downside ratio, and 100 percent appreciation potential, buy it. You will find that your investment results will improve over the years as you continue to use this technique.

On occasion, the stock market cycle will come to a point where you can no longer locate a 3 to 1 upside/downside ratio and 100 percent appreciation potential in addition to equal or higher quality. When this occurs, consider buying short-term bonds as up to 20 percent of the most speculative part of your portfolio. These will provide income while your club waits for a major stock market correction, after which stocks will again be attractive. At the onset of a new upward movement, you may consider several challengers of less quality. As the market advances, you should also enhance the quality of your holdings.

ERRORS TO AVOID

Avoid these two common errors:

1. Do not hold lesser-quality stocks as a bull market winds down, or your results will be erratic. Only stronger companies survive the depths of the downturn that follows a boom. By raising quality with each Challenge Tree exercise, you increase your chances for better results.

2. Do not assume that simply because a company has doubled in value, it cannot continue to appreciate. Superior growth companies do. Why settle for a 50 to 100 percent profit when holding growth stocks for a longer period could mean a gain of 200 percent, 500 percent, or even more?

Determining whether a particular company has further potential requires going beyond the figures. You should be thoroughly familiar with the company from your reading of corporate messages and the business press and be able to make an informed decision as to the company's prospects for the next several years.

THE CHALLENGE TREE AT WORK

An actual Challenge Tree experience illustrates how the procedure works and the results that can be achieved. An investor with $450 made her initial stock purchase in 1957, buying 25 shares of Hoover Ball & Bearing at $18. These shares were sold the following year at $30.875, returning $755.96. The investor then bought 50 shares of Copeland at $13.50 with $675 of the money she made.

A year later Copeland was sold at $23.25. Within a week, the investor purchased 50 shares of Delta for $26, an investment of $1,300. In 1962, she sold 30 shares of Delta for $53.375, receiving $1,601.25. She then bought 100 shares of American Metal Products stock at $14, spending $1,400.

In 1965, her Metal Products stock was selling for $25 and her Delta holdings had grown to 70 shares with splits, selling at $17.25. Her portfolio totaled $5,057.50. She had received dividends totaling $686.43 since the inception of her program, and in just eight years the original $450 had grown to $8,243.93.

By 1983, this investor had a portfolio of 462 Delta, 60 Fruehauf, 239 Occidental, and 249 Asarco, with a total value of $37,031. In addition, she had received dividends totaling $12,978.

Not all Challenge Tree experiences will be this profitable, but this procedure represents an opportunity to significantly improve your financial progress as an investor. The purpose of the Challenge Tree is to provide you with a proven, consistent method for analyzing your holdings and making informed decisions.

APPLYING CHALLENGE TREE TO TWO STOCKS

Let's apply the Challenge Tree to two actual stocks. A club has owned Weis Markets, Inc. for more than ten years. It was first bought at a price, after stock splits, of 8¾. In the past year the stock has sold as high as 34⅜ and as low as 24¼. The Stock Selection Guide shows that the rate of sales growth in the past three years has dropped to under 3 percent. Earnings per share growth have dropped even more, and management has indicated that the current year's earnings will be down. This is also shown by declines in the pre-tax profit on sales and in earnings on equity. The challenging company is First Financial Management Corporation. A club member was attracted to this stock when he noticed that over the past year its price declined from 33¾ to a low of 14¼, yet revenues were growing very rapidly and earnings per share were increasing at 18 percent. In spite of its rapid rate of growth, the company sold at a price/earnings ratio of 16. The investor read reports by S&P, Value Line, and several security analysts. The reports concluded that the corporation was being considered as a bank by the market and was subject to the same suspicion and distrust that all banks were experiencing at that time. Actually, the main business of the corporation is processing credit reports and credit cards for banks and financial companies. It is very different from a bank.

A review of the Stock Selection Guide for Weis Markets makes it clear that sales growth has also recently slowed. Some of this resulted from a lower tax rate. The investor who also keeps a NAIC PERT form on his or her stocks would have noted that the decline in sales growth started in 1987. The profit margins were maintained, and the reduction in the tax rate enabled earnings per share to continue to advance. The Stock Selection Guide on Weis also shows the slowing growth rate is causing a reduced P/E ratio both at the high and the low prices.

The challenging company has caught our attention for two reasons: the very high rate of growth and the substantial decline in price in spite of the fact that the company has continued to increase earnings per share.

DISCUSS THE REASONING

After filling in the Challenge Tree form, the club member goes over the figures and conclusions with the other members to see whether they agree with the conclusion. The price and gain figures come from the Stock Selection Guide, and the members agree that Weis's growth rate has slowed and that First Financial has an exceptional rate of growth. All agree that a conservative projection of a 15 percent compound annual growth rate five years into the future is reasonable.

The club discussed the quality ratings of the two companies a great deal and almost decided to drop the challenging company because of its lesser quality. The members finally agreed that the quality rating of the challenger was not bad in view of its brief history and very rapid growth. Then the club looked at the current stock market cycle. It concluded that the market was in a minor decline and probably had two to three years to go in the current major upward cycle. Therefore, holding a stock with the challenger's quality rating did not pose a problem at this time.

In the next six to eighteen months, Weis will face both a continued weak business period and competition from two new chains in its market. Conversely, First Financial seems likely to continue its advance. In terms of the

"Driving Force" items listed on the Challenge Tree form, First Financial is strongly ahead of Weis. The same is true of the "Evaluating Price" items.

Among other considerations, it is clear that Weis is ahead in quality and financial condition, but the members decided the First Financial's growth potential outweighed these two items. Therefore, the club decided to sell its shares of Weis and use the proceeds to buy First Financial.

CHAPTER 15

DECIDING WHEN TO SELL

Famed investor Warren Buffett has a theory on the best time to sell: "Never." This may be an extreme position, but without question, amateur investors are more likely to sell too soon than to hold their stocks too long.

How likely is it that a decision to sell will prove profitable? Consider that with each sell action you must make not one, but two, right decisions. First, you must decide to sell stock A, and then you must find its replacement. Stock B must offer less downside risk and greater upside potential than its predecessor must in order to justify the action.

CONSIDER COSTS

The decision is not limited to share price. You cannot forget commission, either. A low estimate of the commission involved is 2 percent to buy and another 2 percent to sell. Plus you must add the additional federal and state taxes you and your fellow club members will have to pay on your profits, further eroding your gross profit. You may be startled to learn that, on average, after both commissions and taxes are taken into account, a new stock must register a 37 percent gain before you even begin to make money!

REASONS TO SELL

What are legitimate reasons for selling stocks? Certainly, one is to reap the rewards of years of successful investing and withdraw funds for a new house, a child's education, or other major expense. The other is to improve your port-folio.

You should sell:

1. Because of an adverse management change. New management is not nec-essarily good management. It might be difficult for you to assess the ability of brand-new management, but you consider the opinion of in-vestment professionals, who are probably familiar with the individuals' track records.

2. Because of declining profit margins. This is a leading indicator of corpo-rate problems. Keep in mind the Wall Street saying "There is no such thing as one bad quarter." The company may be in for a year or more of depressed earnings.

3. Because of a deteriorating corporate financial condition. If a company has taken on too much debt, it may face serious trouble meeting interest and principal payments in a slowing economy. Keep up to date on changes in the company's capitalization, and check the impact of leverage, as you learned to do in Chapter 4.

4. Because competition is affecting profits. Nobody has a monopoly on a good idea. When others see the potential for a product or service and enter the business, price cutting, earnings erosion, and even bankruptcy may follow. Although the company's earnings may continue to advance, they could decline in P/E ratio if the EPS growth rate slackens.

   Don't follow the crowd and chase "in" industries. Think for your-self, and look at the ability of management, not the glamour of the business.

   An example: RPM is a specialty chemical company making adhe-sives and coatings. "Not a very exciting business," you might think. Per-haps not, but RPM has chalked up increases in sales and earnings for 37 straight years! And we all know that price is related to earnings.

5. Because of dependence on a single product. In the 1960s, Brunswick Corporation was viewed as a growth stock. When the automatic bowling pin machine was introduced, bowling lanes throughout the country and abroad made sure to buy it. However, once every bowling facility had the equipment, the growth slowed. This was product growth, contrasted with the growth that stems from good management. At Minnesota Min-ing and Manufacturing, the company has traditionally garnered a quar-

ter of its sales from products not on the market five years before. Such a company will probably show slower growth than that of a shooting star, but the growth is longer lasting.

6. Because a stock's quality will change as economic circumstances change. The quality of a stock comprises many factors. To name a few: size, financial condition, consumer acceptance, market share, effectiveness of research, and depth of management. But say raw materials triple in price; the stock's quality attributes are still good, but the changed economic situation has changed its quality as well.

7. Because securities that have proven to be cyclical and that have a recent history of slow growth should be sold when the economy peaks. Buy cyclical stocks during the trough when P/E ratios are relatively high and the market is predicting their earnings recovery. Don't buy when the multiples are relatively low and the stocks seem to be a bargain, as this indicates that earnings are headed for a decline.

8. Because it is important to maintain balance by company size in your portfolio. Remember our recommendation: Keep 25 percent of your holdings in companies with $4 billion or more in sales, 25 percent in small companies with sales under $400 million and with rapid growth rates, and 50 percent in medium-sized companies.

SELLING DON'TS

Set these rules for yourself concerning selling:

1. Don't sell just because the price hasn't moved. One of the cardinal requirements for successful investing is patience. Don't concentrate on the price, as a trader would. Rather, focus on the fundamentals, as a long-term investor should. If the basics remain attractive, over time you need not worry about price.

2. Don't sell because of a paper loss. You might think it is smart to sell out when a decline in price of 10 or 20 percent is posted. But a stock well worth keeping can go down that far in a declining market.

3. Don't sell because of a paper profit. You might be tempted to sell when a stock doubles, yet many stocks post gains of 2,000 percent, 3,000 percent, and even more over a 10-year span. Think how much you'd miss out on if you sold in the first year! Again, concentrate on the study of

fundamentals. As long as the stock meets the criteria you have established, hold on to it.

4. Don't sell on temporary bad news. A perfect example is Metromedia, which once enjoyed an earnings gain of 40 percent in a quarter when newspapers in two of its major markets—New York and Los Angeles—were on strike. Advertisers flocked to Metromedia's TV stations, and management pointed out that earnings probably would be less in the same quarter a year hence. Sure enough, they were. And the price of the stock fell sharply, even after management's caveat. But, as management has also predicted, earnings resumed their upward trend, and so did the stock price.

5. Don't sell just to take action. This is sometimes appealing if you feel frustrated that something isn't happening quickly enough. Be patient and wait out the market.

6. Don't sell a stock that has fallen so far that your remaining downside risk is minimal compared to the upside potential.

If you are unsure about whether to sell, why not hedge your decisions? Sell a part of the holding and keep the rest. You'll be diversifying your portfolio, which can be especially important if a single issue has become too large a part of your holdings. In a small portfolio (under $100,000 in size), a single issue should not account for more than 20 percent of total value. In a large portfolio (at least $100,000 in size), no single holding should represent more than 10 percent of the total value.

To sum up, selling may be the most difficult decision you face as an investor. Take full advantage of the Portfolio Management Guide and PERT. If sales and earnings gains continue to meet or exceed your minimum requirement, and if the pre-tax profit margin is rising, consider selling only if the price multiple earnings ratio exceeds one and a half times the historical average high price/earnings ratio. And even then, you may find reasons why you should continue to hold the stock. Don't sell too quickly—remember Warren Buffett.

PART

Winning with an Investment Club

TWO

CHAPTER 16

STARTING A CLUB

When you form an investment club, your first task is to identify prospective members. You'll probably find plenty of people intrigued by the idea of pooling money together to invest.

WHAT TO LOOK FOR

There are three elements to the successful start-up club. Only when those elements come together are you assured of success.

First, the venture must be an enjoyable social activity as well as an educational and money-making program. You will want to attract people who are compatible and able to function as a team. You are embarking on an activity that could last a lifetime; your fellow adventurers should wear well.

The second requirement is to ensure that all members are committed to the same investment philosophy. The single most frequent cause of early dissolution of investment clubs is conflicting investment philosophies. A club cannot exist if it's divided between long-term investors who want to follow NAIC principles and others who are determined to act as traders, moving in and out of the market. For many inexperienced first-timers, the allure of fast profits and active trading is irresistible. Successful investment clubs adhere to the more conservative point of view that wealth building is a slow process, particularly in the beginning years. The popular conception of investing is that you frequently buy and sell. Many prospects have that idea. It is important that the club make clear to all prospects that its policy is to buy carefully and then hold.

Third, the club will thrive best when members are committed to active participation. The reality is that some members are not willing to contribute more than their monthly dues; they gladly leave to others the work of investigating prospective purchases and sales. (Of course, as a result, these inactive individuals learn little or nothing about investing.) Almost every club has a few of these members. You need to make sure you have enough energetic, dedicated people that the investigative requirements can be managed by them. In time most club members build their own security accounts outside of the club. The monthly club meeting is a valuable source of ideas for these members.

Remember that an investment club works so well because several people share the work. Research takes time and, by splitting it up, you benefit from the shared responsibility of membership.

WHERE TO LOOK

Make up a list of people to approach. Consider friends from every facet of your life: neighbors, members of your church, or those you know from civic and charitable organizations. If you know someone who works as a volunteer and takes that responsibility seriously, you have a most attractive prospect. You will probably want to invite coworkers to your meeting, but don't limit the range of possibilities to this or any other single group. The most successful clubs are made up of individuals from a variety of backgrounds and experience. Generally, try to limit the number of individuals from any one place of employment to no more than half the total membership.

Don't feel obligated to include an accountant and an attorney; most clubs succeed without either. Above all, don't seek out a financial expert, whether a registered representative, an investment analyst, or a long-time successful investor. Other members will tend to lean on such an individual and will know no more after years of membership than they did on joining. Furthermore, the collective judgment of a number of reasonable people can be much sounder than the opinion of a single source, however knowledgeable that individual might be.

Travel time to meetings limits the geography of your search, so your club should be localized. Think about where you will be meeting, and who could reach the site(s) in an hour or less.

In the final analysis, investment club members need only be individuals willing to work to gain knowledge, with an above-average desire to learn for themselves about the world of securities. Members should also regard their investment program as a lifelong process. Investing experience is not a requirement for success, as hundreds of high-performance NAIC clubs can attest.

HOW MANY MEMBERS?

Ideally, a club should be big enough for members to divide the work without it becoming burdensome for any individual, yet small enough to give everyone a sense of direct involvement and personal interest. For most clubs, this number averages fifteen. Another advantage of holding the count to around fifteen is that meetings can remain informal and not become so unwieldy that decisions are difficult to reach. What's more, if membership exceeds fifteen, the number of appropriate meeting places will be limited.

Whatever your target total, seek out three or four extra people, because inevitably some portion of your prospective membership will decide not to join. So if you're looking for fifteen and twenty people express interest, chances are you'll be right on target.

Invite everyone who's interested to an exploratory meeting to learn more, and be sure to get enough informational membership guides from NAIC to pass out to every prospect, so that all will have a better idea of what lies ahead. Don't seek a final commitment from anyone until afterward.

BEFORE THE MEETING

Send a reminder to each of the prospects, enclosing reprints of the Introduction and Chapter 1 of this book. Also include a copy of the suggested Club Operating Agreement (Chapter 17).

Ask each person to review the materials prior to attending, and to come prepared with questions and comments as well as possible names for the club.

Arrange for an experienced investment club member to attend your initial session. If this is impractical, try to attend an existing club's meeting as an observer, to gain useful background and get answers to any questions you may have. If there is a NAIC Council in your area, attend a meeting to make contact with experienced club members.

AT THE MEETING

First, briefly go over the materials furnished to the prospects. Explain what the benefits of joining an investment club are, what will be expected of members, and how the group will be organized. Remind each person that the club is not a get-rich-quick operation. Emphasize that the time to decide whether one belongs in a club is before joining.

Next, ask for questions. When all inquiries have been satisfied, ask a show of hands to determine how many people are interested in joining the group. If most are interested, proceed with the organization, and consider the Club Operating Agreement. (Most clubs form as a partnership; Chapter 17 spells out the many points to be considered in setting up the organization.) To save time, propose that the club adopt NAIC's agreement for a six-month trial period. After that, proposed changes should be considered by the membership. Operating procedures could be adopted in the same way.

Pick the time and place for monthly meetings, and establish the date of the next get-together, when initial deposits will be made. Decide on the amount to be collected from each member, being sure that the sum is not excessive for anyone. Emphasize that this is risk capital. Although members should have every expectation of making money, they should also be prepared to suffer losses without experiencing hardship. Ideally, members should not expect to withdraw money from a beginning club for several years. Of course, every individual does have the right to close out his or her account at any time, but hopefully members will join with the expectation that monthly deposits will be left at work in investments for the foreseeable future.

Your members should be aware of a few market realities. It often takes time—months or even years—before investments become profitable. Remember that it takes a considerable rise in value to cover commissions and taxes. And if a prolonged market downturn occurs—presenting an extended opportunity to buy stocks at bargain prices—members won't be able to liquidate their holdings at a profit until the downturn ends.

Typically, members contribute $20 to $50 monthly. Although it's not necessary, you might consider allowing exceptionally high contributions for the first year of operation. After that time, some members might want to contribute more than others do, and some may need to withdraw a portion of their funds. These variations may be handled quite easily under NAIC's recommended bookkeeping procedures. The method not only permits the receipt of varying deposits, but allows for withdrawals as well. Flexibility is important, because people have different requirements, and no one can predict the future.

New members can be added at any time without being asked to match the financial commitment of long-time members. The accounting system maintains the correct representation of members' equity in accord with deposits and withdrawals over time. Thus, you will be in a position to attract interested individuals on a continuing basis as vacancies occur.

Discuss the idea of working with a broker. Traditionally, investment clubs have depended on good advice from brokers who agree with the club membership's basic philosophy. Today, some clubs do not believe they need advice beyond the research efforts of members, and use discount brokers for placement of orders. Discount brokerage firms offer no advice, but will place buy and sell orders for lower fees than traditional full-service firms. We recommend that you and your fellow club members explore all of your options together and decide which course is best for you. If you are all inexperienced, you might think about using a full-service brokerage firm for at least the first year or two, reviewing your options again when you've gained more experience.

In selecting a broker, you—as the organizer—should seek recommendations in advance from established clubs or experienced individual investors. If you decide to use a full-service broker, be sure to find a broker who is compatible and receptive to your club's overall investment philosophy, and is willing to conduct business within your guidelines. Some brokers may try to get you to speculate and take more chances than you wish to take.

You might end up with several broker prospects, and you'll want to call or visit more than one broker before the initial meeting so you can make recommendations to the group.

Before signing a broker-club agreement, review Chapter 18, "Working with a Broker."

SELECT CLUB OFFICERS

Most clubs form as partnerships to minimize taxes and to give themselves maximum operating and reporting efficiency. The *presiding partner* is responsible for setting the time and place for meetings, appointing committees, presiding at meetings, and overseeing the activities of the club. The *assistant presiding partner* not only takes the place of the presiding partner when the latter is unable to serve, but usually also leads the investment education program.

The *recording partner* keeps minutes of proceedings and notifies members of the time and place of meetings. Typically, the recording partner assumes responsibility for notifying absent members of club actions by mailing copies of minutes.

The *financial partner* maintains the club's financial records and places buy and sell orders with the broker. Record keeping includes an accounting of club receipts and disbursements and calculation of each member's share of interest in the club. The financial partner also prepares a monthly liquidating statement and files an annual informational tax return with the federal government. Your financial partner should obtain NAIC's club accounting kit and should follow the instructions carefully from the outset of your operations to ensure that the records are both complete and accurate. The kit will make the entire financial reporting job much easier.

If your club has access to a computer, a Windows- or Macintosh-based club accounting software program is also available. The program is designed to work hand-in-hand with the copyrighted *NAIC Club Accounting Manual.* For additional information on the NAIC Club Accounting Software program, review the NAIC Membership Guide, which is free upon request.

ADDITIONAL CONSIDERATIONS

With officers identified, you will want to come up with a name for your group. Pick a first as well as a second choice, in case another club is already doing business under your first-choice name and is using the same broker you want to work with.

Clubs select names denoting geographic location, business affiliation, or the purpose of the group. Others pick names "just for fun." Here are some examples: Money Mad Matrons, Tuesday Tycoons, Engine 63 (a group of firemen), Gamma Gals (sorority sisters), Money Tree, and Bowlers' Investment Club. Use your imagination, but try to be accurate. A group of Chicago women called themselves the "Gold Coast Clippers," thinking they'd be clipping coupons. Only later did they discover that delightful task is reserved for bondholders!

Consider affiliation with NAIC. Membership in this national group could be the single most important step your club takes. Share with members the contents of the catalog *NAIC Membership Guide.* Of course, NAIC membership is voluntary, and you may use any or all of the available services as you choose. However, bear in mind that NAIC materials have guided the growth of thousands of clubs over the past four decades. Make all of your members aware of the materials available from NAIC. Some will use them more than others and possibly contribute more to the club's success.

As head of the educational effort, the assistant presiding partner is responsible for exposing other members to the contents of NAIC's stock selection and portfolio management information. Ideally, he or she delegates members to report on different portions of the material. This background will prove useful to members as they assume responsibility for reporting on prospective buys or monitoring securities already purchased. NAIC also has a video that portrays the operation of a model club meeting.

ORGANIZE YOUR STUDY PROGRAM

NAIC offers the investment club Monthly Study Program, a series of twelve articles designed to help clubs. Using these articles at your next twelve meetings will help you focus on issues that will arise during a club's first year. It is provided on request and at no cost to affiliated clubs. Simply write NAIC, give your membership number, and ask for the Monthly Study Program.

The assistant presiding partner should outline what will be expected from each member during the first year. The success of the club depends on the willingness of its members to contribute their time and talent, as well as money.

In advance of the first monthly meeting, the assistant presiding partner delegates a member to prepare a report on a corporation using the NAIC Stock Check List (see Chapter 7), while another member is asked to evaluate the same security using the Stock Selection Guide (see Chapters 8–10). Solicit ideas from the group about companies to look into as possible purchases, but also be prepared with ideas of your own. Launch the club properly. Acting on a hot tip is not the way to begin. Whenever a member mentions a hot tip, ask him or her to prepare a Stock Selection Guide on the company for consideration at the next meeting. (See Chapter 2, "Finding Companies to Study.")

Stock selection is complex, and it takes practice to master the technique. In the beginning, every term will be unfamiliar and every instruction difficult to follow. That's true of any new body of knowledge. However, climbing this learning curve is important because the skill you will develop is valuable.

One new member wrote to NAIC headquarters in despair recently, proclaiming in her letter that "It is 4 am and I just finished my first 'ten minute' analysis!" (Now called the Visual Analysis). She wrote back a month later and said that her time per company was down to thirty minutes.

You might be able to find an experienced club member to help you master NAIC tools, or you may be able to obtain help from a Regional Council in your area. If both of these alternatives fail, you should read over the information in Chapters 7–10 of this book, which are devoted to the Stock Check List and Stock Selection Guide. You will be pleasantly surprised at how quickly you can become comfortable with these tools as you progress. For extra help with the Stock Selection Guide, NAIC has developed a videotape and a home study course that you can purchase.

With so much accomplished at the organizational meeting, your new club will be off to a fast start. At your first regular meeting, you will hear one or more reports on a prospective buy and make your first investment decision as a group. You might decide to purchase a security right away or wait until the next stock study is presented. Remember, don't rush or feel pressured to make an immediate decision; the market will still be there when you're through studying. Whether you buy at once or decide to hold off until the next meeting, you are on the proper path to knowledgeable investing.

CHAPTER 17

THE CLUB AGREEMENT

*E*very investment club needs to define a shared investment philosophy. However, it also needs sets of operating rules, acceptable to all members, that comply with all regulatory and tax requirements.

The Mutual Investment Club of Detroit is one of America's oldest investment clubs. The agreement used by this landmark club works because of its simplicity. It is also designed in response to the members' needs. A review of this club's agreement will give you some excellent ideas for formulating your own agreement. This chapter illustrates the historical experience of one club, and should not be considered as legal or tax advice. You are encouraged to consult with your own legal and tax advisers.

In choosing between two possible forms—corporation or partnership—Mutual looked to these five questions:

1. *Taxes.* Under which type of organization would members pay the least in taxes from the time money was first earned until it was received by individual members?

2. *Personal liability.* Which type would minimize members' financial risk?

3. *Transfer of securities.* With which form can securities be transferred with the least need for supporting resolutions?

4. *Organizational costs.* Which type would minimize the cost of setting up the club?

5. *Maintenance costs.* From the standpoint of both time and money, which type would be more economical over the life of the club?

TAXES

In 1960, the Treasury Department issued a ruling (which remains effective as of the date of this publication) that clubs are taxable as partnerships rather than corporations unless they have four or more of the following characteristics:

1. A group of associates
2. A common objective to carry on a business and divide the resulting gains
3. Continuity of life
4. Centralization of management
5. Limited liability
6. Free transfer of interests

The Treasury Department ruled that investment clubs have the first two characteristics, but generally do not have the remaining four. The application of these characteristics to a particular club requires the legal interpretation and consultation with an attorney.

Mutual reviewed partnership tax law and found that a partnership as a whole would not have to pay any taxes, but that individual partners would be responsible for reporting their own shares of the club's annual income on their personal tax returns. Each partner would owe no further tax on that previously reported income if and when he or she elected to withdraw from the club or the club disbanded.

Mutual saw that even with some of the advantages of being a corporation, only a partnership avoided paying two taxes on the same income (a corporate-level tax on the corporation's earning and an individual income tax on the distribution of corporate earnings as dividends to the shareholders). The members concluded that their tax bills would be less if the club operated as a partnership rather than as a corporation.

Most clubs don't seriously consider trying to get S corporation status. This is a form of corporation that enjoys corporate advantages but is taxed as a partnership. It applies only on the federal level. States continue to tax S corporations as corporations.

The S corporation designation is available only if your club meets these requirements:

1. You have no more than seventy-five shareholders.
2. All shareholders are individuals (as opposed to other partnerships or corporations).

3. All shareholders are residents of the same state, and all are legal residents of the United States.

4. You have only one class of stock.

Once you elect to be taxed as an S corporation, there is a time limit on when you can reverse your decision.

PERSONAL LIABILITY

Under the corporate form, personal liability is usually limited to each member's investment in the club—in other words, you cannot be sued for more than the value of your shares. In Mutual's case, no obvious personal liability limitation existed under the partnership form, and some members feared they would be liable for the personal debts of other partners. However, the club's attorney advised that personal liability would be restricted to acts of a partner performed within the scope of his or her authority and in the course of conducting partnership business. In addition, the individuals of virtually all investment clubs could be held liable for the wrongful actions of the club's agents committed while conducting club business. However, an investment club conducts only one business activity, buying and selling securities, and has only one party in its transactions, its broker. You should consult with an attorney to determine the scope of each partner's personal liability.

In addition to consulting with their attorney, Mutual members were reassured about personal liability by the 1958 study published by the *University of Pennsylvania Law Review.* In this study, research stretching back to the turn of this century uncovered no individual involved in a lawsuit stemming from investment club membership. However, this same article anticipates litigation as the investment club movement grows. To date, NAIC is unaware of any such litigation.

A *limited liability company* is a form of organization that is now legal in all fifty states. NAIC has had little experience with this form, but it appears that it may be satisfactory for use by an investment club. To use this form of organization, the club must form under the law of its state. Generally, application, registration, and annual fees are required to be paid. It is believed that this may be used by clubs whose members have a real fear of the personal liability provisions of a general partnership, and we strongly recommend that the club seek competent professional advice in the state where it is operating. NAIC can supply the legal reference to the Act and contact information for each state.

TRANSFER OF SECURITIES

NAIC worked with the Securities Transfer Association to make operating investment clubs more convenient. This led to the establishment of Rule 3.0610. This rule permits clubs operating as partnerships to transfer securities directly into and out of the club's name with the signature of only one partner. Normally, there is no need for any supporting papers. If your brokerage firm asks for supporting papers for all partners' signatures for transactions, refer it to the above rule number.

Endorsement of your security certificates should read: "ABC Investment Club, a partnership, Jane Any Member, partner."

You reduce the chances of any member misusing club funds by circulating the brokerage firm's monthly statement at every club meeting. Be sure you verify that each month's payments have been deposited to the account, that no unauthorized disbursements have been made, and that securities ordered have been purchased. Set a policy that the financial partner is to circulate the broker's most recent monthly statement to all members at each monthly meeting.

ORGANIZATIONAL COSTS

The Mutual Investment Club of Detroit learned that as a Michigan corporation, it would have to pay a fairly large registration fee to the state. As a partnership, Mutual was required merely to register with the county under the Michigan Assumed Names Act and pay a $10 fee. Registration forms for corporations were lengthy and complicated. The partnership form, in contrast, required only a list of partners' names and addresses.

This information made the partnership alternative even more attractive. Check with your state's licensing board, Department of Corporations, Department of Revenue, or similar regulatory agency to find out the degree of complexity involved in establishing your club either as a corporation or partnership.

MAINTENANCE COSTS

Mutual discovered that as a corporation it would need to file an annual report with the state and pay a franchise fee based on its capital and surplus. As a partnership, it merely had to renew its registration under the Michigan Assumed Names Act every five years. Again, find out beforehand what reporting requirements apply to each type of organization.

The club also asked its attorney about Securities and Exchange Commission (SEC) and state securities commission registration requirements, and learned that there were no filing requirements to be met in either case. However, some states consider an investment club membership to be a security, and certain steps are required for exemption from registration under the state securities laws.

Currently, at least three states (Wisconsin, Illinois, and New Mexico) impose securities filing requirements. You should check the security filing requirements in your state. In Wisconsin, for example, an exemption is granted for clubs organized as general partnerships. Limited partnerships and corporations starting with fifteen or fewer members are also exempt. In Illinois, clubs qualify for an exemption if membership never exceeds seventy, no more than thirty-five members join within a twelve-month period, and sales do not total more than $100,000 within a twelve-month period. General solicitation and advertising for members is not allowed, and new members must be reported within thirty days. This report is the only action required of clubs operating in Illinois that use the Partnership Agreement shown in this chapter. In New Mexico, clubs adopting the Agreement are usually eligible for exemption (be sure to check for yourself, as rules can change). Request a copy of Section 58-13B-27 NMSA 1978, and then file a letter responding to Section questions and request an exemption. The SEC has stated that a club with twenty-five or fewer members would be assumed not to be in violation of any of its rules requiring registration.

Each club is responsible for knowing about and complying with any federal, state, or local regulations pertaining to investment clubs. You should consult an attorney for guidance. In any event, the agreement developed by Mutual may prove helpful in your decision making process. However, it is only an example and should not be considered legal or tax advice. Copies of the Agreement have been given to the SEC, the fifty state security commissions, the Internal Revenue Service, the Securities Transfer Association, and the major securities industry exchanges and associations. None of these agencies express an opinion on the Agreement.

Now, let us look at the agreement itself (Figure 17-1).

Figure 17-1
Partnership of the Mutual Investment Club of Detroit

Partnership Agreement
of
The Mutual Investment Club of Detroit

THIS AGREEMENT OF PARTNERSHIP, effective as of____(date)____, by and between the undersigned, to wit:

(Name of all partners)

NOW, THEREFORE, IT IS AGREED:

1. **Formation.** The undersigned hereby form a General Partnership in accordance with and subject to the laws of the State of Michigan.

2. **Name.** The name of the partnership shall be Mutual Investment Club of Detroit.

3. **Term.** The partnership shall begin on____(date)____ and shall continue until December 31 of the same year and thereafter from year to year unless earlier terminated as hereinafter provided.

4. **Purpose.** The only purpose of the partnership is to invest the assets of the partnership solely in stocks, bonds, and other securities ("securities") for the education and benefit of the partners.

5. **Meetings.** Periodic meetings shall be held as determined by the partnership.

6. **Capital Contributions.** The partners may make capital contributions to the partnership on the date of each periodic meeting in such amounts as the partnership shall determine, provided, however, that no partner's capital account shall exceed twenty percent (20%) of the capital accounts of all the partners.

7. **Value of the Partnership.** The current value of the assets of the partnership, less the current value of the liabilities of the partnership (hereinafter referred to as "value of the partnership") shall be determined as of a regularly scheduled date and time ("valuation date") preceding the date of each periodic meeting determined by the Club.

8. **Capital Accounts.** A capital account shall be maintained in the name of each partner. Any increase or decrease in the value of the partnership on any valuation date shall be credited or debited, respectively, to each partner's capital account in proportion to the sum of all partner capital accounts on that date. Any other method of valuating each partner's capital account may be substituted for this method, provided the substituted method results in exactly the same valuation as previously provided herein. Each partner's capital contribution to, or capital withdrawal from, the partnership, shall be credited, or debited, respectively, to that partner's capital account.

9. **Management.** Each partner shall participate in the management and conduct of the affairs of the partnership in proportion to the value of his capital account. Except as otherwise determined, all decisions shall be made by the partners whose capital accounts total a majority of the value of the capital accounts of all the partners.

10. **Sharing of Profits and Losses.** Net profits and losses of the partnership shall inure to, and be borne by, the partners in proportion to the value of each of their capital accounts.

11. **Books of Accounts.** Books of account of the transactions of the partnership shall be kept and at all times be available and open to inspection and examination by any partner.

12. **Annual Accounting.** Each calendar year, a full and complete account of the condition of the partnership shall be made to the partners.

Drawing up an agreement like this one will provide your club with a written statement of your procedures and processes.

Figure 17-1 (Continued)
Partnership of the Mutual Investment Club of Detroit

13.   **Bank Account.**   The partnership may select a bank for the purpose of opening a bank account. Funds in the bank account shall be withdrawn by checks signed by any partner designated by the partnership.

14.   **Broker Account.**   None of the partners of this partnership shall be a broker. However, the partnership may select a broker and enter into such agreements with the broker as required for the purchase or sale of securities. Securities owned by the partnership shall be held in the partnership name unless another name shall be designated by the partnership.

Any corporation or transfer agent called upon to transfer any securities to or from the name of the partnership shall be entitled to rely on instructions or assignments signed by any partner without inquiry as to the authority of the person(s) signing such instructions or assignments, or as to the validity of any transfer to or from the name of the partnership.

At the time of a transfer of securities, the corporation or transfer agent is entitled to assume (1) that the partnership is still in existence, and (2) that this Agreement is in full force and effect and has not been amended unless the corporation or transfer agent has received written notice to the contrary.

15.   **No Compensation.**   No partner shall be compensated for services rendered to the partnership, except reimbursement for expenses.

16.   **Additional Partners.**   Additional partners may be admitted at any time, upon the unanimous consent of all the partners, so long as the number of partners does not exceed twenty-five (25).

16A.   **Transfers to a Trust.**   A partner may, after giving written notice to the other partners, transfer his interest in the partnership to a revocable living trust of which he is the grantor and sole trustee.

16B.   **Removal of a Partner.**   Any partner may be removed by agreement of the partners whose capital accounts total a majority of the value of all partners' capital accounts. Written notice of a meeting where removal of a partner is to be considered shall include a specific reference to this matter. The removal shall become effective upon payment of the value of the removed partner's capital account, which shall be in accordance with the provisions on full withdrawal of a partner noted in paragraphs 18 and 20. The vote action shall be treated as receipt of request for withdrawal.

17.   **Termination of Partnership.**   The partnership may be terminated by agreement of the partners whose capital accounts total a majority in value of the capital accounts of all the partners. Written notice of the meeting where termination of the partnership is to be considered shall include a specific reference to this matter. The partnership shall terminate upon a majority vote of all partners' capital accounts. Written notice of the decision to terminate the partnership shall be given to all the partners. Payment shall then be made of all the liabilities of the partnership and a final distribution of the remaining assets either in cash or in kind, shall promptly be made to the partners or their personal representatives in proportion to each partner's capital account.

18.   **Voluntary Withdrawal (Partial or Full) of a Partner.**   Any partner may withdraw a part or all of the value of his capital account in the partnership and the partnership shall continue as a taxable entity. The partner withdrawing a portion or all of the value of his capital account shall give notice of such intention in writing to the Secretary. Written notice shall be deemed to be received as of the first meeting of the partnership at which it is presented. If written notice is received between meetings it will be treated as received at the first following meeting.

In making payment, the value of the partnership as set forth in the valuation statement prepared for the first meeting following the meeting at which written notice is received from a partner requesting a partial or full withdrawal, will be used to determine the value of the partner's capital account.

The partnership shall pay the partner who is withdrawing a portion or all of the value of his capital account in the partnership in accordance with paragraph 20 of this Agreement.

Figure 17-1 (Continued)
Partnership of the Mutual Investment Club of Detroit

19. **Death or Incapacity of a Partner.** In the event of the death or incapacity of a partner (or the death or incapacity of the grantor and sole trustee of a revocable living trust, if such trust is a partner pursuant to Paragraph 16A hereof), receipt of notice of such an event shall be treated as notice of full withdrawal.

20. **Terms of Payment.** In the case of a partial withdrawal, payment may be made in cash or securities of the partnership or a mix of each at the option of the partner making the partial withdrawal. In the case of a full withdrawal, payment may be made in cash or securities or a mix of each at the option of the remaining partners. In either case, where securities are to be distributed, the remaining partners select the securities.

Where cash is transferred, the partnership shall transfer to the partner (or other appropriate entity) withdrawing a portion of all of his interest in the partnership, an amount equal to the lesser of (i) ninety-seven percent (97%) of the value of the capital account in the partnership being withdrawn or (ii) the value of the capital account being withdrawn, less the actual cost to the partnership of selling securities to obtain cash to meet the withdrawal. The amount being withdrawn shall be paid within 10 days after the valuation date used in determining the withdrawal amount.

If a partner withdrawing a portion or all of the value of his capital account in the partnership desires an immediate payment in cash, the partnership at its earliest convenience may pay eighty percent (80%) of the estimated value of his capital account and settle the balance in accordance with the valuation and payment procedures set forth in paragraphs 18 and 20.

When securities are transferred, the partnership shall select securities to transfer equal to the value of the capital account or a portion of the capital account being withdrawn (i.e. without a reduction for broker commissions). Securities shall be transferred as of the date of the club's valuation statement prepared to determine the value of that partner's capital account in the partnership. The Club's broker shall be advised that ownership of the securities has been transferred to the partner as of the valuation date used for the withdrawal.

21. **Forbidden Acts.** No partner shall:

(a) Have the right or authority to bind or obligate the partnership to any extent whatsoever with regard to any matter outside the scope of the partnership purpose.

(b) Except as provided in paragraph 16A, without the unanimous consent of all the other partners, assign, transfer, pledge, mortgage or sell all or part of his interest in the partnership to any other partner or other person whomsoever, or enter into any agreement as the result of which any person or persons not a partner shall become interested with him in the partnership.

(c) Purchase an investment for the partnership where less than the full purchase price is paid for same.

(d) Use the partnership name, credit or property for other than partnership purposes.

(e) Do any act detrimental to the interests of the partnership or which would make it impossible to carry on the purpose of the partnership.

This Agreement of Partnership shall be binding upon the respective heirs, executors, trustees, administrators and personal representatives of the partners.

The partners have caused the Agreement of Partnership to be executed on the dates indicated below, effective as of the date indicated above.

Name: _____   Name: _____

Dated: _____   Dated: _____

Name: _____   Name: _____

Dated: _____   Dated: _____

COMMENTARY ON THE PARTNERSHIP AGREEMENT OF THE MUTUAL INVESTMENT CLUB OF DETROIT

Paragraphs 1, 2, and 3: Self-explanatory.

Paragraph 4: The purpose of the club is strictly limited. An important reason for such limitations is to reduce the actual or apparent authority of any partner.

Paragraph 5: Most clubs meet regularly, such as on the first business day of each month or the third Thursday. Regularity makes it possible for members to plan schedules and avoid conflicting engagements.

Paragraph 6: Since dollar cost averaging is one of the basic investment principles followed by NAIC clubs, most partners make a regular capital contribution at each meeting. In the majority of new clubs, partners normally deposit the same amount. In older clubs, partners frequently deposit varying amounts. For the convenience of the treasurer, a valuation unit of $10 is selected, and partner deposits are usually required to be made in multiples of $10 to facilitate bookkeeping.

Many clubs start out under the assumption that the membership will remain constant and all members will continue to contribute the same amount. However, change is inevitable. From the outset, you should use a recording system flexible enough to provide for varying capital contributions. New members will be easier to attract if only a modest regular monthly payment is suggested or required. On the other hand, some clubs are concerned that one particular partner might become a majority owner. Commonly, clubs provide that no partner may add to his or her capital account beyond a certain percentage of the total (often 20%).

Paragraph 7: The assets of an investment club constantly fluctuate. New capital coming into the club must be valued in proportion to the value of the partnership at the time of deposit. Otherwise, the new funds would immediately acquire a value greater or less than existing funds, depending on the club's current worth. To help determine the value of new deposits, a Valuation Statement is prepared for each meeting. To provide adequate time for compiling this statement, a cutoff date well in advance of the meeting date (e.g., ten days, last business day of the previous month, etc.) should be determined. Calculations are made effective as of that date. The Valuation Statement is detailed in Chapter 21 of this book.

Paragraph 8: Self-explanatory.

Paragraph 9: Most clubs provide that members will have a voice in the club's operation in proportion to their financial commitment. Generally, the members with the greatest financial interest have been members longer, and they have more experience. An investment club is a business and, like other businesses, seems to function best when decision making power relates to risk capital employed.

Paragraph 10. Under current federal tax law, if the partnership earnings and losses are distributed on other than a pro rata basis, serious tax consequences could result. For detailed procedures for determining and reporting profits and losses, see Chapter 22.

Paragraph 11: NAIC offers accounting help to clubs in both text and software forms.

Paragraph 12: See Chapter 22 for a more detailed discussion.

Paragraph 13: Many clubs do not have a bank account but deposit all funds with the broker and usually invest the available funds each month. Some clubs have the financial partner maintain a separate personal account for the club.

Paragraph 14: Initially, the Mutual Investment Club of Detroit did not allow a broker to be a member of the club, but it has since changed this policy. The club may handle its relationship with a broker in one of several ways. Refer to Chapter 18 for a detailed description of these procedures and a listing of the advantages and drawbacks of each.

Clubs generally restrict broker contact to one member, who calls for suggestions about stocks to study and transmits buy and sell orders.

Paragraph 15: Self-explanatory.

Paragraph 16: In the experience of NAIC, the strongest clubs have between ten and twenty members.

Paragraph 16A: Placing investment club equity in a revocable living trust provides two primary advantages to members choosing this option: Probate expenses are avoided and the assets in the trust are immediately available for use as designated in the trust document.

Paragraph 16B: Sometimes a member loses interest in the club, consistently missing meetings and not doing his or her share of the work.

Such a member will often just resign, so this paragraph's provision is seldom used.

Paragraph 17: Self-explanatory.

Paragraph 18: See Internal Revenue Code, Section 708, for further information on the continuation of a partnership as a taxable entity.

Paragraph 19: Same procedure as in paragraph 18 and paragraph 20. The remaining partners should exercise care to ensure that the deceased or incapacitated partner's account is paid in cash or stock to the proper claimant. Many clubs provide for the deposit of the deceased or incapacitated partner's funds in a separate bank account in cash, or to a brokerage account in stock, until advice is received as to ownership. An attorney can be consulted if there is any doubt about to whom payment should be made.

Paragraph 20: When a partner withdraws only part of the value of his capital account in the partnership, the partner has the choice of whether to receive cash or securities or a mix of the two.

Most partners seeking a partial withdrawal will choose to receive cash rather than securities since the tax consequences will usually be more favorable that way (see the following paragraph for further explanation). If cash is requested, the partnership must sell enough securities to satisfy the request and allocate any capital gain to all the partners in the current year. The partner withdrawing a portion of the capital account then reduces his or her tax basis by the amount of the cash distribution. If the partner has used up his or her tax basis, the distribution is then considered taxable income.

If the partner in a partial withdrawal chooses to receive securities, the club transfers securities of its choosing with a current value equal to the value being withdrawn. Any subsequent sale is at the discretion and expense of that partner. If the partner receives securities, under current federal tax law the partner withdrawing a portion of the value of his or her capital account is subject to federal income tax on the difference between the partnership's tax basis in the securities withdrawn and the value of the securities, but only on the partially withdrawing partner's subsequent sale of the securities on the open market.

When a partner requests full withdrawal of the entire value of his or her capital account in the partnership, the remaining members have the choice of satisfying the request in cash or securities or a mix of the two. If they choose to transfer cash, they must decide which securities to sell, divide any capital gain among all the partners, and then transfer the cash. The withdrawing partner recognizes a pro rata share of taxable income before the distribution. After the distribution, the withdrawing partner allocates his or her tax basis to the securities received in proportion to their value. Tax between the tax basis distributed on their receipt and the eventual sale is payable at the time of sale.

For the most benefit to remaining members, payment should be made by transferring securities with a substantial paper profit to the withdrawing partner. Currently, the Internal Revenue Code does not classify such a transfer as a taxable transaction, so the remaining members do not incur taxable gain as they would if the securities were sold and cash paid to the withdrawing partner. The withdrawing partner will not have a taxable transaction if the securities are held, but once they are sold, he or she will have to recognize a taxable capital gain of the difference between the net selling price of the securities and his or her adjusted tax basis in the partnership assigned to the stock.

Transferring securities allows your club to postpone taxes on securities with capital gains while not increasing the tax liability of the withdrawing partner. Prior to the withdrawal date, that partner might consider opening an account with the same broker who handles the club's account. The securities can then be transferred and sold in the member's account on the same day, ensuring that he or she receives the current price. See Chapter 7 of *NAIC's Accounting Manual* for a discussion of the advantages of transferring stock to a partner making a full withdrawal.

Transaction costs (mainly broker commissions) may run as high as 10 percent in smaller clubs, while in larger clubs they may amount to only 3 percent or even less. When cash is distributed in a partial withdrawal, brokerage commissions as incurred (or 3 percent, whichever is the larger amount) are charged to the partially withdrawing partner, and the net proceeds are then distributed to that partner. Because securities fluctuate in value, the date used to determine the partner's capital account value should be set after the date of sale of securities used to satisfy the partner's request.

Paragraph 21: Self-explanatory.

The Partnership Agreement adopted by the Mutual Investment Club was a broad agreement designed to facilitate the club's general operation. To cover the detailed operation of the club, motions were passed by the partners from time to time. Following are the first minutes of the Mutual Investment Club. (Each club should discuss detailed operating procedures with its attorney in the light of its own needs and desires.)

OPERATING PROCEDURE
MUTUAL INVESTMENT CLUB

Duties of Partners

Annually, at the first meeting in February, partners shall elect the following positions and assign duties as described below by a majority vote:

1. *President.* The President's duty is to preside over meetings, set meeting dates and locations, appoint committees, and see that resolutions passed by the partnership are carried out.

2. *Vice-President.* The Vice-President takes the place of the President when the President is absent or incapacitated. The Vice-President shall assign companies to report on at Club meetings to each partner and shall be responsible for insuring that the Club's study program is properly carried out.

3. *Secretary.* The Secretary's duty is to keep a record of the actions authorized by the partners and notify partners of meetings and other activities.

4. *Treasurer.* The Treasurer's duty is to keep a record of the Club's receipts and disbursements and partners' interests in the Club. The Treasurer will give partners receipts for payments, place the buy and sell orders authorized by the partners with the Club's broker, and prepare the Club's monthly valuation statement. He/she will see that the needed tax information is compiled and file the necessary reports.

Guests

Partners may invite guests to any meeting of the Club as long as advance clearance is obtained from the host of the meeting. When consideration is given to adding partners to the Club under paragraph 16 of the Club's partnership agreement, anyone considered shall have been a guest for at least two prior meetings.

Meetings

The Club shall hold a meeting on the second Tuesday of each month at a place designated by the Club. Written notice of each meeting shall be given to each partner by the Secretary at least one week before the meeting. Special meetings may be called by the President upon similar notice to the other partners.

Procedure

The monthly valuation statement shall be effective as of a regularly scheduled date and time preceding each monthly meeting.

In maintaining the records of each partner's capital account in the Club, the unit value method as outlined in Chapter 21 of this book will be used.

Additional deposits in the Club may be made by members in multiples of $10.

The Vice-President shall contact investment counsel immediately preceding the monthly meeting and secure investment counsel's suggestions on new companies to consider, and any comments on stocks owned by the Club. He shall report this information at the meeting. The Vice-President shall appoint at least two partners at each meeting to prepare a report on the NAIC Stock Selection Guide on a security for presentation to the partnership at the following meeting. The Vice-President shall remind each person assigned to prepare a NAIC Stock Selection Guide of his assignment one-week before the meeting.

Buy and/or sell action may be taken after a period of discussion by the members, and when voted by a simple majority of the members' interests.

End of motion.

AN ALTERNATIVE AGREEMENT

With the creation of the Individual Retirement Account (IRA) (a federal income tax planning vehicle to defer tax on income), the Mutual Investment Club of Detroit sought a means of allowing members to invest their IRAs in the club. To accommodate IRA requirements, Mutual had to arrange for an approved IRA custodian (bank or trust company) to become a member of the club. Further regulations required that member to be a limited partner. Mutual became a limited partnership in 1982 after more than forty years of operating with its original agreement.

The trustee of an IRA account (typically a bank) may only be a limited partner, and therefore has no voice in the management of the club. In a limited partnership, a general partner may own no more than 20 percent of all the general partnership units, while both limited and general partners are unrestricted in their ownership of limited partnership units.

When a partner wishes to establish an IRA account in the club, and the other members agree to it, the partnership agreement should be altered as shown in Figure 17-2.

If a member has an IRA account in the club, he or she typically maintains a general partner account also. During the year members usually make deposits only to their general partner accounts. Since the trustee of the IRA account probably charges a fee for each transaction, members try to limit the number of transactions they make in IRA accounts. Some accumulate cash and make only one IRA deposit per year. Others make deposits into their general partner account and transfer funds to the IRA account annually.

If your club runs into problems in finding a bank to handle the trustee account, NAIC can put you in touch with a financial institution to perform the task. You may also consider using a regular or discount brokerage firm that provides this service (usually for a small annual fee).

Until recently it was very difficult to buy stock for your IRA account through a dividend reinvestment plan or NAIC's low-cost investment program. NAIC now has a simple, low-cost way to make such purchases. Members will receive details on request.

Figure 17-2
Limited Partnership Agreement for the Mutual Investment Club of Detroit

Limited Partnership Agreement
of
Mutual Investment Club of Detroit Limited Partnership

THIS AGREEMENT OF LIMITED PARTNERSHIP, effective_____(Date)_____, by and between the undersigned as General Partners, to:

(Names of General Partners)

and_____(Name)_____ Bank, Trustee of the Individual Retirement Trust Accounts, Master Trust agreement.

(If the Club is a new partnership, it would begin at paragraph 1, below. If it is a Club converting from a general to a limited partnership, it should include wording appropriate to the law of its own State similar to the following, through "NOW THEREFORE, IT IS AGREED.")

WHEREAS, the Mutual Investment Club of Detroit has been in existence as a general partnership for over forty-six (46) years and has executed numerous partnership agreements based upon various changes in partners, but such partnership has continued as one tax entity since its formation; and

WHEREAS, the partners of the Mutual Investment Club of Detroit desire to organize such partnership as a limited partnership as such term is defined by the Michigan Revised Uniform Limited Partnership Act, MCL 449.1101 *et seq.* and, therefore, the partners desire and hereby do cancel the previous partnership agreement but continue as the same tax entity.

NOW, THEREFORE, IT IS AGREED:

1. **Formation.** The undersigned hereby form a Limited Partnership (the "partnership") in, and in accordance with the laws of the State of Michigan. All partners shall be general partners except those admitted to serve as Trustees of IRA Accounts on behalf of the general partners with such trustees to be referred to as "limited partners."

2. **Name.** The name of the partnership shall be: Mutual Investment Club of Detroit Limited Partnership.

(Paragraphs 3 through 5 of the preceding agreement would be unchanged.)

6. **Capital Contributions.** The partners may make capital contributions to the partnership on the date of each periodic meeting in such amounts as the partnership shall determine, provided, however, that no general partner's capital account shall exceed twenty percent (20%) of the capital accounts of all the general partners.

(Paragraphs 7 and 8 of the preceding agreement would be unchanged)

9. **Management.** Each general partner shall participate in the management and conduct of the affairs of the partnership in proportion to the value of his capital account. Except as otherwise determined, all decisions shall be made by the general partners whose capital accounts total a majority of the value of the capital accounts of all the general partners.

(Paragraphs 10 through 15 of the preceding agreement would be unchanged.)

16. **Additional Partners.** Additional partners may be admitted at any time, upon the unanimous consent of all the general partners, so long as the number of general partners does not exceed twenty (20).

By creating a limited partnership, club members are able to invest their IRAs and defer taxable income.

Figure 17-2 (Continued)

16A. **Transfers to a Trust.**   A general partner may, after giving written notice to the other general partners, transfer his interest in the partnership to a revocable living trust of which he is the grantor and sole trustee.

16B. **Removal of a Partner.**   Any partner may be removed by agreement of the general partners whose capital accounts total a majority of the value of all partners' capital accounts. Written notice of a meeting where removal of a partner is to be considered shall include a specific reference to this matter. The removal shall become effective upon payment of the value of the removed partner's capital account, which shall be in accordance with the provisions of full withdrawal of a partner noted in paragraphs 18 and 20.

16C. **Limited Partners.**   If any general partner establishes an IRA (under section 408 of the Internal Revenue Code), the trustee of such account may be admitted to the Partnership as a limited partner. No limited partner shall have the obligation or the right to participate in the management of the Partnership or in Partnership decisions, and shall have no liability with respect to partnership obligations, and the provisions of this Agreement relating specifically to General Partners shall not apply to Limited Partners. No general partner may own more than 20% of the value of all the general partners' capital accounts. Both general and limited partners are unrestricted in their purchase of limited partnership units. Unless otherwise required by law, Limited Partners shall not be counted as partners in applying the limitation on the number of partners allowed under this Agreement. Limited partners shall not have the power to grant the right to become a limited partner to an assignee of any part of the partnership interest.

17.   **Termination of Partnership.**   The partnership may be terminated by agreement of the general partners whose capital accounts total a majority in value of the capital accounts of all the general partners. Written notice of the meeting where termination of the partnership is to be considered shall include a specific reference to this matter. The partnership shall terminate upon a majority vote of all general partners' capital accounts. Written notice of the decision to terminate the partnership shall be given to all the general partners. Payment shall then be made of all the liabilities of the general partnership and a final distribution of the remaining assets, either in cash or in kind, shall promptly be made to the general partners or their personal representatives in proportion to each general partner's capital account.

(Paragraph 18 of the preceding agreement would be unchanged.)

19.   **Death or Incapacity of a General Partner.**   In the event of the death or incapacity of a general partner (or the death or incapacity of the grantor and sole trustee of a revocable living trust, if such trust is a general partner pursuant of Paragraph 16A hereof), receipt of notice of such an event shall be treated as notice of full withdrawal.

(Continue with the preceding agreement to paragraph 21B and at the end add:) No limited partner shall have the power to assign, transfer, pledge, mortgage or sell all or part of his interest in the partnership.

(After paragraph 21e continue:)

This Agreement of Limited Partnership hereby declared and shall be binding upon the respective heirs, executors, trustees, administrators and personal representatives of the parties.

The parties have caused this Agreement of Limited Partnership to be executed on the dates indicated below, effective on the date indicated above.

General Partners

Name:_____   Name:_____

Dated:_____   Dated:_____

Limited Partners

Name:_____   Name:_____

Dated:_____   Dated:_____

IRA accumulations can become substantial over time. One general partner of the Mutual Investment Club of Detroit Limited Partnership has invested $2,000 into his IRA limited partner account in the club every year since 1982. As of early 1992, his total IRA deposits of $22,000 had grown to $43,800, an average annual increase of more than 12 percent. If he manages to sustain this rate of growth, his IRA account will be worth $124,879 by the year 2000. His contributions by then will total $36,000.

As of early 1992, this same member's account included $9,534 in dividends and realized capital gains. If the Mutual Investment Club of Detroit had not become a limited partnership and therefore provided members the benefit of IRA accounts, those dividends and capital gains would have been subject to federal income tax at that time and would not have still been in the account building future value.

CHAPTER 18

WORKING WITH A BROKER

*P*icking the right broker is not always an easy task. You need to go about your search the same way you would if you were looking for an attorney, accountant, real estate agent, or other professional. Many factors contribute to your choice, but compatibility is the most important feature.

For new clubs, the cost factor looms particularly large. Even if costs are not a big concern, experienced investors inevitably end up working with a discount brokerage rather than a full-service firm, because they don't need the advice and, more to the point, they don't want to be pressured into decisions. Commission-based brokers often call their clients (including investment clubs) and promote a particular security—regardless of whether it would be a good purchase for the club or not.

As a first essential step, you need to find a broker who knows how clubs work and who is willing to advise you, rather than trying to push you into buying the brokerage firm's stock of the day.

Next consider cost. Minimum commissions are often the same for both major discount and full-service brokers. Once you begin investing in larger blocks, the discounts become more significant.

An alternative is the "deep discount" brokerage firm. The price gap between the deep discounters and the rest of the brokerage business is widening. A survey by Mercer, Inc. lists thirty firms offering the lowest commissions on a number of different trades and is available for $34.95 from the firm at 80 Fifth Avenue, New York, NY 10011. What you need to know is this: If you are looking for modest commissions and don't care about brokerage advice, get comparisons from several brokerage firms and select the one offering the best bargain rates. Also look for firms offering flexible services, such as custodial accounts for IRAs.

Keep in mind two other avenues for keeping the costs of investing as low as possible. The first is to take advantage of a special program offered by several major full-service brokers. It is not advertised; you must ask whether it's available at a particular firm. Here is how it works: You mail in your money and your market order, and the order is executed at market opening the day after receipt. The firm's commission is prorated over the number of shares executed on behalf of program participants. Therefore, it's impossible to know in advance what your exact cost will be. No service is offered with the program; you interact with a clerk, not a broker.

The second way to limit transaction costs is with NAIC's own Low-Cost Investment Plan, a boon to clubs with monthly receipts under $500. NAIC has joined the dividend reinvestment program of a number of corporations. You forward your money to an escrow agent in care of NAIC for investment in a particular company or companies. Once your first purchase of a certain stock has been made, you send future investments directly to the corporation's dividend reinvestment agent. NAIC's plan permits clubs to save as much as 10 percent in commissions the first year, an amount sufficient to spell the difference between profit and loss in many cases.

Here's the record of a four-year-old club that initially invested exclusively through NAIC's Low Cost Investment Plan (Figure 18-1). As of early 1996, the group held twenty-two different securities. The club has been profitable since its beginning.

In the fourth or fifth year of operation, a club may wish to move to a full-service broker to gain another perspective on the market as well as to broaden investment choices. On the other hand, you might become more confident in your club's ability to make good decisions without the advice of a broker, and confirm your desire to remain with a deep discount firm.

Whether you select a full-service or a discount firm, there are some procedures you will always have to follow. All members of the club have to sign an agreement when your account is opened. The agreement varies from firm to firm, but in all cases authorization must be given to the designated individuals to place buy and sell orders.

Figure 18-1
Harvestors Investment Club

Date	Cumulative Total Paid in by Members	Cumulative Total Value of Club	Total Paid out to Withdrawing Members
1-31-88	$ 460.00	$ 460.00	—
1-31-89	9,105.00	9,300.15	$ 604.69
1-31-90	17,365.00	18,831.46	2,103.93
1-31-91	27,510.00	29,591.12	3,264.34
1-31-92	37,795.00	52,402.43	8,326.26
1-31-93	18,193.63	88,893.36	11,000.00
1-31-94	21,489.13	109,957.86	5,670.57
1-31-95	17,599.07	158,790.41	16,354.52
1-31-96	28,338.49	168,843.57	18,642.66

FULL-SERVICE BROKERS

If you select a full-service broker, remember the most essential and necessary element in the relationship: The broker must understand your investment philosophy and help you to achieve your goals. If the broker tries to force decisions on you, the relationship won't work.

As part of the relationship, your broker should be willing to provide your club with extra services not necessary for individual customers: custody of securities, dividend collection, and forwarding of stockholder notices. Some brokers want a service charge for these extras. The broker probably also expects that several, and possibly all, of your members will eventually open personal accounts with him or her.

Respect the broker's objectives. Remember that the broker is in business to make money. During the hours the market is open, brokers are consumed with placing buy and sell orders or soliciting such orders from customers. Ask whether there is a particular time, either early morning or late afternoon, that is the best time to talk.

Also, out of respect for the broker's requirements, don't expect him or her to deal with more than one individual—usually the financial partner—on behalf of the club. About twenty-four hours before the club meeting, ask the broker for any recent information on stocks in your club's portfolio, as well as the stocks being studied for possible purchase.

Do not ask the broker what stock to buy; that is your club's decision. (However, once your decision has been made, you may wish to ask your broker's opinion before placing your order. If he or she has valid objections, you should listen carefully and then poll club members before proceeding.)

Information gained from your broker in advance of the meeting should be recorded and shared with club members before any investment actions are taken. As soon as possible after the meeting, the club's contact person should place the authorized order with the broker. Don't hesitate to call during trading hours with a buy or sell order. That is the best time. However, if you want to talk at length with your broker, wait until after hours and try to schedule such discussions in advance.

When your club has selected a stock to study, ask the broker for copies of Standard & Poor's or Value Line sheets.

REQUESTING MATERIAL

Be fair in requesting material from the full-service broker; help him or her minimize the expense of handling your account. There is no need to order more than the two to four Standard & Poor's sheets required for next month's reports. Stock reports you need later should be ordered when the material is current. Mail your sheet order request to your broker, and enclose a self-addressed stamped envelope.

You should never call the broker for prices; these are listed in *The Wall Street Journal* and other financial publications, as well as in the financial section of your local newspaper. Some computer services provide instant online prices.

Once you have made a purchase, your financial officer should transmit one check to your broker, having deposited members' payments in his personal account or the club's bank account. Be prompt; payment must reach the broker within three business days following issuance of the buy order. The broker is subject to a fine if he or she fails to require on-time payment. If you don't meet the deadline, your broker could be required to place your club on a restricted list and possibly be forced to collect funds from you in advance of accepting your orders.

Don't ask your broker to attend all your meetings; you are in business to learn by doing, not to defer to the opinions of others you consider to be more knowledgeable than yourself. Invite the broker to your annual meeting only.

The broker should be asked to give you suggestions on your study program for the months ahead. However, remember that you started your club to make your own decisions with your fellow members. The broker should be asked only to comment generally, and should not be expected to assume responsibility for your investing success. That is your task.

REGISTRATION OF SECURITIES

The most practical form of registration currently available for your stock certificates is known as "street name." Under this form of registration, the broker establishes an account in the club's name, or in the name of an agent or agents specified by the club. Every month, as the club purchases securities, they are registered in the broker's name or "street" form. He or she will submit to the club a monthly statement itemizing transactions and listing securities in the club's account. However, you will not receive stock certificates. This is the most convenient form of registration, because you won't have to safeguard certificates or pay to have them stored.

Dividend payments are sent directly to the broker and credited to your club account. Stockholder notices received by the broker, such as annual and quarterly reports and proxy statements, should be forwarded to you promptly.

Your club can receive annual and quarterly reports directly from corporate investor relations departments if you send a written request. Explain that your shares are held in street name, and that you will advise the company when you sell and ask to be removed from the mailing list.

When securities are held in street name, you are not allowed to participate in a corporation's dividend reinvestment program. To do so, you will have to ask your broker to deliver securities in the club's own name. When securities are registered in street name, you cannot physically hold your own stock certificates. However, the industry is moving toward electronic record keeping in the interest of cost reduction, and stock certificates are becoming arcane. The SEC has lent its support to this effort. Recently, a major brokerage firm began imposing a fee on clients who request that securities be registered and shipped to them in certificate form. The charge is $15 per certificate; when a single order is placed, the fee is capped at $30. This policy may accelerate the trend away from the use of stock certificates.

A new stock registration form is now awaiting approval from the Securities and Exchange Commission (SEC). It is referred to as the IRO (Individual

Registration Option) and offers advantages to individuals and corporations. Under IRO, the club's securities are registered in the club's name directly with the corporation. Certificates may be obtained at no cost from the corporation, and securities in IRO are eligible for dividend reinvestment plans. Securities can be released to the broker with a phone call. Corporation reports are mailed on time directly to the owner. Since the securities are directly registered with the corporation, no danger exists from the possible bankruptcy of the broker holding your securities in street form.

CHAPTER 19

CONDUCTING THE MONTHLY MEETING

*T*he monthly meeting is the focal point of club activity. Your group is a business and should be run like one, with the social aspects a necessary and important side element. Clubs that hold well-run, organized meetings consistently enjoy superior investment results—and that's not just coincidence. Success results from skillful organization and planning. NAIC has a video that shows how a model club meeting would be conducted.

The presiding partner prepares club get-togethers and ensures that each meeting is run effectively. Members should come away from the meeting with a sense that their time at club meetings is well spent. Participants should be allowed to express themselves without being pressured; the presiding partner should encourage open discussion and thoughtful consideration of all issues, while making sure business moves along at a good clip.

The meeting should be only as long as necessary to thoroughly cover all essential business. No one enjoys exhausting, long meetings. Except under the most unusual circumstances, two hours should be sufficient for taking care of business at the monthly meeting.

START PROMPTLY

The presiding partner should call the meeting to order at the appointed hour. Don't keep everyone waiting for a few stragglers. Reward the majority of your members for being there on time.

The presiding partner presents the agenda, including a list of specific items of old or new business that are to be covered. After reading the minutes of the last meeting, the financial partner presents each member with a copy of the club's current valuation statement and reviews highlights of his or her discussions with the club's broker. Any important comments concerning securities the club already owns or is considering for purchase should be explained and passed along to the members. Any stocks the broker has suggested will be identified and assigned to particular members for study, assuming the club wants to follow up on the recommendation.

The assistant presiding partner next calls on each member following a stock in the club's portfolio to circulate any information he or she has gathered, including whether the Portfolio Management Guide shows that the stock is a candidate for a purchase, hold, or sale.

Then members who have researched possible stocks to purchase present their findings. Each report should be prepared manually or by computer on a Stock Selection Guide (or, in the case of new clubs, a Stock Check List). Copies of the form should be distributed so that all members have a chance to review the analysis.

LET EVERYONE SEE

One option is to use a presentation-size Guide, if the Club has the capability of displaying it so that all can see. Remember, it's virtually impossible to assimilate all these figures unless the listener is also able to see them. If all members have equal access to the financial data, full discussion and better decision making will follow. As the members give their stock selection reports, an officer should record key data on each possible purchase on a giant Stock Comparison Guide. As an alternative, information can be collected in advance of the meeting and copies of a Stock Comparison Guide prepared for distribution to each member. If you do this, the Guide should not be made available until the reports are completed. Otherwise, some members won't listen carefully to the reports and will instead base their decision strictly on the data before them.

When all the different stock reports have been summarized on the form, other members are allowed to propose stocks previously studied but never purchased. However, original reports should be updated to include current data. At this point, the club is ready to make a decision on the best stock to purchase. It is helpful for the investment program leader to indicate which of the prospects ranks highest on the basis of each of the statistics. This emphasis helps members avoid the trap of buying the best report rather than the best stock.

Discourage members from making decisions for the wrong reasons. For example, some members of new clubs are intent on buying as many shares as possible, so they'll gravitate to the lowest-price stocks. In terms of value, low-price stocks could be expensive while higher-price stocks may offer considerably more for your money. Members should take into account not only new securities, but also previously considered securities.

VOTING

After a motion is made, the club is ready to vote. If the motion fails, additional motions are permitted until the club comes to a decision. Occasionally the club may take more than one action—buying two different securities for example, or buying one and selling one.

The important point is that the club should not consider any security that does not have an accompanying report. This minimizes the possibility of selecting stock based on emotion rather than reason and succumbing to "hot tips."

The presiding partner next opens the meeting to discussions of old and new business. During this time, the club's contact with NAIC should announce conventions, local Council meetings, and other items of interest. Also any annual reports received from NAIC should be passed along to the investment program head.

The assistant presiding partner then asks for suggestions for new companies or industries to be considered at the next meeting and makes assignments for the following month's stock study presentations. Each month, NAIC's *Better Investing* magazine features a stock to study. Many clubs automatically include this security in their review. The stock to study is not a recommendation, but NAIC's selection committee takes care to pick companies that have the prospect of doubling in five years.

It's not mandatory to act immediately; you can study the stock the following month. Sound company fundamentals are the key to investment success, not picking for price movement. So don't be too concerned about the precise timing of your decision.

After a year of operation, the club should update the Stock Selection Guides on securities in the portfolio and possibly look at fewer new companies as the club devotes more time to current holdings. As more and more funds go into the existing portfolio, it may be wise to spend time reviewing the entire portfolio. See the last section of Chapter 12 for a suggested procedure for an annual review of the total portfolio.

ENJOY THE MEETING

Once the formal business is concluded, club members can turn their attention to having a little fun—enjoying refreshments, talking informally, and getting to know each other better. Relaxing before going home helps you to end each meeting on a friendly basis.

You should welcome guests to your meetings, including prospective members as well as people who might want to form a club of their own. Some clubs appoint a membership committee responsible for identifying and attracting qualified people to the club. Both business and personal factors cause members to leave the group. Without replacements, the club will ultimately wither and die. If there's a waiting list of prospects, well and good; however, few clubs enjoy such luxury. The best plan is to encourage people to attend more than one meeting, so they know the extent and type of effort required. This will also help current members and prospective members get to know each other and find out if they are compatible.

One person on the membership committee should be assigned to help each newly elected member become familiar with club procedures and tasks. The group suffers along with the newcomer who is left to fend for himself. Encourage new members to ask questions and make it easy for them to get answers.

New members should be encouraged to attend the classes your nearest NAIC Council has on the use of NAIC's stock study procedures. Your club may have one member who will spend time helping a new member complete a NAIC Stock Selection Guide and Report. Even in the liveliest group, meetings tend to fall into a routine. As part of your collective goal to expand your investment knowledge, consider finding interesting guest speakers to address your club. Assign one club member the primary responsibility of enlisting a speaker every third or fourth meeting. Consider economists from local universities, financial writers in your area, bank executives, financial planners, stock market employees, and regulators, among others. Once you begin thinking about the range of prospective interesting speakers, you will probably be able to come up with an endless supply.

CHAPTER 20

KEEPING INTEREST HIGH

*K*eeping members interested may be the most challenging part of forming a club—perhaps even more difficult than earning a profit from your investments.

At the outset, everyone will be filled with enthusiasm. However, over time, particularly in a declining market, members' interest may flag. If you allow the club to dissolve at this crucial point, the potential to achieve long-term gains will vanish. In contrast, if club members can be persuaded to continue even during long down periods, you are virtually certain to purchase stocks at bargain prices and profit handsomely when prices move upward again.

Fortunately, there are countless ways to rekindle the spirit of members until the amount invested becomes large enough that everyone's attention remains focused. Involve all of the members; after you get to know everyone, you will know who is best suited for outside activities, such as a field trip or party. Your outside activities do not have to be related to investing, although a field trip to a financial institution such as a stock exchange could be very interesting.

EDUCATIONAL PROGRAMS

The most knowledgeable members are usually also the most committed to the club's continuing success. Look for every possible opportunity to increase the knowledge of all your club members. Encourage members to take night classes conducted by your local NAIC council, read newly published investment trade books, subscribe to market-oriented magazines, and seek out informative guest speakers to address meetings.

Invite each member to regularly read at least one business publication. *The Wall Street Journal, Barron's, Business Week, Forbes,* and *Fortune,* as well as NAIC's own magazine, *Better Investing,* are all good resources. NAIC recommends that everyone in your club read *Better Investing* as a matter of routine. Such features as "A Stock to Study" and "The Repair Shop" are invaluable educational tools for investment clubs.

Some clubs name a club economist who reports regularly but briefly to the membership on economic trends. If possible, the economist should be someone who will benefit professionally from the research—a purchasing agent or sales/marketing executive, for example. The economist should monitor the impact of economic trends on specific industries and companies, focusing on companies that the club either owns stock in or is considering.

For example, your club economist could develop up to eight reports on industries or companies worthy of consideration as potential investments. He or she may discuss the international and national economic outlook on a quarterly basis. Sources of data for the economist range from business publications of general interest to monthly newsletters on economic matters published by leading banks. Government publications such as the Department of Commerce's *Survey of Current Business* are also useful.

NAIC RESOURCES

Many clubs set aside a fifteen- or twenty-minute period in every meeting for instruction. This book offers a wealth of material appropriate for mini-lessons; the chapters on investment philosophy, the Stock Selection Guide, and portfolio management can keep you busy for months. Appendix D, "Sources of Further Information," can serve as a springboard for volunteers to prepare and present commentaries on subjects of special interest to them.

One or more members should plan to attend the annual National Investors Congress of NAIC. This event offers all investment clubs a great forum to exchange ideas; it also provides you the chance to meet with many other investment club organizers and members. Conversations with fellow investment club members from across the country are always one of the more pleasant and instructive side benefits of attendance. The Congress is always held in a major city, so attendance can also serve as a vacation for you and your family. For club members who are computer oriented, the annual CompuFest will provide a host of ideas.

You may also think about entering your club's investing record in NAIC's Annual Performance Survey. (See each year's May edition of *Better Investing.*) After you have been notified of your ranking, compare your portfolio with those of the winning clubs. If you use a computer, you can project what your continued deposits plus compounded earnings will be worth five, ten, fifteen, or even twenty years ahead.

NAIC COUNCILS

If a NAIC Council operates in your area, we encourage you and your fellow members to attend the annual Investors Fair. This event includes presentations from four or five companies of different sizes. You will have the chance to talk one-on-one with corporate officials in companies whose stock you might consider buying.

Each January issue of *Better Investing* lists all Investors Fairs for the year. You may wish to attend not only the fair in your own community, but also all other fairs within your state or close by. One member might enjoy the assignment of attending all Council meetings and reporting to the club. Most of the meetings are devoted to NAIC stock study and portfolio tools. New members in experienced clubs could find Council attendance particularly helpful.

You may also consider inviting a Council leader to attend one of your meetings to critique your portfolio and your procedures.

OTHER RESOURCES FOR EDUCATION

Following are some additional ideas for you and your fellow club members to improve your investment knowledge base:

Invite your broker to your annual meeting to discuss your holdings and evaluate the club's current investment opportunities.

Go on a field trip to the broker's office. Take an after-trading-hours tour of the premises to discover how your orders are processed and how to become familiar with resources available in the library.

If you live in or near a city with a stock exchange, or if you can arrange a visit to one, take advantage of the visitors' gallery to learn firsthand how the market works.

Arrange a visit to a local company in which you own shares, to see firsthand the people who work in supplying the company's product or service.

Designate a member to attend the annual meeting of a local company in which you have invested and to report back on management's message, business discussed and voted on, opportunities or problems brought up and reported on, and questions raised by other stockholders.

Take a field trip to your local library, and let the business department head review available references for investors.

If there is a chapter of the Financial Analysts Society in or near your community, call and ask about upcoming meetings. You may be allowed to attend as a guest and learn meaningful information about companies of interest to your club. You will be interested in hearing the questions investment professionals pose to management.

Invite as a guest speaker an experienced member from a successful club with a significantly longer operating history than your own. Ask him or her for a critique of your portfolio.

Ask a local economist, banker, company executive, or college professor to visit your club to discuss the regional, national, and international economic outlook. Also invite a corporate representative to discuss his or her company and industry.

OTHER ACTIVITIES

Invite a friend to visit your club. If there are no openings in your club, express your willingness to help your friend get a new club launched.

Publish an annual report, including the year-end valuation statement; members' names, addresses, and phone numbers; and the club's operating agreement. Distribute it to families of members, friends, your broker, and any acquaintances who have expressed an interest in investment clubs.

Hold your annual meeting at a special location such as an elegant restaurant or meeting hall.

Stage one or two special events during the year, such as a Christmas party or summer picnic, and invite nonmember friends and family.

Hold an annual retreat for a day or a weekend to let members review the club's performance away from daily distractions. Establish goals for the coming year. At subsequent retreats, review the club's attainment of prior goals before setting new ones.

Initiate an investment competition for a set time period with an established sum of imaginary money. Give a prize to the member achieving the greatest profit.

Award a prize to the member who picked the most profitable investment of the year. Give another award to the member who did the most during the year to further the club's goals.

Sponsor an annual guessing game to allow members to forecast the Dow Jones Averages, club results, gross domestic product, and any other statistics of interest. Reward the best guesser.

Stage a joint cocktail party with one or more other investment clubs.

Have one meeting per year for a purely social pursuit.

Consider contributing one month's contributions to a charity or toward participation in a local social event rather than investing the money. If you come up with an especially fun alternative, write to the Editor of *Better Investing*. Your idea may be featured in the magazine and benefit clubs nationwide.

As you can see, there are many ways to keep up the interest in your club. The very best way of all, of course, is to obtain superior investment results. To review, here are a few guidelines for creating a successful club:

- Follow a structured yet flexible agenda.
- Set goals, both short- and long-term, and track the club's performance toward achieving them.
- Require involvement of all members.
- Reward member participation.
- Support the continuing education of all members.
- Maintain a disciplined approach to stock study and selection and to portfolio management procedures.
- Think creatively: "How can we continue to meet the needs of our club?"
- Encourage member involvement in Council activities and national NAIC Congresses.
- Promote a spirit of enthusiasm, excitement, and enjoyment.
- Use available aids such as computers, videotapes, and overhead projectors to facilitate member participation and understanding.

CHAPTER 21

RECORD KEEPING

One of the first tasks for your newly formed club is setting up the books. You need to come up with a system to track every cash transaction and to calculate every member's share of the whole. You can accomplish this important task in four ways:

1. By hand, with one or more club members using NAIC's Accounting Manual and prepared forms.
2. Electronically, with one or more members using NAIC Club Accounting Software.
3. By hiring an outside bookkeeper or accountant to maintain the books for the club.
4. By using a combination of 1 and 3, with an outside service doing the monthly valuation statement and members' records and a club member keeping cash records.

Under each of these alternatives, the financial partner is ultimately responsible for club record keeping—even if that means only overseeing everyone else's reports. The financial partner might also work with a co-treasurer or assistant.

We recommend, in the interest of protecting yourself as well as the club, that every member of the group be somewhat familiar with the process of record keeping. Every member should also be prepared to audit the work of the financial partner if asked to do so. The NAIC Council nearest you offers periodic programs on record keeping and tax reporting. At the very least, the club's financial partner and members of the audit committee should attend these sessions.

This discussion of record keeping is aimed at all members of the club and deals only with the valuation of members' interests. For a more complete explanation of club accounting, study NAIC's Accounting Manual. NAIC's Club Accounting Software is designed to be used with the Accounting Manual.

GETTING A TAX IDENTIFICATION NUMBER

The first step is getting your Tax Identification Number. Write or phone (1-800-TAX FORM) the nearest U.S. Department of Treasury Internal Revenue Service office and ask for Form SS-4, Application for Employer Identification Number. This is a simple sheet of paper that asks for an officer name, address, and Social Security number, club name, and some general information. You will then be assigned a Tax Identification Number, which is used on all tax filings. You need to provide this number to your broker and the transfer agents for the securities your club buys. All security transactions and all dividend income received are reported to the IRS under this number. When individual members report their share of the income on their individual tax returns, the Tax Identification Number is included so that the reported amounts can be cross-referenced to the club's return.

We recommend the unit value system for keeping track of members' proportionate equity in the club. At first review, the system may seem unnecessarily complicated to new clubs. But when you compare it with other methods, you will ultimately agree that this is the most accurate and reliable method to use.

You might wonder, "Why do we have to go through complex calculations when all the members contribute the same amount each month?" In virtually every club there comes a time when one or more members will want to make a more substantial contribution than the minimum amount required. The unit value system permits this and allows the larger contributor to remain in the club with all members' interests fairly valued.

The system allows for flexibility. When a member wants to withdraw funds, the unit value system enables you to calculate and reset proportionate shares without trouble. Likewise, a member might not be able to contribute every month; you need a system that allows adjustment of proportionate ownership in a way that is accurate and fair to all.

The unit value system also permits the club to accept a new member at any time without requiring him or her to make a lump-sum payment to match the funds already contributed by long-time members. You have to realize that, for several reasons, you won't be able to maintain identical share values between all members. With this system in use, your club can attract and retain all the members you want without imposing a financial barrier.

CLUB ACCOUNTING IS DIFFERENT

The valuation of an investment club member's interest is different from valuation in other businesses, because the worth of club assets is constantly fluctuating due to stock market changes. In addition, most clubs are partnerships, so each person owns part of the total assets rather than shares of stock, as in a corporation. All of the assets must be valued whenever members deposit additional funds, which is monthly in most clubs. Each member's account consists of two parts: the accumulation of cash deposits and a valuation record of his or her deposits, which includes the sum of profits and losses.

Preparation of a Valuation Statement is the first step in valuing new capital deposited in the club. This statement lists the assets of the club at their market value as of the valuation date. As a convenience to the financial partner—or out of necessity, if an outside accountant or bookkeeper is being used—the Valuation Statement customarily is prepared several days before the membership meeting. Most clubs base valuation on the closing price of listed securities or the bid price of the over-the-counter securities. Sample statements are shown later in this chapter.

TWO METHODS

You can develop a record of each member's interest in one of two ways. Under the first method, each member's account is credited or debited with the proportionate amount of value change in the club's assets since the last statement. An example of this method appears in Figure 21-1.

The total value of the club and members' accounts as of January 21 is $43,652.45. The club's Valuation Statement total for the February meeting is $42,925.54. During the month since the January valuation, the club's asset value dropped $726.91. This decline is distributed to the members based on each one's proportionate financial interest in the club.

Figure 21-1

	(1)	(2)	(3)	(4)	(5)	(6)
			Distribution of (Decrease)			Member's Balance,
	Value of Acct.,	% of Total	or Increase	Member's New	Deposited This	End of Feb. 28
Member	Jan. 21	Value	in Value	Balance	Month	Meeting
Adam	$ 5,456.56	12.5	$ (90.86)	$ 5,365.70	$ 10.00	$ 5,375.70
Mary	6,782.40	15.5	(112.69)	6,669.71	20.00	6,689.71
Charlotte	5,456.56	12.5	(90.86)	5,365.70	10.00	5,375.70
David	5,456.56	12.5	(90.86)	5,365.70	10.00	5,375.70
Edward	6,221.10	14.3	(103.94)	6,117.16		6,117.16
Frances	3,015.14	6.9	(50.16)	2,964.98	50.00	3,014.98
Georgiana	4,627.42	10.6	(77.05)	4,550.37	30.00	4,580.37
Harry	6,636.71	15.2	(110.49)	6,526.22	20.00	6,546.22
	$43,652.45	100.0	$(726.91)	$42,925.54	$150.00	$43,075.54

In the illustration, column 1 lists the balances forward from column 6 on the previous month's Valuation Statement. Column 2 translates the figures in column 1 into percentages of the total. Column 3 distributes the loss of $726.91 by applying the percentages obtained in column 2. Column 4 is the sum of columns 1 and 3. Column 5 lists the members' deposits made at the February 28 meeting. Column 6 is the sum of columns 4 and 5 and represents the new balance forward, to be transferred to column 1 in March.

With this method, each member can see what he or she would receive if the club were liquidated as of the valuation date.

Most clubs prefer the second method, because fewer calculations are required. This is the method described in the Club Accounting Kit and used in the computer program. With this method, you establish a "unit of value" for determining ownership in the club. This amount is typically $10. Each new deposit made by a member is valued to reflect the changes from the prior deposit.

Each member's account consists of a record of cash deposited and "valuation units" credited to his or her account. Any member's liquidating value can be readily computed at any time by multiplying the member's total valuation units owned by the fair market value of a unit.

Let's look at an illustration. Assume that a club has twelve members. At the initial meeting, each member invests $10. The valuation unit is set at

$10, so each member is credited with 1 valuation unit. When a member invests $20, he or she will receive 2 valuation units; an investment of $25 will bring 2.5 valuation units.

This method eliminates the need to compute percentages, since cash, whether earned from investments or newly deposited, is assigned a value based on the unit value—$10 in our example. To determine the total proportionate value of any account at any time, simply divide the number of units in the account by the total units held by the club.

Another way to look at the valuation unit method is to apply it to market buying power. When a stock is selling for $10 a share, you can buy one share with one unit of the same value. When the stock rises to $11, however, the regular contribution is not enough to purchase a whole share; your $10 will buy only .909 shares ($10 divided by $11). You cannot actually buy fractional shares in the market; you and your fellow club members will pool your funds to make full-share purchases. We raise this point only to illustrate how the unit value system simplifies the tracking of proportionate ownership in the club for each member—even when different amounts are contributed over time.

The Valuation Statement assigns a varying portion of a valuation unit in return for the fixed sum invested; the portion changes as contributions vary and as market values grow or shrink.

SAMPLE STATEMENTS

The first Valuation Statement for a twelve-member club might look like the one shown in Figure 21-2. The statement reflects the club's condition at the beginning of the second meeting. Each $10 paid in by members at the second meeting will purchase 1.081 valuation units in the club. Assuming that every member pays in $10, 1.081 units will be added to each member's account, making a total of 2.081 units for each member (assuming no other transactions, like dividend income or expenses, took place) and 24.972 units for the entire club. To determine the value of one unit, divide the total current value of the club by the total number of valuation units in the club.

Assuming all members of the club make another investment at the second meeting, the Valuation Statement at the beginning of the third meeting would appear as in Figure 21-3.

Maintain a record of both the total number of valuation units in the partnership and the total number of units owned by each member. You will need

Figure 21-2

Investment Club 600 Valuation Statement Prepared July 12, 199X, for
Club Meeting July 19, 199X

Company	No. of Shares	Cost per Share	Total Cost	Price per Share This Date	Total Value
Moore Steel Co.	20	$5.58	$111.55	$5.125	$102.50
Cash on hand					8.45
Total value of club this date					$110.95
Total number of valuation units to date					12.00

(This is the number of units at the beginning of the July meeting)

Value of each unit this date ($110.95 ÷ 12 units)	$9.25
Number of units each $10.00 deposited at July 19 meeting will purchase ($10.00 ÷ $9.25)	1.081

to keep total club figures on one sheet and set up a separate sheet for each
member's account value.

CONVERTING TO THE UNIT VALUE SYSTEM

Many clubs that have operated under a different procedure may decide to convert to the unit value system. Here is NAIC's recommended procedure for
conversion:

1. Prepare a Valuation Statement as shown in this chapter.
2. Divide the total value of the Valuation Statement by $10, and take the
   quotient as the number of valuation units in the club.
3. Allocate these valuation units to your members.
   a. When everyone has an equal interest, divide the total number of
      valuation units by the total number of members to determine the
      valuation units for each member.
   b. When interests are unequal, calculate the percentage of the value of
      each member's account to the total value of the club. Determine the
      number of each member's valuation units by applying his or her
      percentage of ownership to the total number of valuation units.
4. After determining the total number of valuation units for the club and
   the number for each member, with the unit value set at $10 received, cal-
   culate this month's receipts. For each $10 received, add one valuation
   unit to each member's account and to the grand total.

Figure 21-3

Investment Club 600 Valuation Statement Prepared August 9, 199X, for Club Meeting August 16, 199X

Company	No. of Shares	Cost per Share	Total Cost	Price per Share This Date	Total Value
Moore Steel Co.	20	$5.58	$111.55	$5.50	$110.00
XG Products, Inc.	22	4.91	108.15	4.25	93.50
Cash on hand					20.30
Total value of club this date					$223.80
Total number of valuation units to date					24.972*
Value of one unit ($223.80 ÷ 24.972)					$8.96
Number of units $10.00 purchases ($10.00 ÷ $8.96)					1.116
Members' total investment					$240.00

* The "total number of valuation units to date" of 24.972 is derived as follows:

Valuation units as of beginning of July meeting	12.000
Twelve members deposit $10.00 each at July meeting, each purchasing 1.081 units (12 × 1.081)	12.972
Total units at beginning of August meeting	24.972

5. For future meetings, divide the total of your liquidating statement by the new total of valuation units, determining the value of one unit. Divide $10 by the new unit value; the resulting figure will be the number of units that $10 will purchase at the next meeting.

MAINTAINING CONSISTENT RECORDS

The financial partner can verify the consistency of club accounts by confirming that the sum of all the individual records matches the total shown in the Valuation Units Control Ledger (Figure 21-4). The Valuation Units Control Ledger records on one sheet all members' actual cash deposits in the club and the members' total number of valuation units.

The first three rows represent regular deposits by members.

The information listed in columns 1 through 4 is recorded before the meeting from the Valuation Statement. Some clubs show the statement date in column 1; others list the meeting date; and some clubs list both dates, since only columns 2, 3, and 4 reflect data as of the Valuation Statement date. The remaining columns represent actual contributions received from members at the meeting.

Figure 21-4

VALUATION UNITS CONTROL LEDGER

FORM 1 DATE	2 VALUATION STATEMENT TOTAL	3 UNIT VALUE	4 NO. UNITS $10.00 OR $ PURCHASES	5 TOTAL PAID IN THIS MONTH	6 MEMBERS' ORIGINAL INVESTMENT	7 MEMBERS' ORIGINAL INVESTMENT PLUS EARNINGS DISTRIBUTED BY PARTNERSHIP	8 UNITS PURCHASED THIS MONTH	9 TOTAL UNITS
(1) 6-21-9X	—	10 00	1.00 0	120 00	120 00	120 00	12.0 0 0	120.0 0
(2) 7-19-9X	1 10 95	9 25	1.0 81	120 00	240 00	240 00	12.972	24.972
(3) 8-16-9X	223 80	8 96	1.1 16	120 00	3 60 00	360 00	13.392	38.364
(4) 12-20-9X	749 79	9 86	1.014	1 20 00	840 00	840 00	12.168	88.236
	THIS IS THE DATE THE VALUATION STATEMENT WAS PREPARED OR DATE OF THE CLUB MEETING	THIS IS THE TOTAL CLUB VALUE AS SHOWN ON THE MONTHLY VALUATION STATEMENT	THIS IS THE AMOUNT IN COL. (2) ÷ TOTAL IN (9) FROM PRECEDING MONTH	THIS IS THE RESULT OF DIVIDING $10 BY THE ENTRY IN COL.(3)	THIS IS THE ACTUAL CASH PAID IN BY THE MEMBERS	THIS IS THE ACCUMULATED TOTAL OF ACTUAL CASH PAID IN BY MEMBERS	THIS IS THE SAME AS COL. (6) UNTIL THE FIRST DISTRIBUTION OF CLUB EARNINGS TO MEMBERS	COL. (8) IS PRODUCED BY MULTIPLYING COL. (4) BY NUMBER OF UNITS DEPOSITED IN COL. (5) (12 X 1.014)	THE SUM OF THE LAST ENTRY OF COL. (8) AND THE PREVIOUS ENTRY IN THIS COLUMN

TO RECORD DISTRIBUTION OF LOSS FOR YEAR OF $11.88 OR $.1346 PER UNIT AS FOLLOWS:

(5) 12-31-9X	8 57 01	971	1.02 9	—	840 00	828 12	(1.2 2 4)	87.01 2
	VALUATION TOTAL AT 12-31-9X	$ 85 7.01 ÷ 88.236	$10.00 ÷ 9.71			$840.00 – $11.88	FROM DIST. OF EARNINGS SHEET $11.88 ÷ 9.71 =1.224	88.236 LESS 1.2 2 4 87.01 2

TO RECORD DISTRIBUTION OF 199X+4 EARNINGS TOTALING $348.92 OR $.4538 PER UNIT

(6) 12-31-9X+ 4	10648 37	13 85	0.72 2	—	7400 00	8 075 34	25.19 3	79 4.0 28
(7) 3-18-9X+5 (TOTALS BEFORE WITHDRAWAL OF FRANK VESTOR)					876 0 00	9 435 34		87 8.96 4
(8) 3-18-9X+5 (WITHDRAWAL OF FRANK VESTOR)						4 11 40	(32.965)	84 5.99 9
(9) 3-18-9X+5 (NEW BALANCES)					876 0 00	9 023 94		84 5.99 9

Row 4 shows how club records might appear after a year of operation, shortly before the annual distribution of earnings is recorded.

Row 5 demonstrates the distribution of the loss at the end of the first year. The earnings are assigned to each member's account since the income (loss) is taxable (deductible) and must be reported by the individual members on their personal tax returns. As long as a member leaves the account money on deposit, it is treated as part of his or her tax-paid invested capital—assuming that member has reported the profits on his or her tax return and paid taxes on them.

Row 6 shows the distribution of a gain with earnings of $348.92 added to column 7. This column represents total cash invested in the club by partners plus realized earnings left in the club after payment of taxes.

The earnings of $348.92, divided by the unit value from column 3, $13.85, reflect a total of 25.193 valuation units being purchased by the year's total earnings. The 25.193 units are recorded in column 8 and added to create a new total in column 9.

The distribution of earnings is divided among all the members in proportion to their investment in the club. The next chapter describes a convenient form and procedure for making this distribution.

After row 6 is completed, a new unit value for funds deposited by members at the meeting is calculated based on the December 31 statement. This is done by dividing the total liquidating value by the new unit total of 794.028. Entries corresponding to those in the Valuation Units Control Ledger are made in each Individual Valuation Units Ledger, as shown in Figure 21-5, line 7 for Frank N. Vestor.

Each partnership club is required by tax law to distribute taxable income to members at the end of each calendar year. While most members do not withdraw that income, once taxes are paid on it, it becomes part of their tax-paid investment in the club. The distribution of units is not required by law.

Row 8 of the Control Ledger illustrates the withdrawal of funds by a member. He withdraws 32.965 units worth $12.48 each at the time, for a total of $411.40. Tax regulations require that the tax base be reduced by the value withdrawn, which in this case is $411.40 in cash. The "Members' Original Investment" column (column 6) is a historical record, and we suggest that this record be left intact. You should not use the withdrawal to adjust the original deposit amount.

Figure 21-5

INDIVIDUAL VALUATION UNITS LEDGER

NAME **FRANK N. VESTOR   5478 Sixth Street, Detriot, MI 48225**

	DATE PAID	UNIT VALUE	NO. UNITS $10.00 OR $ PURCHASES	PAID IN THIS MONTH	TOTAL PAID IN TO DATE	TOTAL PAID IN TO DATE INCLUDING SAVINGS REINVESTED	VALUATION UNITS PURCHASED THIS DATE	TOTAL VALUATION UNITS
(1)	6-21-9X	10.00	10.00	10–	10–	10–	10.00	10.00
(2)	7-19-9X	9.25	10.81	10–	20–	20–	10.81	20.81
(3)	8-16-9X	8.96	11.16	10–	30–	30–	11.16	31.97
(4)	12-20-9X	9.84	10.16	10–	70–	70–	10.16	73.53
	To record distribution of loss for year of $11.88 or $.1246 per unit as follows							
	7.353 units x $.1346 equals total loss of $.99 per member							
(5)	12-31-9X			(99)	70–	69.01	(0.102)	72.51
(6)	1-15-9X+2	9.81	10.19	10–	320–	343.52	10.19	329.65
	To record distribution of 199X+4 earnings at rate of $.4530 per unit							
(7)	12-31-9X+4			37.04	680–	929.69	2.674	842.98
(8)	3-18-9X+5 (Total before withdrawal)				750–	999.69		893.71
(9)	3-18-9X+5 (Withdrawal of 32.965 units)					(411.40)		(32.965)
(10)	3-18-9X+5 (Total after withdrawal)				750–	588.29		564.06

For partial withdrawals, no tax liability is incurred until the member has drawn out more than his or her tax-paid investment in the club.

TAX CONSEQUENCES OF PAYING IN CASH OR STOCK

A member withdrawing either all or part of his or her account value may be paid in cash or stock. The tax consequences of how a departing member is paid off should be taken into consideration. IRS rules differ depending on whether the withdrawal is full or partial. See NAIC's Accounting Manual and Chapter 22 of this book for details about these rules and recommended methods for handling the transaction.

The transfer of stock is advantageous to both club and member if the member is making a full withdrawal. The club transfers the stock to the partner and the stock picks up the member's tax basis in the club, less any cash received. Since this is not a taxable transaction until the member sells the stock, this method is becoming increasingly popular. A letter to the broker stating the time of transfer, number of shares, and name of the member is all that's required. If the withdrawing member wants cash, he or she merely instructs the broker to sell. The club liquidating statement on which the value of the withdrawal is calculated should be of the same date as the letter to the broker authorizing the transfer.

Some clubs seek out people, either present members or new members, who are willing to contribute enough to pay the departing member's interest in the club. These individuals pay enough into the club to cover the amount that the club will pay the withdrawing member. The newcomer should never pay money directly to the member leaving the club.

Only in the first case, when a club sells securities it owns to pay a withdrawing member, does a tax liability arise for the remaining members. The club fares best, taxwise, by selling stocks with a loss and transferring stocks held at a profit. Withdrawing members are liable in all instances for any profit in their accounts, although they do not assume tax liability for shares transferred to them until they elect to sell them.

Most clubs have no stipulations on the frequency or amount of partial withdrawals that members are allowed to make. While the vast majority of club members look on their contributions as a means of long-term savings, an occasional need will arise for cash. Normally, the same requirements of notice and fee apply to both partial and complete withdrawals.

NO LUMP SUM REQUIRED OF A NEW MEMBER

When a new partner joins the club, no large initial deposit is needed to catch up with other members. Under the unit valuation system, the new member may make the same or a similar monthly contribution as other members. The valuation unit determined each month will relate the value of his or her holdings to those of other members. Of course, a new member's valuation will be considerably lower than that of long-standing members.

HELP FROM NAIC

NAIC's Club Accounting Software is designed to help anyone with a PC become a full-fledged club treasurer. At least 512 KB of RAM is needed, but 640 KB is recommended. A hard disk is also advised, but a minimum of 720 KB of disk storage will suffice. The software supports CGA, Hercules, EGA, and VGA monitors, as well as both color and monochrome. Any Hewlett-Packard LaserJet, Epson-compatible, or wide-carriage printer may be used. For further information, contact NAIC, P.O. Box 220, Royal Oak, MI 48068, ATTN: Computer Software.

CHAPTER 22

REPORTING TAXABLE INCOME

Tax reporting is a chore for every individual, corporation, and partnership. It requires keeping complete, meticulous records, comprehending endless forms and regulations, and meeting deadlines. Investment clubs, like other entities, have to be aware of the tax rules that apply to them and to their members.

Instructions on tax computation and reporting requirements can be found in NAIC's Accounting Manual. Our purpose here is to introduce you to the overall tax and reporting requirements you assume when you start an investment club.

At the end of each taxable year, a partnership calculates the profit/loss earned during the year. It does not pay federal income taxes, but reports the overall results, as well as each member's portion of the total, to the IRS. This applies to income from dividends, interest, and capital gains. Club members are personally liable for payment of their share of the club's income.

One rule that many people have trouble understanding is the difference between profit and withdrawal. As a partnership, your club is only the conduit for the collective transactions of all members. If it earns profits through dividends, interest, and capital gains, those are divided up and reported according to each person's share of the total. You are liable for the taxes on your share.

For example: Let's say that no one in your club withdraws any money during the year. You all agree to leave your earnings on account to reinvest. You are still taxed on your share of the profits; just because you didn't withdraw those profits doesn't mean you can get around paying taxes on them.

The same rule applies if you withdraw more than your tax basis in any one year. Suppose that last year your share of club earnings was $400, but you have accumulated a large amount of money over the years, so you withdraw $5,000. You are only taxed this year on your $400 earnings. The $5,000 withdrawal is a different matter. The sum of deposits you have made in the club plus earnings you have paid taxes on is your tax basis in the club. Any withdrawal less than your tax basis is tax free. Any amount over your tax basis is taxed as a long-term capital gain as long as the club is more than one year old. Most states that collect an income tax duplicate the federal rules somewhat, although some states have different rules for reporting income. Be sure to check with your state taxing agency for any special rules. Also, the rules for taxation and treatment of withdrawals apply to individual accounts only. If your investment club account is part of an IRA or other tax-deferred retirement account, special penalties and taxes may apply to withdrawals.

FILING REQUIREMENTS

Partnerships must file tax forms 1065 and K-1 for each member.

When the club's income is calculated, it is divided among the members based on their proportionate shares. Because members hold interests of varying amounts and the club income falls into two different tax classes, this process requires a number of computations. Investment club income typically comes from two sources:

1. Dividends from securities owned by the club
2. Capital gains from sales of securities

Some clubs may also have interest income, which must be accounted for separately.

The dividend income is taxable as ordinary income. If your club had both short-term gains and short-term losses during the year, they are combined, and only the net short-term gain, if any, will be taxed as ordinary income. As this edition is written, long-term capital gains are taxable as ordinary income, at a maximum tax rate of 28 percent or 20 percent, depending on the holding period prior to sale. This—like all tax rules—is subject to change in the future, so check with your tax advisor before filing your returns. Long-term gains and losses are netted and reported as a single item.

In the Earnings Distribution Statement that follows (Figure 22-1), one member—Fred Hill—withdrew part of his funds during the year. Fred's earnings up to the point of his withdrawal have been subtracted from the total taxable income for the year to determine the remaining taxable amount for each member. The importance of such an adjustment becomes increasingly evident as the earnings of the club grow larger. Consider a case where several members withdraw all of their capital. Without this adjustment, the remaining partners have to pay taxes on earnings that were distributed to other partners. They would consequently pay far more taxes than they should.

To prepare the Distribution Statement, list all of the partners' names in column 1. In the next column, copy the number of valuation units listed in each partner's account from the Individual Valuation Units Ledger. The total of column 2 should be the same as the total number of valuation units shown in your Valuation Units Control Ledger.

The illustrated Income and Expense Statement (Figure 22-2) provides the figures to be placed on row 9 in the Earnings Distribution Statement. Total dividend income is listed at $279.15, short-term capital gains at $45.25, long-term capital gains at $202.93, total expenses at $161.17, and net profit at $366.16.

FRED HILL'S CALCULATION

Fred Hill made his partial withdrawal on November 26. The distribution of income and expenses earned up to the withdrawal on November 26 is shown in row 10. The club calculated these figures at the time Fred made his withdrawal. To calculate these items for Fred, take the sum of each item at the time of the withdrawal and divide it by the total number of valuation units in the club. The result is the amount per unit. Then multiply these answers by the number of units Fred withdrew to determine the total of each. The remaining balances to be distributed are shown in row 11 of the Distribution Statement. If more than one withdrawal had been made during the year, each one would be listed and deducted from the club's taxable income for the year in row 10. Only the earnings that remain to be distributed to current members would be shown in row 11. Notice that Fred Hill's capital account still needs to be adjusted for the earnings attributed to him up to the point of withdrawal and for the remaining earnings to year end.

Figure 22-1
Earnings Distribution Statement

(1)	(2) No. of Valuation Units	(3) Dividends	(4) Short-Term Capital Gains	(5) Long-Term Capital Gains	(6) Total Club Expenses	(7) Year's Net Profit	(8) Val. Units Purchased If Profit Is Held
(9) Taxable income for year		279.15	45.25	202.93	($161.17)	366.16	
(10) Partial withdrawal by Fred Hill on Nov. 26		8.83	2.19	9.94	(3.72)	17.24	
(11) Taxable income remaining to be distributed		270.32	43.06	192.99	(157.45)	348.92	
(12) Per unit		0.3516	0.0560	0.2510	(0.2048)	0.4538	
Bob Smith	63.510	22.33	3.56	15.94	(13.01)	28.82	2.0811
Arthur Black	63.510	22.33	3.56	15.94	(13.01)	28.82	2.0811
Mary Brown	63.510	22.33	3.56	15.94	(13.01)	28.82	2.0811
Paul Hill	63.510	22.33	3.56	15.94	(13.01)	28.82	2.0811
Fred Hill *	52.111	27.15	5.11	23.02	(14.39)	40.89	2.9523
Rosilyn Rhodes	63.510	22.33	3.56	15.94	(13.01)	28.82	2.0811
Joe Rodgers	63.510	22.33	3.56	15.94	(13.01)	28.82	2.0811
Faye Dearson	63.510	22.33	3.56	15.94	(13.01)	28.82	2.0811
Donald Luis	63.510	22.33	3.56	15.94	(13.01)	28.82	2.0811
Nellie Neil	63.510	22.33	3.56	15.94	(13.01)	28.82	2.0811
Ed Echels	63.510	22.33	3.56	15.94	(13.01)	28.82	2.0811
Frank Vestor	81.624	28.70	4.57	20.49	(16.72)	37.04	2.6746
TOTAL	768.835	279.15	45.25	202.93	($161.17)	366.16	26.438

Value of unit before distribution $13.85

Value of unit after distribution $13.39

* Fred Hill's account was adjusted for a combination of taxable items earned prior to November 26 (the date of his partial withdrawal) and those earned to year end. For example, on November 26, Fred Hill's account was assigned $8.83 in dividend income. At year end, an additional $18.32 of dividend income (52.111 units × .3516) was earned on his units owned, for a total of $27.15.

Figure 22-2
Investment Club 671
Income and Expense Statement
January 1, 199X thru December 31, 199X

INCOME:

Dividends	$279.15	
Sale of securities:		
Net short-term	45.25	
Net long-term	202.93	
Total income		$527.33

EXPENSE:

Expenses of checking account	$65.72	
Dues to National Association of Investment Clubs	19.50	
Postage, paper, and supplies	25.31	
Subscriptions to business publications	35.00	
Miscellaneous	15.64	
Total expense		161.17
Net profit		$366.16

You are now ready to calculate the total profit per valuation unit (column 7, row 12), derived by dividing the adjusted net profit for the year—$348.92 (column 7 total)—by the total number of valuation units—768.835 (column 2). The total profit per unit is $0.4538. Since this figure includes income from dividends, short-term capital gains, and long-term capital gains as well as expenses to be deducted from taxable income, it's necessary to break it down to these items. The IRS does not permit partnerships to report just "net" income or loss.

In columns 3, 4, 5, and 6, you follow the same procedure. The column total is divided by the total number of valuation units to get the total per unit. Round the answer to the fourth decimal point to reduce the amount of penny adjusting required later. To find each individual's share of dividend income (column 3), multiply the number of units owned by the amount per unit—$0.3516. When all of the figures have been inserted in each column, add the columns to double-check that the individual figures add up to the column total. Since you are working with fractional amounts, you might need to adjust individual results by a penny or two to arrive at the exact column total.

DISTRIBUTING EARNINGS TO INDIVIDUAL ACCOUNTS

Members generally leave their earnings in the club rather than taking annual withdrawals, and the earnings are then distributed to individual accounts as additional valuation units. In our example, we assume that the club's total value is $10,648.37 and that there are 768.835 valuation units in the club. Therefore, the value of a unit is $13.85.

To convert the earnings in column 7 into the valuation units shown in column 8, we divide each figure in column 7 by the $13.85 unit value. We now have a new total of 795.273 valuation units (768.835 plus 26.438) with a per unit value of $13.39 ($10,648.37 divided by 795.273).

It is necessary to distribute the cash value of earnings per year to each member's account in order to reflect the additional tax-paid investment of club members. Since members report this income on their personal tax returns, it becomes part of their tax-paid investment (tax basis) in the club, just like their monthly deposits.

When the club's books are closed at year end, the total profit of $366.16 will be put into the surplus account (unrealized gains disbursed). From this account, it will then be transferred to the paid-in-by-members account and into the individual account of each member.

MEMBER TAX RETURNS

Each member of the club is given a copy of the Earnings Distribution Statement that contains all of the information he or she needs to file a personal tax return. However, members also must be given a K-1 form to keep with their tax records.

Keep all of these tax regulations in mind:

1. Unrealized gains and losses (paper gains and losses for securities still held by the club) are not taxable. Taxes become due—or losses can be deducted—only in the year securities are sold.

2. Capital gains are currently treated like ordinary income. The maximum tax rate on long- and mid-term capital gains is currently set at 28 percent and 20 percent, respectively.

3. Capital losses are offset by short-term and long-term capital gains. The net amount, when a profit, is taxed at the previously mentioned rates.

4. There is a limit to the total amount of net capital losses you can deduct each year. Excesses are carried over and applied to future capital gains, up to the annual deduction limits.

5. Capital gains are offset against capital losses to reduce tax liabilities.

6. If you own more than one lot of a security (shares bought at different times), you should sell high-cost lots in order to reduce gain or increase loss. Sell low-cost lots to increase gain or reduce loss. If it is impossible to establish which securities are being sold through certificates themselves, identify them by designation when the sale is made. Specify in writing to your broker from which purchase you wish stock to be sold, identifying the shares by purchase date, cost, or both, and see that you receive a detailed written confirmation of the order from your broker.

7. Part or all of the cash dividends paid by certain companies may be classified as return of capital and not taxable. Be sure to determine whether the dividends your club receives are taxable.

8. In general, stock dividends (dividends paid in the form of additional shares rather than in cash) are not taxable. Tax is postponed until the stock dividend is sold at a gain, when it is subject to capital gains tax.

9. Cash received in lieu of a fractional share of stock dividend is treated as a sale and a capital gain or loss.

10. In calculating gains on stock sold, the IRS allows you to add commissions you have paid to the purchase price, and to deduct them from the sale price.

11. Costs incurred in connection with investing, such as subscriptions to financial publications, are deductible as itemized miscellaneous deductions for each individual. However, the total on Form 1040, Schedule A, in the category of "Miscellaneous" has to be more than 2 percent of the individual's adjusted gross income, or there is no deduction.

WHERE TO RECORD ITEMS ON FORM 1040

This section describes each member's reporting requirements for investment club transactions.

Dividend income is entered on Schedule B of Form 1040 if over $400 is earned, or on line 9 if under $400 is earned. Write down your share of club dividend income, with the description "Share of qualifying corporation dividends received from investment club partnership, $." Any amount paid to the club as dividend income and then reclassified by the issuing corporation as "return of capital" (usually from utilities and insurance companies) is reported in a separate column on the Earnings Distribution Statement and reported by members on their personal returns.

Returns of capital are deducted from total dividend income at the bottom of Schedule B. (They are also deducted from the cost of the security in the club's records.)

When issuers have withheld tax from the club's dividend payment, total dividends are recorded on the Earnings Distribution Statement. The total withheld is recorded in the section of your return where other withheld amounts are listed (the reverse side of Form 1040.)

Capital gain income and loss are reported on Schedule D of Form 1040. Short-term capital gains are entered under part I of Schedule D on the line for partnership items. Long- and mid-term capital gains are entered in part II. The individual's share of club expenses shown in column 6 of the Earnings Distribution Statement is listed as a separate item in the Miscellaneous Deduction section of Schedule A as "Share of investment club expenses, $."

If your club received interest income during the year, it is shown as a separate item in the Income and Expense Statement and in a special column of the Earnings Distribution Statement. You report interest on Schedule B, part I of Form 1040 if over $400 and on line 8a of Form 1040 if under.

INDIVIDUAL RETIREMENT ACCOUNTS

Investment club members are allowed to use the club account for their IRAs. NAIC has detailed information on the procedure. Refer to Chapter 17.

FILING FORM 1065

Partnerships file a partnership return (Form 1065) each year. Form 1065 should be filed promptly and completely. Include a copy of the K-1 form for each member. You can get the form from your nearest IRS office or calling 1-800-TAX-FORM.

The IRS may fine each partner for late or incorrect returns. If the club receives notice of a fine, promptly prepare and send a letter to the IRS office explaining why the form was not filed in a timely manner, and ask that the fine be forgiven. If the request is not granted and you receive a second fine notice, rewrite your letter in response to the second letter and specifically request that your letter is forwarded to the next level of authority. Persist until you find the right person at the IRS with authority to forgive the fine.

All contacts with the IRS should be made in writing; keep copies of correspondence in your files.

STATE AND LOCAL RETURNS

You might be required by state and local law to file state income tax, city income tax, and intangible property tax returns. In some locations, partnerships have the option of paying taxes as an organization and exempting individual members. It usually costs less to pay such taxes at the club level rather than individually. Check with your tax advisor to be sure that you understand all state and local reporting and tax requirements.

CHAPTER 23

APPRAISING YOUR FINANCIAL RESULTS

"If you don't know where you're going, any road will get you there." This bit of cynical wisdom holds a lot of truth, and in your investment club, setting specific money and time goals are the only way to know whether you are succeeding. We recommend setting the goal of doubling your money in five years. Why? Because, with proper research and diligence, you can reach this goal. Investment clubs that have subscribed to our philosophy of stock selection have proven repeatedly that this goal is realistic.

The five-year interval spans the average time between market peaks. It may take as little as three years, or as long as eight years, but five years is the standard we use for measuring peak to peak. Because our selection guidelines show you how to judge the value of stocks, you will be able to maximize profits by applying value tests—not only to stocks you're thinking of buying, but also to stocks you already own.

We suggest you apply these three tests to judge how well your club is doing:

1. Determine your actual rate of return by using the procedure outlined in this chapter.

2. Evaluate your results against a broadly based market index, such as the S&P 500, which represents the bulk of the total value of NYSE-listed common stocks.

3. Evaluate your results against those of other clubs of the same age by entering NAIC's annual performance survey. Entry forms are in each May issue of *Better Investing*. Each club is rated on its lifetime earnings rate as well as last year's rate and the club's comparison with the S&P 500 index.

"Success" doesn't demand that you meet or exceed your established standard; setting that goal is only a means of giving yourself a measurement and a focus. As long as your club produces a higher rate of return than you could have achieved through other forms of investing, you're doing a creditable job. And if you're actually earning at the NAIC recommended rate—doubling your money between market peaks—then your club has joined the thousands that have found out for themselves that these ideas work.

PROCEDURE FOR CALCULATING RETURNS

The method we recommend for calculating your rate of return (Figure 23-1) is based on the assumption that member contributions have been made every month in unvarying amounts, exclusive of reinvested dividends. This calculation was developed by Dr. Thomas O. Walton, chairman of the Mathematics Department at Kalamazoo College, under the auspices of Smith-Hague & Co. The method recognizes that the true return on an investment is a combination of dividends and market appreciation.

Figure 23-1
Compound Annual Rate of Increase

Number of Years	3%	4%	5%	6%	7%	8%	9%	10%	12%
1	1.016	1.022	1.027	1.032	1.038	1.043	1.048	1.053	1.064
2	2.063	2.084	2.105	2.126	2.148	2.169	2.191	2.212	2.255
3	3.141	3.189	3.237	3.286	3.336	3.385	3.436	3.487	3.590
4	4.251	4.338	4.426	4.516	4.607	4.699	4.793	4.889	5.084
5	5.395	5.533	5.674	5.819	5.967	6.118	6.273	6.431	6.758
6	6.573	6.776	6.985	7.200	7.422	7.650	7.886	8.128	8.633
7	7.786	8.069	8.361	8.664	8.979	9.305	9.643	9.994	10.732
8	9.036	9.413	9.806	10.216	10.645	11.092	11.559	12.047	13.084
9	10.323	10.811	11.323	11.861	12.427	13.022	13.648	14.305	15.718
10	11.649	12.265	12.916	13.605	14.335	15.107	15.924	16.788	18.666

Use this chart to determine your annual rate of return, and evaluate your results against returns for NYSE stocks and the success rates of similar clubs.

Here is a list of the steps to follow:

1. Determine the market value of the individual capital account as of the close of the last fiscal year.

2. Determine the total annual individual investment by multiplying the monthly contribution by 12, not including reinvested dividends.

3. Divide the amount in step 1 by the amount in step 2 to the third decimal place.

4. Determine the number of fiscal years over which the annual contribution has been made.

5. Locate the row in Figure 23-1 corresponding to the number of years in step 4.

6. In the row for the number of years, find the number closest to the quotient referred to in step 3.

7. Read up to the head of the column for the percentage figure representing the compound annual rate of increase in the value of the individual capital account.

8. Examples:
   a. Monthly contribution = $10

      Value of individual capital account at end of last fiscal year = $912.12

Figure 23-1 (Continued)
Compound Annual Rate of Increase

14%	16%	18%	20%	22%	24%	26%	28%	30%	32%
1.074	1.085	1.095	1.105	1.116	1.126	1.136	1.146	1.156	1.166
2.299	2.343	2.387	2.431	2.477	2.522	2.567	2.613	2.659	2.705
3.695	3.803	3.912	4.023	4.137	4.253	4.370	4.490	4.612	4.736
5.278	5.497	5.711	5.933	6.163	6.399	6.642	6.894	7.152	7.418
7.098	7.460	7.834	8.225	8.634	9.060	9.505	9.970	10.454	10.958
9.170	9.738	10.339	10.975	11.649	12.361	13.113	13.907	14.746	15.631
11.602	12.333	13.295	14.275	15.327	16.453	17.658	18.947	20.326	21.799
14.231	15.446	16.783	18.235	19.815	21.527	23.385	25.398	27.579	29.941
17.280	19.003	20.899	22.987	25.290	27.820	30.601	33.656	37.009	40.688
20.777	23.128	25.756	28.690	31.969	35.622	39.693	44.225	49.268	54.874

Number of fiscal years contribution was made = 6

Multiply $10 by 12 = $120

Divide $912.12 by 120 = 7.601

Locate the number closest to 7.601 in the row for 6 years (the closest number is 7.650). Read up to 8 percent, which equals the annual rate of increase.

b. Monthly contribution = $20

Value of individual capital account at end of last fiscal year = $2,017.58

Number of years contribution was made = 7

Multiply $20 by 12 = $240

Divide $2,017.58 by 240 = 8.406

Locate the number closest to 8.406 in the row for 7 years, which is 8.361. Read up to 5 percent.

You should note that these answers are approximate and not precise. A ballpark figure is sufficient to indicate whether your results are in the right direction and whether they are sufficient to bring you close to your goal.

If you meet with initial success, don't allow yourself or fellow club members to become overconfident. As the English novelist Samuel Butler said, "Money is like the reputation for ability—more easily made than kept." And don't be discouraged if you are not ahead of the game from the start. Clubs typically lose money the first year or two, until reinvested capital gains and dividends begin to have an effect. Remember that you are in the market for the long term.

Commenting in *The Wall Street Journal,* Charles R. Schwab, founder of the major discount brokerage, reminded readers that researchers have convincingly demonstrated that stocks provide superior returns over extended holding periods. Despite this evidence, most people contributing to employer-sponsored defined-contribution plans direct their retirement funds into fixed-rate investments. Schwab wrote, "I find this disturbing. By taking the low-risk, low-reward path, millions of Americans are limiting their financial future. . . . Take charge of your financial future. No one else can do it for you."

PART

More About
NAIC

THREE

CHAPTER 24

OBJECTIVES AND PROGRAMS

NAIC is founded on the belief that investors succeed when they establish clear programs and standards and when they follow those programs and standards according to sensible rules. NAIC takes the same advice. We have two important purposes. The first is to encourage people to own stocks directly. The second is to provide a learn-by-doing investment program for everyone who wants to be a self-reliant investor, alone or as a member of an investment club.

ENCOURAGING INDIVIDUAL OWNERSHIP

Approximately 60 million Americans invest as individuals in this country today, and they hold nearly $1.8 trillion in stocks. Yet the individual investor's influence in the market appears to be in decline when you look at the overall market. During the past ten years, individual net purchases and sales of common stock have declined drastically as a percentage of total market volume. In the 1950s the individual investor was responsible for 80 percent of New York Stock Exchange trading. Now, the situation is reversed: 80 percent of today's trades are institutional investors; less than 20 percent are individual trades. Similarly, the percentage of individual investors' financial assets in equities plummeted from 43 percent to 18 percent during the past two decades. A rebound from that low began in 1988, but the level is currently approximately 25 percent.

We believe that institutional investors cannot provide the level of market diversity and liquidity achievable by the actions of many individuals. For this reason, NAIC has joined with over 400 American corporations in sponsoring the "Own Your Share of America" campaign. The initiative is designed to encourage direct individual share ownership by pointing out the advantages to individuals and public companies, and by simplifying the methods of transfer and ownership of shares.

NAIC also intends to lobby for legislation favorable to individual investors. NAIC backs a capital gains tax program that would do the following:

1. Exempt the first $25,000 of capital gains annually from taxation for individual investors.

2. Grant a lifetime exemption of $500,000 on an individual's overall equity investment.

3. Allow an individual investor to roll over capital gains without taxation until retirement age, and then pay gains as they are realized, in a way similar to deferral rules for investment real estate.

4. Index the tax base of capital gains to offset the effects of inflation.

HELPING WITH INVESTMENT TOOLS

People launch investment programs with a variety of goals in mind. As an investor, you may want to accumulate capital to start a business of your own. Or you might want to fund higher education for your children. Virtually all investors have in mind a financially secure retirement, free of the money worries that plague those who failed to plan for the future. Of course, no investment club program should be undertaken until an adequate savings account for emergencies and suitable insurance coverage have been established.

The accompanying table (Figure 24-1) shows the savings of capital at the rate of $200 per month during the ages 40 through 59 and withdrawal at $5,000 per year plus 3 percent inflation during the ages 60 through 79, with income compounded annually at 7 percent. After nineteen years of withdrawals, a sizable portion of the total assets is still available. In order to plan realistically for your retirement, we recommend that you calculate your own retirement needs based on higher or lower deposits and withdrawals, and based on interest rates you believe to be realistic.

Figure 24-1
Retirement Statistics

	Saving $2,400 Annually			Withdrawing $5,000 Annually plus 3 Percent Inflation	
Age	Save	Principal	Age	Withdraw	Principal
40	$2,400	$2,400	60	$5,000	$106,996
41	2,400	5,136	61	5,150	109,335
42	2,400	8,064	62	5,305	111,684
43	2,400	11,196	63	5,464	114,039
44	2,400	14,548	64	5,628	116,394
45	2,400	18,134	65	5,796	118,745
46	2,400	21,971	66	5,970	121,087
47	2,400	26,077	67	6,149	123,414
48	2,400	30,471	68	6,334	125,719
49	2,400	35,172	69	6,524	127,995
50	2,400	40,202	70	6,720	130,235
51	2,400	45,584	71	6,921	132,430
52	2,400	51,343	72	7,129	134,572
53	2,400	57,505	73	7,343	136,649
54	2,400	64,098	74	7,563	138,652
55	2,400	71,153	75	7,790	140,567
56	2,400	78,702	76	8,024	142,384
57	2,400	86,779	77	8,264	144,086
58	2,400	95,421	78	8,512	145,660
59	2,400	104,669	79	8,768	147,089

The illustration makes our point that even those investors who wait until middle age to begin an equities investment program can create an important supplement to other sources of retirement income, such as employer pension plans and Social Security.

The NAIC investment philosophy certainly helps you to achieve financial security in the future. We also offer a complete array of services for you individually and as an investment club member. These include:

NAIC Councils. Operating in more than 100 areas around the nation, Councils provide local NAIC members a nearby educational resource. Programs range from instruction in the use of NAIC stock study tools to large Investors Fairs, complete with presentations by corporate officials and investment professionals.

Low-Cost Investment Plan. This is a simple, nearly cost-free opportunity to invest in one or all of the stocks of participating companies' dividend reinvestment plans, offering the opportunity to make monthly additional cash contributions to your equity holdings.

NAIC Growth Fund, Inc. This is a closed-end mutual fund set up for investment using NAIC principles.

NAIC Stock Service. Another low-cost program for accumulating wealth in equities. This program allows you to purchase stocks and consolidate all your holdings in one account, receiving monthly statements.

Investors Congress. This is an annual convention featuring lectures, workshops, and seminars by investment professionals, as well as the chance to swap ideas with other investors and take post-meeting tours.

World Federation of Investors Meeting. Held biennially, this get-together in a major overseas business center affords a world view of investing. A post-meeting tour is available for NAIC members wishing to extend their trip.

Investors Expo. We sponsor an annual exposition designed for the public, with corporate displays, workshops, seminars, and other investing information for beginning and advanced investors.

Investment Education Institute. A separate organization established by the Trust. It has worked primarily with the Business School at Wayne State University on investment education subjects. Each year it awards a Distinguished Service Award in Investment Education to selected individuals who have made major contributions to investment education, and has started a youth investing program.

NAIC Computer Group. About 85 percent of NAIC's membership owns or has access to a computer. Organized to increase investment education through computers, the Computer Group offers NAIC members, for an additional fee, a newsletter, computerized stock studies, regional seminars, an online investor forum, and discounts on NAIC investment software. The annual CompuFest highlights the group's many activities.

NAIC Investor Advisory Service. A subscription service providing the individual or club detailed information including a completed Stock Selection Guide study of three corporations each month as investment recommendations.

Better Investing Magazine. One of the nation's most widely read financial publications, *Better Investing* is included in NAIC dues and contains ideas on stocks to study, investment techniques, and investment club news.

Other NAIC Aids

NAIC Stock Study Course

NAIC Accounting Manual & Accounting Kit

NAIC Stock Check List

NAIC Stock Selection Guide and Report

NAIC Stock Selection Guide

NAIC Giant Stock Selection Guide

NAIC Stock Comparison Guide

NAIC Ratio Calculator

NAIC Portfolio Management Guide

Challenge Tree Comparative Form

PERT (Portfolio Evaluation Review Technique)

NAIC Youth Study Course, Investing for Life

NAIC Mutual Fund Handbook

NAIC Model Investment Club Video (VHS)

NAIC Stock Selection Guide Video (VHS)

A more comprehensive and detailed description of NAIC publications, services, and supplies, along with an order form, are listed in the NAIC Membership Guide, available from NAIC on request.

CHAPTER 25

HISTORY AND ORGANIZATION

*T*he National Association of Investors Corporation is primarily a volunteer organization, with only a small paid staff. The work of NAIC would be impossible without the ability and dedication of those volunteers who serve in so many capacities and in so many locations without compensation.

NAIC was formed in 1951 by representatives of four Michigan investment clubs. One of these, the Mutual Investment Club of Detroit, remains active today. More than 400 of NAIC's member clubs are at least twenty-five years old.

The Association is an independent Michigan not-for-profit organization, free of control by any individual, company, or financial institution.

The trust agreement that marked the organization's beginnings provided for a board of trustees to govern NAIC. The trustees set up a not-for-profit corporation (the N.I.A. Corporation) to be governed by directors elected by the membership. This structure remains in place.

NAIC has three classes of membership: individuals, investment clubs, and corporations. Members pay dues to and are members of the National Association of Investors Corporation, which extends membership to any appropriate Council. NAIC belongs to the World Federation of Investment Clubs, Inc., and thus NAIC members belong to the worldwide group.

The Trust established a separate corporation to operate NAIC Advisory Service. A nominee partnership was established to expedite the transfer of securities in NAIC's Low-Cost Investment Plan.

Figure 25-1

NATIONAL ASSOCIATION OF INVESTMENT CLUBS TRUST

Owns Stock of National Association of Investors Corporation
Owns Stock of the NAIC Investment Advisory Corporation

Board of Advisors

THE NAIC INVESTMENT ADVISORY SERVICE

NAIC GROWTH FUND, INC.

NAIC ASSOCIATES
Nominee Partnership

LOW COST STOCK PURCHASE PLAN

NATIONAL ASSOCIATION OF INVESTORS CORPORATION

A Michigan Not-for-Profit Stock Corporation

An Operating Organization Providing Services to Members

PUBLICATIONS

INVESTMENT EDUCATION INSTITUTE

TRADE ASSOCIATION TYPE ACTIVITIES

NICHOLSON AWARDS

INVESTORS INFORMATION REPORTS

FIDELITY BOND

NAIC COMPUTER GROUP

SOFTWARE

BITS

NAIC CORPORATE ADVISORY COMMITTEE

NATIONAL INVESTORS CORPORATION

A Michigan Not-for-Profit Membership Corporation

INVESTORS EXPO

ANNUAL INVESTORS CONGRESS

REGIONAL COUNCILS

WORLD FEDERATION OF INVESTMENT CLUBS, INC.

A Non-Profit Membership Corporation

MEMBERS

INDIVIDUALS | INVESTMENT CLUBS | CORPORATIONS

Indicates Membership Flow
Indicates Control Flow
Indicates Services Flow

238

In 1990, acting on the suggestion of many members, the Trust established the NAIC Growth Fund, Inc. This is a closed-end investment fund dedicated to NAIC investment principles.

There are two advisory groups assisting different divisions of NAIC. The Board of Advisors counsels the Trust and the National Association of Investors Corporation on matters of policy and investment education. The Corporate Advisory Committee works with the National Association of Investors Corporation and the N.I.A. Corporation in conducting the Investors Expo and in developing new programs and projects.

The accompanying chart (Figure 25-1) depicts the flow of control, membership, and services in the organization.

GLOSSARY

*A*bout the abbreviations: cf. stands for Latin *confer,* meaning "compare." q.v. stands for Latin *quod vide,* meaning "which see," a cross-reference.

Accelerated depreciation.   Provision for recovery of the cost of an asset whose value will decline over a period of time. This is accomplished through deductions against income, with larger deductions taken in earlier years.

Accounts payable.   A current liability; debts owed by a company to its suppliers that must be paid within the course of a year.

Accounts receivable.   A current asset; debts owed to a company by its customers that the company expects to collect within the course of a year.

Accrued taxes.   A current liability; taxes owed by a company to various governmental bodies.

Accrued wages.   A current liability; money owed by a company to its employees.

Accumulated profits.   Same as retained income (q.v.).

Acid test ratio.   The sum of a company's cash, accounts receivable, and marketable securities divided by its total current liabilities. A test of financial liquidity.

Amortization.   Reduction of debt through periodic payments consisting of interest and part of principal.

Area method.   A way of drawing the trend line on the Stock Selection Guide chart so that there is an equal amount of area above and below the trend line. (cf. mid-point method and best judgment method.)

Asked.   The price demanded by a willing seller. (cf. bid.)

Asset.   Something of value owned by a company. May be tangible, such as a piece of machinery, or intangible, such as goodwill. (cf. current asset and fixed asset.)

Authorized stock.   The total number of shares that a corporation, as indicated in its charter, is authorized to sell. May or may not be the same as outstanding stock (q.v.).

Averages.   Selected lists of stocks or bonds whose price action is considered representative of the market as a whole. The best-known averages are the Dow Jones and Standard & Poor's.

Balance sheet.   A financial statement detailing, as of a certain point in time, a company's assets, liabilities, and capital. Assets minus liabilities equals net worth, or the equity of the company's stockholders. The balance sheet indicates a company's financial strength and solvency.

Bear.   An investor who anticipates a market decline.

Bear market.   A declining market.

Best judgment method.   A way of drawing the trend line on the NAIC Stock Selection Guide chart, based on the analyst's use of his or her best judgment. (cf. area method and midpoint method.)

Beta.   A coefficient that measures volatility relative to the total market, usually as represented by the S&P 500.

Bid.   The price offered by a willing buyer. (cf. asked.)

Big Board.   Nickname for the New York Stock Exchange, the nation's largest.

Black Monday.   October 19, 1987, when the Dow Jones Industrial Average dropped over 500 points.

Bond.   An instrument of debt. In issuing bonds, a corporation agrees to pay holders a stated rate of interest until principal is repaid on a specified date.

Bondholder.   A creditor. In buying corporate bonds, an individual acquires no portion of ownership in the company, but assumes less risk than a stockholder (q.v.).

Bond ratio.   That portion of a company's capital structure consisting of bonds, found by dividing the face value of bonds by the total value of bonds, preferred stock, common stock, capital surplus, and retained earnings.

Book value of common stock.   The value of common stock of a company, found by adding the par value of the common stock, retained earnings, and surplus reserves. Book value per common share may then be determined by dividing this sum by the number of outstanding common shares. Book value has no relation to market value.

Broker.   A firm or individual who arranges a transfer of securities between a buyer and a seller, charging a fee for the service.

Business cycle.   The phases of transition in a free economy, consisting of prosperity, recession, depression, and recovery.

Buy zone.   The computed range on NAIC forms that signals favorable buy prices for the analyzed security.

Capital gain or capital loss.   Profit or loss from the sale of a capital asset, such as securities.

Capitalism.   An economic system that permits private, rather than public, ownership of the means of production, and free pricing of products.

Capitalist.   Anyone who provides funds for the conducting of a business.

Capitalization.   The total value, as stated in a company's books, of bonds and preferred and common stock outstanding. (cf. capital structure.)

Capital structure.   The total of bonds, preferred stock, reserves, and retained earnings. (cf. capitalization.)

Cash dividend.   The earnings of a corporation directed by the board to be paid to the stockholders in cash. (cf. stock dividend.)

Cash flow.   The net income of a company, with the addition of any non-cash deductions from income such as depreciation and depletion. Since cash flow represents the actual amount of money generated by a company, it is considered by some analysts to be a more meaningful figure than net income.

Cash flow statement.   A report showing a company's cash flow over selected periods of time. This statement offers the best evidence of a company's debt-paying ability.

Challenge Tree.   An NAIC form used to compare the merits of holding a stock against those of a prospective purchase.

Cheap stock.   Not necessarily a low-priced stock, but one that is selling at a lower price/earnings ratio than would appear justified by corporate results.

Combined yield.   The total return from a stock, consisting of cash and stock dividends and price appreciation.

Common stock.   A representation of ownership in a corporation. Typically, common stockholders elect the company's board of directors, whose responsibilities include declaring of dividends. In case of dissolution of the company, common stockholders have last claim on assets.

Common stock ratio.   That portion of a company's capital structure consisting of common stock. The stated value of common stock, any paid-in capital, and retained earnings divided by the total value of bonds, preferred stock, common stock, paid-in capital, and retained earnings.

Consolidated statement.   A statement that includes figures for a company and all of its subsidiaries.

Corporation.   An entity created by law with perpetual life and limited liability of shareholders.

Cost of goods sold.   The cost of labor, materials, and overhead that properly may be assigned to units produced. (cf. selling, general, and administrative expenses.)

Cost of products sold.   Same as cost of goods sold (q.v.).

Cost of sales.   Same as cost of goods sold (q.v.).

Creditor.   An individual or entity that lends money to a company, e.g., a bondholder, buyer of commercial paper, or extender of trade credit.

Curb.   Nickname for the American Stock Exchange.

Current asset.   An asset that can be converted into cash within a year. Current assets are listed in the balance sheet in order of their ease of convertibility to cash: cash, government securities, accounts receivable, and inventories.

Current liability.   A liability of a company that must be paid within one year.

Current ratio.   A firm's current assets divided by its current liabilities.

Cyclical growth stock.   A stock that is very dependent on the business cycle, and reaches new highs in sales and earnings in each succeeding period of prosperity.

Debenture.   A bond not secured by any specific property but backed only by the general credit of the issuing company.

Deferred charge.   Also known as *deferred expense* or *prepaid expense,* an asset that represents payment for a good or service properly chargeable to a future period. Payment of a premium on an insurance policy with several years to run is a common deferred charge.

Deferred expense.   Same as deferred charge (q.v.).

Depletion.   A charge against earnings derived from a natural resource. Depletion recognizes exhaustion of the resource through its continued conversion into a salable product. Lumber and oil companies are among those listing depletion on their balance sheets. The provision for depletion may exceed the cost of the natural reserve.

Depreciation.   Recovery of the cost of an asset that will be worn out over a period of time. (cf. accelerated depreciation and straight-line depreciation.)

Dilution.   The effect on earnings and book value per share when the number of shares issued by a company increases disproportionately to growth in company earnings or assets. New shares can be created by the conversion feature in some bonds, debentures, and preferred stock; additional shares can also result from stock dividends, stock splits, options and warrants, and, of course, a new issue. If the book value of new shares is less than that of the old shares, dilution has occurred.

Dividend.   Payment a company makes, in cash or stock, to its shareholders from retained earnings.

Dividend yield.   Found by dividing the cash dividend per share by market price per share. Lower yields are associated with growth companies, higher yields with more mature companies.

Dollar cost averaging.   Buying a set dollar amount of a security at stated intervals. Over a period of time, the average cost will be lower than the average price of the shares, since more shares will be purchased when the price is low and fewer when the price is high.

Dow Jones Average.   (Dow Jones Industrial Average). Average of the prices of thirty leading industrial stocks. Dow Jones Transportation and Utility averages are also widely watched.

Downside risk.   On NAIC forms, the difference between present price and estimated low price for the next five years.

Earned surplus.   Profits that have been kept in the business rather than being distributed as dividends. Also called *undistributed earnings or profits, accumulated profits, retained earnings,* or *retained income.*

Earnings per share.   Of paramount concern to the common shareholder, earnings per share is found by dividing net income after any preferred dividends by the number of shares of common stock outstanding.

Earnings plowback.   Reinvesting earnings in a business rather than paying them out to stockholders in the form of dividends.

Earnings report.   A financial statement (also called *income statement* or *profit and loss statement*) that shows a company's operating results over a period of time and gives evidence of the company's profitability.

Economies of scale.   Savings realized by larger corporations, which are able to spread fixed costs over a larger number of units produced.

Equity capital.   Funds furnished by the owners of a business.

Exchange.   A meeting place for the representatives of buyers and sellers of securities.

Ex dividend.   From the Latin, meaning "without dividend." When a stock is selling ex dividend, the buyer does not receive the soon-to-be paid dividend; rather, it remains the property of the seller.

FIFO.   Abbreviation for *first in, first out;* a method of inventory valuation. Inventory issued is priced at the cost of the oldest inventory on hand (cf. LIFO.)

Financial leverage.   Same as leverage (q.v.).

Financial risk.   One of the important types of risk confronting investors, it acknowledges that companies may suffer adversity that would affect their ability to make payments to investors and/or creditors. (cf. interest rate risk, purchasing power risk.)

Financial statement.   A report depicting a corporation's financial condition as of a given date or financial results for a given period. The most common financial statements are the balance sheet (q.v.), earnings report (q.v.), and cash flow statement (q.v.).

Fiscal period.   A span of time selected as an accounting period. The fiscal year often coincides with the calendar year, although it need not. Companies may follow the business year, closing their books when business activity is slackest. An example is retailers, who close their books in January (following the Christmas selling season).

Fixed asset. Property of a company that will not be used up or converted into cash within a year's time.

Fixed asset turnover. A measurement of efficiency, found by dividing fixed assets before depreciation into net sales. The more rapid the turnover, the better.

Fixed cost. A business expense that continues even if production ceases. (cf. variable cost.)

Fixed income investments. Those investments, including bonds and (usually) preferred stock, for which the company is committed to paying a specific amount of return to investors.

Fixed liability. A debt of a company that will not be paid for a year or more.

Form 1065. A tax form that must be filed by all investment clubs operating as partnerships.

Forms 10-K and 10-Q. Filing requirements of the Securities and Exchange Commission. The 10-K may contain more financial information than the annual report, while the 10-Q offers more data than interim reports.

Formula investing. Investing by prearranged design. Dollar cost averaging (q.v.) is a popular type of formula investing.

Free enterprise. Same as capitalism (q.v.).

Funded debt. Debt carrying a provision that cash must be set aside each year to provide for payment of the debt at maturity.

Funding. A company's conversion of short-term debt into long-term debt.

Goodwill. An asset that arises from business combinations accounted for under the purchase method; represents the cost to a purchaser in excess of the fair value of net assets (equity) of an acquired business. This amount appears in the parent company's balance sheet as an intangible item that is amortized as an expense over a period not to exceed forty years.

Government bond. An evidence of U.S. government debt, considered to offer the lowest possible financial risk (q.v.).

Government securities. U.S. government obligations (bills, notes, and bonds) in which companies invest excess cash. The investments are classified as cash equivalents or marketable securities, depending on their maturities. Federal agency obligations issued by the Federal Home Loan Mortgage Corporation (Freddie Mac) and the Federal National Mortgage Association (Fannie Mae) are also included in this category.

Gross domestic product. The new statistic offered by the U.S. government to supplant gross national product. The value of goods and services produced in the United States during a specified period of time. An important indicator of the state of the nation's economy.

Gross profit. Net sales minus cost of goods sold. The higher the gross profit margin (q.v.), the better.

Gross profit margin. Gross profit (q.v.) divided by net sales. Also called gross margin.

Gross sales. Sales before deductions for returns and allowances. (cf. net sales.)

Growth stock. The stock of a company whose growth is faster than that of the economy as a whole.

Hidden asset. An asset, such as a trade secret, that does not appear on a company's books.

Hold zone. On NAIC forms, the calculated price range where securities are neither a buy nor a sell.

Hot tip. A story suggesting a favorable development for a company. You're likely to get burned if you follow such advice. NAIC's rational approach to investing requires that figures support the story.

Income stock. A stock offering a liberal yield.

Inflation. A period during which the purchasing power of the dollar is declining.

Insolvency. The state that exists for a corporation when liabilities exceed assets and it is not able to pay its debts.

Inspection method. Same as best judgment method (q.v.).

Interest. Payment to a creditor by a borrower for the use of money.

Interest rate risk. One of the important types of risk confronting investors. Acknowledges that changes in the interest rate may affect the market value of a security. (cf. financial risk and purchasing power risk.)

Inventory. The raw materials, goods in progress, and finished goods of a company.

Inventory turnover. A measurement of efficiency, found by dividing the cost of goods sold for a period by average inventory at cost for the same period. The faster the turnover, the better.

Invested capital. Same as capital structure (q.v.).

IRA. Abbreviation for Individual Retirement Account, a means of deferring taxes on investment income, dividends, and price appreciation. IRAs may be held in investment club accounts.

Leverage. The use of nonequity capital in the hope of increasing the return on equity (q.v.).

Liabilities. The claims of creditors. (cf. current liability, fixed liability.)

Lien. A claim of a creditor against property of a company. Bonds may be secured by liens against real estate or equipment.

LIFO. Abbreviation for *last in, first out;* a method of inventory valuation. Inventory issued is priced at the cost of the newest inventory on hand. (cf. FIFO.)

Limited liability. Restriction of liability to the amount invested. Stockholders enjoy limited liability.

Liquid assets. Current assets that can be quickly converted into cash.

Liquidating value. In an investment club, the total number of valuation units multiplied by the dollar value per unit. The current market value of the club.

Liquidity. The ease with which a company's assets can be converted into cash. A business is said to be liquid when it holds a high proportion of liquid assets.

Listed security. A security that has met the requirements for trading on one or more of the nation's stock exchanges. (cf. off-board security.)

Long-term capital gains. Gains on securities held more than one year. (cf. short-term capital gains.)

Long-term capital losses. Losses on securities held more than one year. (cf. short-term capital losses.)

Long-term debt. On the balance sheet, borrowed funds that are due for payment after one year, usually over several years.

Long-term liabilities.   Obligations that fall due after one year, including long-term debt, deferred income taxes, and deferred credits.

Lower of cost or market.   A conservative rule of accounting that prices an item at the lower of its current market value or the price paid for it.

Market price.   The price at which transactions in a security take place.

Market timing.   The strategy used by the speculator who hopes to buy low and sell high by going in and out of the market.

Market value.   Current value of an asset; its sale price on the open market. Used in financial statements to value marketable securities and inventories.

Maturity.   The date on which an obligation falls due.

Merchandise turnover.   The same as inventory turnover (q.v.).

Midpoint method.   An approach to determining the trend line on the NAIC Stock Selection Guide chart where the average figures for the first and last five-year periods are used to locate the trend line. (cf. area method, best judgment method.)

Mortgage.   One form of long-term debt on the balance sheet. Represents an obligation of a company secured by specific assets, generally plant, property, and equipment.

Multiple.   Another term for price/earnings ratio (q.v.).

Net before taxes.   Same as pre-tax profit (q.v.).

Net income.   Profit after taxes.

Net interest margin.   The profit margin for financial institutions, found by dividing net interest revenues by average earning assets.

Net sales.   Gross sales (q.v.) minus returns and allowances. Synonymous terms are revenues, gross income, and receipts.

Net working capital.   The difference between current assets (q.v.) and current liabilities (q.v.).

Net worth.   All assets minus all liabilities of a corporation; equivalent to stock, paid-in capital, and retained earnings.

New York Stock Exchange.   The largest auction market securities exchange in the nation.

Nonoperating income and expense.   Income and expense of a corporation not connected with the principal business. Sale of property is an example of non-operating income; payment of interest to bondholders is an example of non-operating expense.

Notes payable.   A current liability on the balance sheet for money owed usually to a bank by a company, as evidenced by promissory notes.

Odd lot.   Less than a round lot, which is the established unit of trading in a security. For most issues, from one to ninety-nine shares constitutes an odd lot.

Off-board security.   Same as unlisted or over-the-counter security, one not listed on a stock exchange.

Operating expenses.   Selling, general, and administrative expenses; those costs of doing business that cannot properly be charged against units produced.

Operating profit.   Gross profit minus operating expenses.

Operating ratio.   A measurement of efficiency, calculated as cost of goods sold plus selling, general, and administrative expenses divided by net sales. The smaller the result, the better.

Ordinary income rate.   The rate at which the federal government taxes a particular level of earned income.

Other income and expense.   Same as nonoperating income and expense (q.v.).

Outstanding stock.   Stock issued and in the hands of owners.

Overhead.   Costs incurred in manufacturing other than those for materials and direct labor. Electrical power is an example.

Over-the-counter market.   Marketplace for securities that, because the issuing companies cannot qualify or do not care to do so, are not listed on any securities exchange.

Paid-in capital.   Capital arising from payments by stockholders, in contrast to earned surplus, which arises from profits.

Pay-out ratio.   The ratio of cash dividends to earnings. Normally, growth stocks pay out a smaller portion of their earnings in dividends than do income stocks.

Peak period month.   A method for computing the trend line on the Stock Selection Guide chart. Under this plan, the trend line goes through the two most recent peaks in performance. (cf. best judgment method, area method.)

Percent earned on equity. Net earnings divided by total capitalization, less any debt. The bigger the return, the better.

PERT. Portfolio Evaluation Review Technique, an NAIC tool permitting investors to keep current on the latest figures on their holdings and to take action as appropriate.

Pink sheets. Report available at brokerage offices that lists current prices for less popular over-the-counter stocks whose worth is not reported in the newspaper.

Plant turnover. Same as fixed asset turnover (q.v.).

Portfolio. All of the securities held by an individual, investment club, or institution.

Portfolio Management Guide. An NAIC tool permitting users to keep watch over the price movement of their holdings.

Preferred stock. Stock with claim on dividends and assets that takes precedence over common stock.

Preferred stock ratio. That portion of a company's capital structure consisting of preferred stock. The stated value of preferred stock divided by the total of bonds, preferred stock, common stock, retained earnings, and capital surplus.

Prepaid expense. A current asset representing an advance payment, generally for services and supplies, that is classified as current on the balance sheet.

Pre-tax profit. Earnings or income before taxes.

Pre-tax profit margin. Profit before taxes divided by sales. The higher the margin, the better.

Price appreciation. The advance in price of a security. Typically, price appreciation results from two factors: increased earnings and a higher price/earnings ratio.

Price/earnings ratio. The market price of a security divided by the earnings per share. Used to determine whether a stock represents value at a given price.

Pro forma. A manner of presenting financial information, showing the combined full-year results of a parent and company acquired during the year.

Profit. Same as earnings or income.

Profit and loss statement. Same as earnings report (q.v.).

Prospectus. In fulfillment of a federal requirement, the prospectus is issued by corporations to give investors considering purchase of a new issue information on solvency, profitability, and other matters.

Purchasing power risk. One of the important types of risks confronting investors. Recognizes that the value of a stock issue may be affected by a change in the value of the dollar. (cf. financial risk, interest rate risk.)

Quality. A rating given to bonds and stocks by a recognized rating service. A requirement for Challenge Tree users is to find a challenging security of equal or higher quality.

Quick asset. A current asset readily converted into cash. Cash, marketable securities, and accounts receivable are all quick assets.

Quick asset ratio. Same as acid test ratio (q.v.).

Ratio analysis. Appraisal of the equality of a prospective investment through computational relationships between various balance sheet and income statement items.

Ratio calculator. NAIC tool for doing ratio analysis.

Ratio chart. A graph, such as the one on the Stock Selection Guide, that depicts relative changes or geometric progressions. Used to plot rates of growth in sales and earnings.

Receipts. Same as sales and revenues.

Receivables. A current asset representing amounts owed to a company that are to be collected within the next year.

Refunding. Replacing one bond issue with another of a lower rate when it is to the financial advantage of the corporation to do so.

Registrar. The agent, usually a bank or trust company, responsible for issuing and distributing shares of stock and bonds.

Relative value. For NAIC investors, the current price/earnings ratio (based on EPS for the latest twelve months) as a percent of the historical average price/earnings ratio.

Reserves. Profits that are set aside for certain purposes.

Retained earnings. Same as retained income (q.v.).

Retained income. Money a company keeps from net profits in order to finance its operations.

Return. Same as yield (q.v.).

Return on book.   Percent earned on book value, or percent earned on equity (q.v.).

Revenues.   Synonymous with sales and receipts.

Risk capital.   Refers to the nature of money that should be invested in the stock market, funds not earmarked for specific near-term purposes.

Round lot.   The established unit of trading in a security, usually 100 shares. (cf. odd lot.)

Rule of five.   A rule for investors stating that for every five stocks purchased, one will experience unforeseen difficulties, three will perform more or less as expected, and one will far exceed what was forecast for it.

Sales.   Same as net sales, revenues, or receipts.

Securities and Exchange Commission.   A federal agency that regulates the securities business and protects the interests of the investing public.

Selling, general, and administrative expenses.   Nonmanufacturing expenses such as salaries of executives, commissions paid to salespeople, and advertising and public relations outlays.

Sell zone.   On NAIC forms, that range of calculated prices indicating that the holding is a candidate for sale.

Semilog chart.   A chart such as the one used in the Visual Analysis section of the NAIC Stock Selection Guide, where the vertical scale is based on logarithms. Equal vertical distances represent equal percentage changes, regardless of the absolute values involved.

Shareholder.   Synonymous with stockholder or shareowner, the owner of one or more shares of a corporation.

Shareholders' equity.   Same as equity capital (q.v.).

Short-term capital gains.   Gains for tax purposes on securities held one year or less.

Short-term capital losses.   Losses on securities held one year or less.

Solvency.   Measure of a company's ability to meet its long-term debt obligations. (cf. liquidity.)

Spread.   The difference between a security's bid and asked prices.

Stock Check List.   An NAIC form to be used until the investor has gained mastery of the Stock Selection Guide.

Stock dividend. Distribution of stock to shareholders as a dividend on shares held.

Stockholder. Synonymous with shareholder, the owner of one or more shares of a corporation.

Stock Selection Guide. An NAIC form designed to assist investors in making a judgment about whether or not to buy a security.

Stock split. The issuance of a number of shares for each share of stock outstanding. The common purpose of a split is to broaden ownership and increase marketability.

Straight-line depreciation. A depreciation method in which the same amount is deducted every year.

Street name. Refers to securities held in the name of the broker rather than the customer.

Sum of the years' digits. A form of accelerated depreciation (q.v.).

Surplus. The difference between assets on the one hand and liabilities and capital stock on the other.

Tax identification number. Mandatory for an investment club. Form SS-4 is submitted for a partnership, and the resulting number is furnished to brokers and transfer agents.

Thin market. A market in which there are few offers to buy or sell a security, characteristic of stocks with a small number of shares outstanding.

Trader. An individual who does a good deal of buying and selling in the hope of realizing short-term profits.

Trading on equity. Same as leverage (q.v.).

Transfer agent. A bank or trust company charged with keeping a record of a company's stockholders and with canceling and issuing certificates as shares are bought and sold.

Treasury bill. A U.S. government obligation that matures within a year of issuance.

Treasury bond. A U.S. government obligation that matures more than five years from the date of issuance.

Treasury note. A U.S. government obligation that matures from one to five years from the date of issuance.

Turnover. The volume of trading in a particular security or in the market as a whole.

Undistributed earnings. Same as retained income (q.v.).

Undistributed profits. Same as retained income (q.v.).

Unit value system. An investment club accounting method that permits varying contributions and partial withdrawals as well as skips in contributions.

Unlisted security. Same as an off-board security (q.v.).

Unrealized gain or loss. On paper and not affected by taxes until taken.

Upside/downside ratio. On NAIC forms, a measurement of risk. Divide the upside potential (q.v.) by the downside risk (q.v.).

Upside potential. On NAIC forms, the difference between the calculated high price and the current price.

Valuation statement. Investment club accounting report that lists assets at market value as of a certain date.

Variable cost. The expense of a corporation that varies with the amount of goods produced. (cf. fixed cost.)

Visual Analysis. That portion of the Stock Selection Guide containing the ratio chart, where sales and earnings trend lines are established and prices recorded.

Wasting asset. An asset that is exhausted in production. (cf. depletion.)

Working capital. The difference between current assets and current liabilities. Generally, the number should be positive.

Working capital ratio. Same as current ratio (q.v.).

Yield. The per-share dividend divided by the per-share cost of the stock.

How to Use the Ratio Chart and Calculator

*T*he chart in Section 1 of the Stock Selection Guide, called a ratio or semilog chart, enables you to determine quickly the rate of growth of a company under study.

The chart is ruled so that a consistent rate of growth appears as a straight line. The compounded growth rates of 5, 10, 15, 20, 25, and 30 percent are drawn on the chart for reference.

On the ratio chart, equal vertical distances represent constant percentage relationships. For example, the distances are precisely the same between 1 and 2, 2 and 4, and 4 and 8—all increases of 100 percent.

The chart includes two complete series of ratio rulings, or cycles. The first cycle begins at 1 and ends at 10. The second cycle begins at 10 and goes to 100.

In assigning values to the numbers on the scale, the value corresponding to 1 must be one tenth of the value corresponding to 10 of the first cycle and one hundredth of the value corresponding to 10 of the second cycle. In other words, as you move up a cycle, you must add one zero to each of the numbers.

You can see that you have a wide range of values at your disposal. Depending on the size of the numbers to be plotted., the unit 1 on the ratio chart might represent 10, 100, or even .0001. Whichever value you assign to 1, all other guide numbers must relate. For example, when the baseline represents

100 million, the unit 4 becomes 400 million, the 6 stands for 600 million, and 10 becomes 1 billion.

Figure B-1 shows a variety of correct ways to assign values to the lines on a ratio chart. The last two columns (G and H) depict cases in which a multiple other than 10 is used. You may wish to confine your choices to those employing a multiple of 10 at the baseline; this makes it easier to ascertain that your relationships are correct throughout the cycles.

Note that a ratio chart makes no provision for zero or negative numbers. The numbers to compare must always be positive. When a company suffers losses, these cannot be expressed on a ratio chart.

Caution is called for in plotting figures. There are ten lines (or divisions) between 1 and 2, 2 and 3, and 3 and 4. But between 4 and 5, 5 and 6, 6 and 7, 7 and 8, 8 and 9, and 9 and 10, there are only five lines. Since there are just half as many lines after the 4 guide number is reached, each line past that point must be assigned twice the value of the lines below. Therefore, if each line between units 1 and 2 equals 1, each line between units 4 and 5 must equal 2.

QUICK CALCULATIONS

After you have recorded data on the Stock Selection Guide, NAIC's Ratio Calculator makes it easy to read many ratios directly from the chart. There's no need for separate and more time-consuming mathematical computations. By using the Ratio Calculator, you may determine price/earnings ratio, pre-tax profit margin, percent earned on invested capital, and dividend yield.

In Figure B-2, the earnings per share of a company have been plotted as well as the high and low stock prices for the year. Earnings and prices are recorded on the same scale, so that wherever EPS and price intersect, the price/earnings ratio is 10 to 1.

To determine the high P/E ratio, place the Ratio Calculator parallel to the price bar. The Calculator's index line should be on the EPS mark. Read the figure on the Ratio Calculator where the top of the price bar falls. This is the three quarters past the 16 line, or 16 and three quarters to 1.

Find the low P/E by reading the figure on the Calculator where the bottom of the price bar falls. The answer is about 8.6.

If we plot the pre-tax profit figures on the chart in the same cycle as sales, we can use the Ratio Calculator to read the percent of pre-tax profit earned each year (Figure B-3).

Figure B-1
How to Number on a Ratio Chart

Figure B-2

Figure B-3

Lay the Ratio Calculator on the vertical time line so that the index line of the Calculator is at the sales point. Read the pre-tax profit percentage from the point on the Calculator. In Figure B-3, the answer is approximately 14.5 percent.

To read the percent earned on invested capital, plot book value per share on the chart in the same cycle as earnings per share. Read the relationship on the Ratio Calculator.

To determine dividend yield, plot dividend per share on the same cycle as price and read the answer off the Ratio Calculator.

APPENDIX C

HOW TO READ NEWSPAPER STOCK TABLES

*S*tock prices are quoted daily in most newspapers. Business publications such as *The Wall Street Journal, Investor's Business Daily,* and *Barron's* offer information that is more detailed. However, your local paper probably contains sufficient data for your use.

Prices typically are presented by marketplace. Listed stocks (those traded on an exchange) may be found in the New York Stock Exchange or American Exchange (AMEX) tables. If a regional exchange operates in or near the newspaper's circulation area, a table may also be found for the Pacific, Chicago, Boston, Philadelphia, or Cincinnati exchange. All told, there are about 10,000 listed equities.

Unlisted stocks are those traded over the counter (OTC), the single largest market for stocks. Generally, newspapers report prices only for the most actively traded OTC stocks or those with a local following. There are, after all, more than 50,000 unlisted stocks!

Equities are traded on the basis of eighths of a dollar, a practice dating back to the Spanish real's reign as a world-class monetary unit. (The real was the basis for the "pieces of eight" of pirate tales.) Increasingly, stocks are traded in sixteenths or even thirty-seconds.

LISTED STOCKS

Figure C-1 shows how the New York Stock Exchange table probably appears in your newspaper. The high and low prices for the previous fifty-two weeks appear first, followed by the name of the stock. In the case of Abbott Labs, the high price was $69.50 and the low was $42.875.

Be alert for codes following or preceding names. An explanation of the codes usually accompanies the tables. The letter *s* following the name indicates the stock has split during the past fifty-two weeks, or paid a stock dividend of at least 25 percent. The high and low prices have been adjusted to reflect the split. The *g* following Abitibi indicates that the dividend is in Canadian funds. The *pf* following AdobeRes indicates a preferred stock. In *The Wall Street Journal,* the stock symbol follows the name for NYSE, AMEX, and NASDAQ OTC stocks. All of the other listings shown are common stocks. Following the name is the tape symbol for the stock (e.g., ABT for Abbott Laboratories).

The dividend column depicts the actual cash amount paid annually. If a letter follows the sum shown, the footnotes at the end of the table will explain its meaning. An *a* means the company paid the amount shown plus an extra dividend. The *e* after the dividend for Adams Express indicates there is no regular dividend, but the amount shown was paid last year. If no figure appears in the dividend column, no dividend was paid.

Figure C-1

52 Weeks Hi	52 Weeks Lo	Stock	Sym	Div	Yield %	PE	Vol 100s	Hi	Lo	Close	Net Chg
6 1/2	2 1/2	ATT Cap yen wt			...	...	15	5 1/4	5 1/8	5 1/8	− 1/2
69 1/2	42 7/8	AbbotLab	ABT	1.00	1.6	25	5738	64 3/4	63 1/4	64 1/4	+ 5/8
14 5/8	11 1/2	Abitibi g	ABY	.50	...	...	4	12 7/8	12 3/4	12 7/8	...
5 5/8	3 3/8	AcmeElec	ACE		...	27	176	4 7/8	4 1/2	4 7/8	+ 1/8
▲ 9 3/4	5 1/4	**AcmeCleve**	**AMT**	.40	4.0	...	951	10	9 3/8	10	+ 5/8
40	25 3/8	Acuson	ACN		...	21	823	30 7/8	30 1/2	30 7/8	+ 1/4
20 1/4	15 1/2	AdamsExp	ADX	1.63e	8.6	...	159	18 7/8	18 3/4	18 7/8	...
9 1/8	3 7/8	AdobeRes	ADB		...	...	2927	5	4 7/8	5	...
20 1/8	12 7/8	AdobeRes pfB			...	...	43	14 1/4	14	14	− 1/4
18	10 3/4	AdobeRes pfA			...	...	42	12	12	12	...
21 3/8	7 1/4	**AdvMicro**	**AMD**		...	13	29751	20 3/4	19 7/8	20 5/8	+ 1 1/8
48 1/2	23 1/2	AdvMicro pf		3.00	6.3	...	300	47 3/4	46 3/4	47 1/2	+ 2

The dividend yield is given as a percentage of the current prices. For example, Abbott Labs pays $1.00. When that sum is divided by the current price ($64.25), the yield comes to 1.6 percent. This is the annual cash return on your investment if the dividend remains the same. Dividend yield is based on cash, not on stock dividends. In the example, no yield is shown for ACE, which pays no cash dividend.

The price/earnings ratio comes next. The P/E is the figure you get by dividing the present price by the latest twelve months' earnings per share. No P/E is shown for AMT, a common stock, because the company did not earn a profit in the last twelve months.

The sales figure tells how many shares were traded in the most recent session. The figure is a composite for all exchanges where the security is listed. The 5738 shown for ABT translates to 573,800 shares. Unless a z appears after the sales figure, it is given in hundreds. The z denotes actual sales.

The next three columns show the high, low, and closing prices for the day. For ABT, the high was $64.75, the low $63.25, and the last price $64.25.

The last column represents the change in price from the previous day's close. ABT gained $0.625.

In our example, all of the net changes are fractional, and price fluctuated only moderately during the day's trading. You can be certain no important news concerning any of these companies became known during the session!

OVER-THE-COUNTER STOCKS

OTC stocks are divided into two groups in most publications. The more actively traded are reported in the same manner as the listed stocks. The less actively traded securities will appear as in Figure C-2. A large number of these infrequently traded stocks are listed in what are called *pink sheets,* since the prices are printed on pink paper. Brokers have these lists.

The dividend follows the stock's name. Sales are presented in hundreds. Only the bid and asked prices are shown. The net change reveals the difference from the previous day's bid price.

Basically, the bid price is what buyers are offering. The asked price represents what sellers are seeking. There is no way to tell the day's trading range. The bid and asked prices, as reported, do not necessarily represent actual transactions, but are intended as a guide to the range within which the securities could have been sold or bought at the time the table was compiled.

Figure C-2

Stock	Div	Vol 100s	Bid	Asked	Net Chg
Alcoln' s		1665	11½	11¾ —	2⅜
Alden	.12e	2	3¾	4⅛	. . .
AllACm		62	2⅛	2½ —	½
AldCap		16	2⅞	3⅛	. . .
AldWste		621	5⅞	6⅛	. . .
Alpha1		392	15½	16 —	¼
Alph1 wtB		100	8	8½ —	½
Alphr un		9	8¼	9¼ —	¼

As a rule, an OTC stock buyer pays the asked price; the seller receives the bid price. The difference or spread between the two constitutes profit for the marketmaking brokerage firm. If the marketmaker for Alden buys 100 shares from a selling investor, the firm will pay $375. If there is a buyer seeking a round lot, the firm sells the shares for $412.50 and pockets $37.50. There may be more sellers than buyers, however, and the firm must then commit capital to inventory the shares until buyers can be found. If a buyer and seller bid and ask the same price, between the published bid and asked price, the transaction may not take place unless a marketmaker accepts the offer.

APPENDIX D

SOURCES OF FURTHER INFORMATION

INVESTMENT ADVISORY SERVICES

Donoghue'$ Money Letter. Published by the Donoghue Organization, Inc. This guide to stock funds, bond funds, and money market funds, issued twice monthly, includes mutual fund asset allocation models for conservative, active, or venturesome portfolios.

Emerging and Special Situations. Published monthly by Standard & Poor's with a New Issues supplement. Advice for those interested in small capital stocks, including a recommended list.

Growth Stock Outlook. Edited by Charles Allmon. Mailed twice monthly and designed for those "who recognize the risk and rewards of investing in vigorously growing companies."

Handbook for No-Load Fund Investors. Published annually by Sheldon Jacobs of the No-Load Fund Investor Advisory Service. A directory of more than 1,300 no-load stock and bond funds, along with ten-year performance data on the funds and a section on how to pick and monitor funds.

Handbook of Common Stocks. Published by Moody's, this quarterly provides overviews of more than 900 stocks with high investor interest, including operating data, stock performance, seven- to ten-year comparative earnings per share, dividend and stock price charts, as well as short-and long-term prospects and a discussion of recent corporate developments.

Handbook of Dividend Achievers.   Published annually by Moody's. Lists companies that have increased their annual dividend payout for ten consecutive years or more.

Handbook Guide to Financial Newsletters.   Edited by Mark Hulbert and issued by the New York Institute of Finance, this reference rates more than 100 investment newsletters by clarity of advice, completeness, relative riskiness, and volatility. The methods and philosophies each newsletter follows are named, and the percent gain or loss on recommended investments is given for both short- and long-term periods.

Industry Review.   Published by Moody's and updated semiannually, this loose-leaf service provides comparative key financial and operating data on more than 5,000 corporations covering 145 industry groups.

Moody's Dividend Record Service.   Published twice weekly, the service covers more than 12,500 common and preferred dividend-paying stocks, mutual funds, foreign securities, and nonpaying issues.

Morningstar Mutual Funds.   Published biweekly in two sections by Morningstar, Inc. The first section classifies 1,242 load and no-load equity and fixed income funds by risk, objective, total return, dividends, and net assets. Portfolio manager changes are included. The second section presents detailed information on 120 or so different funds.

Morningstar Mutual Fund Sourcebook.   Annual coverage of 1,800 funds by Morningstar Inc. One volume is devoted to equity funds and the other to fixed income funds. Information includes investment criteria, performance data, risk-adjusted ratings, and more.

Mutual Fund Profiles.   Published quarterly by Standard & Poor's. Covers 750 funds, comprising general and specialized equity funds, balanced funds, and long-term taxable fixed income mutual funds. Description includes investment policy, performance evaluation, portfolio composition, and five-year historical data.

NAIC Investors Advisory Service.   Three stocks are discussed and recommended for purchase each month. A completed NAIC Stock Selection Guide is furnished for each. Also, this service tracks and ranks 80 stocks by selected investment objectives.

Nelson's Earnings Outlook.   A compilation of estimated earnings per share based on figures supplied by security analysts who follow particular stocks and industries.

No-Load Fund Investor.   Edited by Sheldon Jacobs of the No-Load Fund Investor, Inc. Provides comprehensive coverage of virtually all no-load funds available to the public, plus direct marketed low-loads and closed-ends. Offers performance data for seven periods ranging from the latest month to five years. Includes cash positions and betas.

The Outlook.   Published by Standard & Poor's weekly except on legal holidays. Covers the status of the stock market, lists stock to buy and stocks to avoid, and features a stock from S&P's Master List of Recommended Stocks for Superior Long-Term Total Return.

S&P Earnings Guide.   A compilation of estimated earnings per share based on figures supplied by security analysts who follow particular stocks and industries.

S&P Industry Report Service.   Provides a comprehensive look at thirty-seven business sectors from aerospace to utilities, offering fundamental and investment forecasts by industry and buy and sell recommendations on individual stocks within the groupings. Lists more than 800 companies by industry.

S&P Stock Guide.   A monthly pocket-size alphabetical guide to more than 5,300 common and preferred stocks, both listed and over-the-counter. Offers forty-eight items of information on each. A special section contains data on 600 leading mutual funds.

S&P Stock Report Services.   Popularly known as S&P sheets, the services offer salient statistics on about 4,700 companies listed on the New York, American, and regional stock exchanges, as well as over-the-counter issues.

Stock Market Encyclopedia.   Published quarterly by Standard & Poor's. Includes data on 750 companies: industrials, utilities, transportation and financial firms. A full-page report is included for every stock in the S&P 500.

Value Line Investment Survey.   Published by Value Line Publishing Inc. Follows 1,700 stocks and 97 industries in three sections. Part 1 is Summary and Index. Part 2, Selection and Opinion, analyzes and forecasts the national economy and the stock market. Part 3 is Ratios and Reports.

Wall Street Digest.   Monthly digest of investment advice from leading financial advisors.

NEWSPAPERS AND MAGAZINES

Barron's. A business and financial weekly published by Dow Jones & Company. Contains articles on industries and companies, commentary on stock market activity, information on new issues, a summary of research reports, and a comprehensive statistical section including both current and year-ago earnings information.

Better Investing. Monthly magazine of NAIC containing information designed especially for the self-reliant investor. Features include a stock to study, an undervalued stock, selected portfolios, and regular columnists who provide a variety of investment information and ideas.

Business Week. Published weekly except for one issue in January. Covers the general business scene, with departments focusing on the economy, government, finance, science and technology, and personal business, among other topics. Reviews business books.

FW (formerly *Financial World*). Published biweekly except for a combined December/January issue. Departments include market watch, company watch, economic currents, market comments, and special situations.

Forbes. Published biweekly, except for an extra issue in October. Sections include companies/industries, international, money and investing, law and issues, marketing, computers, science and technology, and personal affairs. Also featured are regular columnists.

Fortune. Published biweekly, with three issues in May and October. Coverage includes the economy, innovation, technology, and money and markets. Departments include personal investing.

Investor's Business Daily. Gives complete market quotes and a variety of statistical information along with news stories.

Kiplinger's Personal Finance Magazine. Published monthly. Topics include spending, taxes, estate planning, investing basics, insurance, and personal finances.

Money Magazine. A monthly publication centering on personal finance. Areas of concern include home ownership, jobs, taxes, insurance, and investing.

The New York Times. The business section, daily and Sunday, is the nation's most comprehensive.

USA Today. A national daily with extensive quotations and business news.

The Wall Street Journal. Published by Dow Jones & Company. Issued Monday through Friday in regional editions, reporting news developments in term of their significance to businesspeople and investors. The third section, Money & Investing, contains regular features such as Heard on the Street, Abreast of the Market, Digest of Earnings Reports, and corporate Dividend News.

Wall Street Transcript. Published weekly by the Wall Street Transcript Corporation. Provides reprints of investment research reports, round-table discussions, and industry features.

INDEXES AND DIRECTORIES

America's Corporate Families and International Affiliates. Published by Dun & Bradstreet in two volumes, linking U.S. and foreign parents with the domestic and international affiliates.

Brands and Their Companies (1992). Edited by Susan L. Stetler and published by Gale Research Inc. In two volumes, providing access to more than 240,000 consumer brands and about 45,000 manufacturers and importers. Brands are presented in alphabetical order.

Bull & Bear's Directory of Investment Advisory Newsletters. Published annually by *Bull & Bear Financial Newspaper, Inc.* Lists 445 newsletters in alphabetical order within each category, including international investments, mutual funds, new issues, and stocks. Included are newsletter titles, addresses, phone numbers, descriptions, subscription rates, frequencies, and trial subscription offers.

Business and Investment Almanac (1991). Edited by Sumner N. Levin and Published by Business One Irwin. A review of the year, including stock market averages, prices/earnings ratios, foreign stock markets, mutual fund performance, and more. Includes an explanation of investment and financial terms.

Business Periodicals Index. Published monthly except July by H. W. Wilson Company, with a bound cumulation annually. An index to the contents of several hundred periodicals, including *Barron's, Business Week, Forbes, Fortune,* and *FW* (formerly *Financial World*).

Directory of Companies Offering Dividend Reinvestment Plans (eighth edition, 1991). Edited by Sumi Kinoshita and published by Evergreen Enterprises. Dividend reinvestment plans listed for more than 1,100 corporations and closed-end investment companies.

Dun's Business Rankings. Published by Dun & Bradstreet. Ranks the top 8,000 firms by sales and employees.

Encyclopedia of Business Information Sources (eighth edition, 1991–92). Edited by James Woy and published by Gale Research, Inc. A guide to more than 21,000 citations covering 1,000 subjects of interest to business people.

Investment Statistics Locator (1988). Written by Karen J. Chapman and published by Oryx Press. Detailed subject index to the most used sources of financial and investment data.

Million Dollar Directory: America's Leading Public and Private Companies. Published by Dun & Bradstreet; offers information on more than 160,000 top businesses.

Moody's Complete Corporate Index. Comprehensive index to 28,000 corporations included in Moody's Manuals. Published twice yearly.

Moody's Manuals. Six volumes of comprehensive statistical and analytical data covering listed and unlisted industrials, public utilities, transportation companies, banks and finance companies, and international businesses.

New York Times Index. Published semimonthly by the New York Times Company, with quarterly cumulations and an annual cumulation. Business listings indexed by industry, individual company, and person.

Predicates F and S Index—United States. Published by Predicates, Inc. monthly, with weekly supplements. Selectively indexes leading business publications for company activities, industry news, and product information.

Principal International Businesses. Published by Dun & Bradstreet; offers up-to-date information on approximately 50,000 leading enterprises in 133 countries around the world.

Reader's Guide to Periodical Literature. Published by H.W. Wilson Company. A cumulative author/subject index to periodicals of general interest. Published semi-monthly in March, April, September, October, and December and monthly in January, February, May, June, July, August, and November. Bound cumulation issued yearly. Includes *Business Week, Kiplinger's Personal Finance, Forbes, Fortune,* and *Money.*

Reference Book on Corporate Managements. Published by Dun & Bradstreet; lists biographies of top corporate executives.

Register of Corporations, Directors, and Executives. Published annually by Standard & Poor's in three volumes. Volume 1 lists 55,000 corporations with address; telephone number; name title, and function of approximately 500,000 officers, directors, and other principals; and a description of company products/services. Volume 2 offers listings of more than 70,000 individuals service as officers, directors, trustees, and partners. Volume 3 consists of indexes.

Stock Market Encyclopedia. Published quarterly by Standard & Poor's. Includes data on 750 companies—industries, utilities, transportation, and financial firms. A full-page report is included for every stock in the S&P 500.

Wiesenberger Investment Companies Service. Published annually. Includes general information about funds as an investment medium, as well as descriptions of and data on investment companies.

INDEX